THE POPE

ALSO BY ANTHONY McCARTEN

DARKEST HOUR

THE POPE

Francis, Benedict,
and the Decision That
Shook the World

Anthony McCarten

FLATIRON
BOOKS
NEW YORK

www.flatironbooks.com

Library of Congress Cataloging-in-Publication Data

Names: McCarten, Anthony, 1961– author.
Title: The Pope : Francis, Benedict, and the decision that shook the world / Anthony McCarten.
Description: First [edition]. | New York : Flatiron Books, 2019. | Includes bibliographical references and index.
Identifiers: LCCN 2018044744 | ISBN 9781250207906 (hardcover) | ISBN 9781250207913 (ebook)
Subjects: LCSH: Popes—Abdication. | Benedict XVI, Pope, 1927– | Benedict XVI, Pope, 1927—Abdication, 2013. | Francis, Pope, 1936– | Catholic Church—History— 21st century.
Classification: LCC BX958.A23 M33 2019 | DDC 282.092/2—dc23
LC record available at https://lccn.loc.gov/2018044744

First Edition: January 2019

10 9 8 7 6 5 4 3 2 1

For my parents: my mother, whose lasting wish was to ride around Heaven on a motorcycle; my father, whose last instruction to me was to "keep the faith"; and for Eva, who showed me the view of Rome from the Villa Borghese.

CONTENTS

PROLOGUE

On February 11, 2013, a seven-hundred-year-old tradition was shattered: Pope Benedict XVI, former protector of doctrine and loyal heir of the long-suffering John Paul the Great, made a startling announcement. After eight years in the papacy, he would, owing to his advanced age, resign, but would retain the title of "Pope Emeritus" for his lifetime.

Within weeks, the great doors of the Sistine Chapel in the Vatican were sealed and the cardinals, drawn into conclave for the second time in less than a decade, were asked to choose a new spiritual leader for the Catholic Church's 1.28 billion followers. When the doors opened again a few days later, the charismatic Argentinian Jorge Bergoglio, who would take the name Francis, had been elected. The world, for the first time since the year 1415, had two living popes.

The reasons for Benedict's cataclysm became fodder for speculation. A pope, surely, *must* die on the job. Wasn't this an integral part of the job description? Not just tradition; it was virtually dogma. As *The Washington Post*, citing a theological expert, explained: "Most modern popes have felt that resignation is unacceptable except in cases of an incurable or debilitating disease—that paternity, in the words of Paul VI, cannot be resigned."

Pope Benedict's resignation was not entirely unprecedented, nor was the dilemma of two living popes. In the long history of the church, three popes have now resigned, while 263 did not. Pope

Gregory XII resigned in 1415 in the midst of a political struggle between Italy and France over who really controlled the Catholic Church. But we have to return to 1294, to Celestine V, to find a pope who decided, of his own volition—out of a "longing for the tranquility of his former life"—to step down.

The reaction at the time to Celestine's bombshell was outrage. There is a passage from the third canto of the *Inferno*, in Dante's *Divine Comedy*, where Virgil is guiding Dante through the Gates of Hell. Before they reach the Inferno they pass into an antechamber filled with a cacophony of agonizing cries of those miserable souls who lived a life "without disgrace and without praise"; in effect, people worse than sinners, who had failed to act, failed to believe, or failed to deliver on promises made. Dante stares at the doomed faces of the terminally bland until, at one point, he sees a man and writes: "I saw and recognized the shade of him who made, through cowardice, the great refusal." That man was, of course, Pope Celestine V, whose defection so horrified the great Italian poet that he immortalized him in his magnum opus.

So, knowing the outrage a papal resignation would cause, why did Benedict, *the* most traditional pope of the modern era, do the most untraditional thing imaginable? Poor health alone is not seen as a valid explanation; in fact, it has usually been an *asset* to a pope, in that it reenacts—for all to see—Christ's suffering on the cross. An additional mystery has to be sorted: How could this ultraconservative protector of the faith, guardian of doctrine, even contemplate resigning when, as he very well knew, he would be surrendering the Chair of St. Peter to the radical Jorge Bergoglio, a man so different from him in character and views?

This book tells the tale of two popes, both possessed of tremendous and inalienable authority: an odd couple whose destinies converged and who influenced each other profoundly.

Let us consider Benedict first, the former Cardinal Joseph Ratzinger, an intellectual German, suspicious of humor, a luxury-savoring introvert and somewhat dandyish dresser—he revived the papal tradition of wearing red velvet slippers, and commissioned and sported a perfume maker to create a signature fragrance for his sole use—who feels the church's *refusal* to yield and change is its greatest strength and is, indeed, the secret of its timeless durability. While sincere about his sacred duties, he's a man completely lacking the common touch. A reclusive theologian wholly without in-the-field experience. Not known to be a fan of any sport. Has never, to our knowledge, spoken a romantic word to another soul.

Francis, on the other hand—or, as we will first encounter him, Cardinal Bergoglio—is a charismatic, fun-loving Argentinian, on the surface a humble man, an extrovert, a simple dresser (he wore the same pair of black shoes for twenty years, still wears a Swatch), and an on-again, off-again advocate of liberation theology, a Catholic movement that seeks to aid the poor and oppressed through *direct* involvement in political and civic affairs. He's a man with the common touch. A man of the people. Once even had a girlfriend. Worked as a bouncer at a tango club. An ardent fan of football.

"Sin" is a theme in both men's lives, more specifically the grace and extra wisdom that come if a sinner can acknowledge their failings and put their sins behind them. How much wiser, how much more valuable as a future teacher and healer and guide, is the person who has a full, firsthand understanding of a particular human weakness or failing or problem, and who has then risen from this place of dark insight to see the true dimensions of this problem. Alternatively, how much less valuable, and even more dangerous, the one who has failed in this regard.

Jorge Bergoglio openly labels himself a sinner, continually points out that this is not some euphemism, some mere turn of phrase. He has sinned. He goes even further, controversially stating that it is not enough to enact the ritual of confession of sins to a priest. One must take practical steps to atone for those sins in one's daily life, make real and deep changes. No one gets a clean scorecard with just a quick visit to a priest in his confessional. One must *act*. As he has said, "Sin is more than a stain that can be removed by a trip to the dry cleaner. It is a wound that needs to be treated, healed."

This logic suggests a true reformist agenda, one that, if permitted, would reach naturally into many other areas of belief and doctrinal teaching. Why, for instance, should a celibate priest feel confident to lecture on sexual matters? Surely the church ought, with similar frankness, to admit that it is not best qualified to impose its views in this arena. How should such celibate, sex-denying men judge their sexually active parishioners, whose experience of life will be much more complete and varied than theirs? As Frank Sinatra once quipped, "Your Holiness, you no play-a da game, you no make-a da rules." Or how, for instance, can a celibate novice on the day of his ordination, when asked to renounce sex for the rest of his life, be wise enough to know what he is saying no to? He cannot know. If this naïf has never explored his own sexual drives, what is he to do should these drives one day make themselves felt? Like so many before him, he will be forced into a double life, with sometimes disastrous consequences, and sometimes many innocent victims. And what makes the church fit to say that only celibate men are fitting vessels for teaching from the pulpit God's ministry? Also, if the story of Adam and Eve is, as Francis has said, merely a parable, not at all to be taken as literal fact, thus pouring considerable water on the whole seven-day creation myth, what else of the sacred scriptures ought to be considered make-believe? Is even the story of Christ rising from the dead and ascending bodily into Heaven also now only a parable? If the spirit of Francis's frankness is logically extended into all areas of faith and dogma, where will the recalibrations end?

The story that follows unfolds largely in a Vatican in crisis, swamped with scandals but denied simple remedies, aware of the need to change but fearful of what losses change will bring, with one pope who—because of his past—feels himself lacking in the moral authority, skills, and strength to deal with these scandals, and a second, new pope, who—because of *his* past—predicates his spiritual leadership of over two billion followers with the admission that he is a sinner.

It is a crucial way station in the journey of an institution that has lasted two thousand years.

An interesting dilemma attends this situation of having two living popes, and it has to do with the concept of papal infallibility.

Let us address it briefly.

For two millennia the church has striven to avoid having two living popes and has almost entirely succeeded. Some pontiffs were even poisoned so that the situation never came up. And the reason? Why does a pope not just serve a term and then step down to be replaced by a younger man? *Infallibility.* The grace of infallibility. The gift of correctness, God's gift to he who sits in St. Peter's chair, the grace of being right, indisputably right—in the present and, most important, in the future, for time immemorial, on all matters of doctrine. When the pope speaks ex cathedra, that is from the Chair of St. Peter, speaking as pope and not as a private individual, his words form part of the Magisterium, that is, the official teaching of the Catholic Church, which has the power and authority of Christ behind it. How could Ratzinger and Bergoglio coexist and *both* be infallible, both be right . . . when they seem to disagree on so much? In fact, it would seem that as long as they both continue to coexist, they must serve as proof eternal that popes are *fallible,* as anytime they disagree, one pope will always be wrong. And a pope who is wrong, and is proven to be so by the mere existence of his twin, his countervailing voice, is no pope at all. For every papal pronouncement, there walks and breathes the rebuttal, the living counterargument—invalidating it. How can they both be God-filled and blessed by the gift of ultimate wisdom . . . and yet disagree?

Given, then, that two papal points of view are, at the time of this writing, both available, Catholics (and even some leaders in the church) are able to choose which pope and which papal position best suits them, Benedictine or Franciscan, making very real the practical dilemma of having *two* men in white. The staunchly conservative American cardinal Raymond Burke, a vocal critic of Francis, told a Catholic newspaper in 2016, "My pope is Benedict." A conservative former papal ambassador to the United States, Archbishop Carlo Maria Viganó, has even called for Francis *to resign.* In what some see as an act of revenge for Francis's replacement of him as papal nuncio (a presumed punishment for Viganó's setting up of a secret meeting with U.S. conservatives opposed to gay marriage), Viganó alleges that he once told Francis about the sexually abusive American cardinal Theodore McCarrick, and that Francis failed to take appropriate action until much later. Whether there is any truth to Viganó's unsupported claim or not, it is unprecedented in modern times for a pope to be so mutinously attacked by his own clergy.

But Benedict himself, in a rare letter released by the Vatican in September 2018, rebuked those who, like Burke, still pledge fealty to him, presenting instead a united front with Francis and sharply criticizing those who argue a discontinuity of theology, calling such anti-Franciscan anger a "foolish prejudice." To return the compliment, Francis has publicly embraced his predecessor, whom he has likened to "having a wise grandfather at home." Are the Burkes and Viganós within the church satisfied, chastened into silence? Not at all. Quite the contrary.

In a world where the disinherited and disaffected strike out at power to often self-destructive effect, the Catholic Church is in very unusual and dangerous waters.

Joseph Ratzinger is a man of tremendous principle. This book will look into his past to decode the sources of his deep conviction that change is more a sign of weakness than of strength.

His election as pope in 2005 surely represented a safe option, under the circumstances as they were. He *was* safe. After John Paul II's theatrics, his outreach, his travel, travel, travel (was there an airport runway in the world left unkissed by his lips?), the mother church needed to rest, to do some housekeeping. Benedict, an eminent theologian, would reassert, protect, and strengthen ancient doctrine. In short, he would make sure overdue reforms remained overdue. This was his strength and value. Even as a child, he kept his bedroom notably tidy. On all the evidence, this son of a policeman believed that only in authority—in rules, in obedience under the law, in the indissoluble—will the faithful find true peace. Doubt, uncertainty, vacillation, and correction breed disaffection, despair, cynicism, and finally contempt. People's souls, he would ask us to agree, ache for certainty. He has spoken repeatedly about what he sees as the greatest threat to this certainty: the spirit of relativism. He has despaired at so many winds of doctrine, so many ideological currents, so many new ways of thinking in recent decades. In such a world, how are we to know who speaks the truth?

What is the truth? The world quakes with rival voices—Marxists, liberals, conservatives, atheists, agnostics, mystics—and in every breast the universal cry "I speak the truth! Only I!"

No, says Ratzinger, there is but one truth. Saith the Lord, "I am the truth." The center of Ratzinger's teaching is that there must be a common reference point, an *axis mundi*, if we are to avert chaos and cataclysm and conflict. One truth, from which we can all navigate—this is the doctrinal position that might liken itself to a compass that points in all directions but needs to take as its starting point True North. Only then can it help travelers plot a journey and direct them on the right path. The same goes for human morality, he seems to be telling us. What is *its* True North? God. Without God, humanity has no agreed reference point, no *axis mundi*. Every opinion is as valid as every other. The truth becomes relative. Kill God and what you actually kill is any hope of absolute truth. Your truth is yours, mine is mine, locking each person into a prison of his or her own interpretation of good and evil.

That is the great crisis of Western life, as Ratzinger perceived it: the curse of relativism. The damage done by it? He saw clearly how, in the English-speaking world at least, fewer and fewer were taking their fire from the flame lit by a two-thousand-year-old Christian faith. Take America. If ex-Catholics are considered a religious group of their own, they are now the fourth-largest religion in the United States. In Britain, more than half of people under forty now say they have no religion. Why have so many quietly, steadily shuffled out of the churches?

There were other, more pressing crises waiting for him when he became pope—so many of them. Crimes were being committed by men of the cloth, by his colleagues, by his staff, fellow workers in the vineyard of the Lord. Crimes involving buttons, often *children's* buttons, zippers, hands, genitalia, mouths; violations, betrayals, secrets, intimidations, lies, threats, trauma, despair, ruined lives; and such evils in a climate of sanctimony, to the scent of ancient incense. Each scandal, in its own way, would rock Benedict and erode his belief that he was the man who could solve it. Finally, he shocked the world. He did the unthinkable. He stepped down. And in doing so, ironically, this great traditionalist robbed the church of a crucial

certainty upon which its remaining faithful had always relied: that
a pope is pope for life.

At the other end of the spectrum, in so many respects, is Jorge Bergoglio, the reformer. No sooner had he become pope number 266
and taken the name Francis than the astonishing ad lib comments
began. His was quickly the name on everyone's lips, as was the universal refrain "The pope just said *what*?" A breath of fresh air, with
a rock star's charisma, there was a touch of John Lennon about him
also (both men have been on the cover of *Rolling Stone* magazine),
with a propensity for jaw-dropping statements to make even his most
ardent fans gasp. To match Lennon's remark that the Beatles were
"more popular than Jesus now," which threw fundamentalists in the
American heartland into a spree of record-burning, there was Bergoglio's astonishing announcement that even heathens can get to
Heaven. *Heathens?* Really? These wooden-god worshippers, these
Sunday slumberers, were they just as likely to be Heaven-bound?
Then what was the point—many of the world's Catholics rightly
wondered—of all those thousandfold hours given over to knee-
numbing prayer, all those sermons and upbraidings from the pulpit,
all those visits to confession with ensuing penance, all those muted
recitations of the Rosary, counting off with thumb and forefinger
each bead on the string, all those Lenten fasts and all that sublima-
tion of natural urges, all that God-demanded love, and finally all
that guilt, so much *guilt* . . . for what? What . . . if not to have some
advantage in securing the ultimate celestial reward? But the new
pope confirmed it: it cannot be the heathen's fault if he or she is
born into a heathen culture. It is therefore quite unfair that only
the God-reared, by accident of birth, should get the best and only
rooms in the Heavenly hotel. With such remarks the new pope
seemed intent on single-handedly reviving the spirit of the 1960s.

But he wasn't done surprising people. To homosexuals he offered
the church's apology, ex cathedra. It is not the church's role to judge
homosexuals, he proclaimed. He even reportedly told one gay man,
Juan Carlos Cruz (a victim of sexual abuse), that "God made you like
this and loves you like this and I don't care. The pope loves you

like this." (Contrast this with Benedict, who called homosexuality "an intrinsic evil.") Pope Francis has not ruled out married priests, either, saying "it is human to want one's cake and eat it, too . . . naturally one wants the good things from the consecrated life and from the lay life also." He is happy to admit the hypocrisy of the church's current position, given that there are married priests already in remote corners of the Catholic empire, in the Greek and Russian branches. And he is happy to acknowledge that St. Peter himself had children. Clement IV and Adrian II were married before they took holy orders. Pius II had at least two illegitimate children. John XII is said to have died in the act. And let's just say all those who took the name Pope Innocent did not exactly live up to the name.

The literal truth of the Bible? Adam and Eve are "a fable." Then what of the Virgin birth, planetary floods, men who literally lived to be eight hundred years old, or the parting of waters with miracle crossings on dry land—all of that? Francis seems to have concluded that—particularly in the West—people no longer require priests to say things that everybody knows are not true and can't possibly be true. And more than that, he has hinted, perhaps the church is even weakened by these claims of literal truth.

The culture of the Catholic Church? Speaking with the authority of the Magisterium, he has dubbed it "narcissistic," too inward looking, concerned with its own survival and enrichment rather than the needs of the poor. He has used terms like "spiritual Alzheimer's" to describe a church that has forgotten Christ's example of mercy and called out "the lust for power of ladder-climbing clerics." He has stated, "Like every body, like every human body, the church is exposed to illnesses, malfunctioning, infirmity. It must be treated. With strong medicine."

Sexual abuse? Leading a church that Bishopaccountability.org, a nonprofit advocacy group that tracks church abuse cases, says has paid out three billion dollars in settlements to victims worldwide, he now speaks of "zero tolerance" of both abuse and, vitally, church cover-ups, charging his bishops, on pain of being found complicit, to report incidents to the police. These new rules of transparency, exposure, and criminal consequences have already begun to produce an extraordinary drop in the number of reported cases of abuse, suggesting that acts of sexual criminality by priests *were* reducible, almost to zero, with the responsible imposition of swift penalties (such as jail terms) and the removal of the church's cloak of protection from sex-fiend priests. How shockingly simple the solution here may yet prove to be, as long as the police are given unrestricted access to church files, and the church matches or betters the anguished efforts of victims for justice to be done. After all, the Catholic leadership has every incentive for doing so: its survival is at stake.

Capitalism? Pope Francis has deemed it a sin, a system of trickle-down suffering. He has been accused of biting the hand that fed.

The environment? He has taken aim at the world's governments for their sinful protection of those who are wounding Mother Earth, destroying our collective home. In a long and carefully researched encyclical, he dismantled the positions of climate-change deniers and self-interested, profit-driven industries.

In short, he has shown himself prepared to make powerful enemies. Already there are grumblings among those in the church who yearn for the simpler certainties offered by Pope Benedict. At times, change seems to be all that Francis represents, and it has always been harder to mount arguments for change than for stasis. Still, his arguments, when simplified and distilled, seem—to me at least—to be that the church should *insist* less, *include* more. It must bring into joyous alignment the beautiful lessons taught in churches and the beautiful lessons taught in schools.

Bergoglio's choice of the name *Francis*, after St. Francis of Assisi, can now be seen for what it was: a statement of revolutionary intent. How far will he go? How far will he be *allowed* to go?

The name derives from Francesco Bernardone. This young man was walking in the wood. He found a chapel—a ruined chapel. One wall had fallen down. He stepped inside. The crucifix was still on the wall where the altar had been. Afterward, Francesco always said it "captivated his senses." It even spoke to him: "Francesco, rebuild my church." Francesco was a practical man; he took this instruction literally, said okay, went up to the quarry on top of Mount Subasio, cut stones, carted them down the mountain, and started to repair the little broken wall. He mistook God's meaning, who wanted something much bigger for him. The lesson? Even the most glorious journey can begin . . . with a mistake.

Let me end this prologue on a personal note.

I am a Catholic. At least, I was raised one, and I am told, and can attest to the fact, that once thus stamped, always stamped.

I was reared on the tale of Jesus Christ, this young Jewish radical hailing from Nazareth two millennia ago, claiming to be the "Son of Man" or, even more audaciously, the "Messiah" and "King of the Jews," sent by his father on a divine mission to rid humanity of the original sin blighting it since Eden, before being caught and crucified, but then rising from the dead two days later, thereafter ascending bodily into Heaven, there to remain until the unspecified day when he would return to announce the end of the entire human experiment. This was my religion. A tall tale, admittedly, but with the insolent logic of truth. Tacitus called Christianity "that most mischievous superstition," and the writer Jorge Luis Borges "a branch of fantastic literature." Still, this was the faith I was born into.

I grew up as the second-to-youngest member of a large household, one so Catholic that two of my sisters would marry—very happily—ex-priests. We knew priests at our dinner table, the odd bishop, and even, once, a cardinal. Our home, in addition to the ritual churchgoing, would once a month be visited by a large statue of the Virgin Mary, in solemn procession throughout the parish, obliging my brothers and sisters and me to observe, under the thumb of my mother, the (to my mind, tedious) recitations of the Rosary, paeans to the Virgin, asking for help, for help, for divine help. Life was certainly tough enough in our working-class town. Money was as scarce as good jobs, so we figured that we could do worse than be on good terms with the Mother of God. Don't argue, just get on your knees, and everything would work out okay with God on your side: this was the drill. We obeyed, falling dutifully, burying our faces in the couch as we mumbled the ancient incantations over and over again: *"Pray for us sinners, now and at the hour of our death . . ."*

Amen.

If you'd care to know my parents' policy on birth control, I am one of eight children (more *coitus* than *interruptus*). Educated first by nuns, I progressed to ordained brothers; was well served by two good Catholic schools. For all my childhood I served the mass, as an altar boy, making my last appearance in red cowl and white surplice at the embarrassingly advanced age of sixteen, early stubble on my chin, the robes then two sizes too small for me, as I carried to the priest cruets of water and wine and then the white and innocent wafers that this Heaven-connected man, this neighborhood magician, would transform into the actual body of Christ. The daily miracle, right before our eyes. The *body* of Christ, abracadabra. Believe it or not.

We were Catholics, or, more specifically, "Irish Catholics" (albeit transplanted to New Zealand via migrant ships four generations before me), the flame of our Irishness kept alight in a remote land by an extended family who did business, and did "the business," only within the closed circle of this one faith and culture. It shaped us. And my life today, a writer's life, owes its roots to the animating beauty of the liturgy, heard first through young ears, an art located in the ornate language that inclined all to think in multiple dimensions and across time and space, never contemplating life without first mulling death. The factual was hitched irreparably to the fictional, and distinguishing between the two was actively discouraged. So what, we were taught, if you could not prove something was true: How did it make you *feel*? Your emotions led you. People wept openly in our small church. Hands were clasped so tightly in prayer, you could see the whites of knuckles. Belief was as necessary for these people as a paycheck. You *had* to believe, to make it through the day. The church in our town, hexagonal and spireless, was at the geographical and psychological center of our lives. If I ever doubted this, my mother would set me straight. If I questioned some aspect of creed, some far-fetched claim made from pulpit or book, I would receive her stock rebuke: "Anthony, a little knowledge is a dangerous thing." That this woman, who left school at fourteen, should so easily quote the poet Alexander Pope (or slightly misquote him, for the operative word is *learning*, not *knowledge*), I offer as proof that, in the absence of schooling, the church served as our university, the priest substituting for professor.

This book, and the feature film of the same name that accompanies it (Netflix, 2019, starring Sir Anthony Hopkins and Jonathan Pryce, directed by Fernando Meirelles), specifically came about with the sudden death of a cousin of mine. Pauline's death caused my eldest sister, a devout Catholic, to text me, suggesting I light a candle, if I was near a church. I was. I was in Rome. So, with Eva, my partner, I went to St. Peter's Basilica in the Vatican and found the famous square thronged with thousands, all there to see the new pope say an open-air mass. The huge face of Francis, projected on a superscreen, conveyed his superstar appeal. And while standing there, listening to his gentle Italian words, I asked Eva if she knew where the *other* pope was, Pope Benedict, the one who had resigned, who had slipped off the international radar. Eva knew. Her father, in Munich, had once worked under Benedict (then Archbishop Ratzinger of Munich) while serving as vice chancellor of that city's Catholic University. Eva informed me that this second pontiff, who retained the title of pope and arguably many of his powers, was quietly living in a monastery just a few hundred yards behind the stage on which Pope Francis now stood, sequestered within the Vatican walls, silent, obedient, old. Two popes, then, within a solid stone's throw of each other! I asked Eva if she knew when the last time was that the world had two living popes. We googled it. The resulting answer, when it resolved on the screen of her smartphone, inspired both book and film.

1

CONCLAVE

Let me go to the house of the Father."

These words were whispered in Polish at 3:30 P.M. on April 2, 2005. A little over six hours later, the Catholic Church was set on an unprecedented new course.

Pope John Paul II was dead. Since 1991, the Vatican had kept his illness secret, admitting only in a 2003 statement on the eve of his eighty-third birthday what had already become clear to the world's then 1.1 billion Catholics. The pontiff's slow and painful deterioration from Parkinson's disease had long been agonizing to watch.

Rome had been ablaze with speculation and rumor since February 1, when the pope was rushed to his private wing in Gemelli University Hospital for the treatment of symptoms of "acute inflammation of the larynx and laryngo-spasm," caused by a recent bout of flu. The press duly assembled for the deathwatch.

Over the following two months, however, John Paul II had displayed more of the same resilience that had characterized his many years of illness. This was, after all, a pope who during his twenty-six-year reign had survived not one but two assassination attempts; he had recovered from four gunshot wounds in 1981 and a bayonet attack a year later. Now, despite multiple readmissions to the hospital and a tracheotomy, he continued to appear at various Vatican windows and balconies to bless the crowds in St. Peter's Square. His voice was barely audible. He missed the Palm Sunday Mass for the first time during his tenure as pope, but, dedicated to the last, he was presented in a wheelchair on Easter Sunday, March 27, and attempted to make his traditional address. He was described as "[looking] to be in immense distress, opening and shutting his mouth, grimacing with frustration or pain, and several times raising one or both hands to his head." It was all too much for the estimated eighty thousand devoted Catholics watching below, and tears flowed freely. The pope managed a brief sign of the cross before being wheeled behind the curtains of his apartment.

Over the following six days the Vatican frequently updated the world on his worsening condition, and those who had been hopeful that he might make a full recovery began to accept that his death was only a matter of time. On the morning of April 1 a public statement advised, "The Holy Father's health condition is very grave." At 7:17 the previous evening, he had "received the Last Rites." John Paul's most trusted friend and personal secretary, Archbishop Stanislaw Dziwisz, administered the sacraments to John Paul II to prepare him for his final journey, by giving him absolution from his sins and anointing him with the holy oils on his forehead and on the backs of his hands, as is done only with priests. (Those not ordained are anointed on the palms of their hands.) Vatican expert and biographer of Pope Benedict XVI, John L. Allen Jr. witnessed this press briefing and described how "the most telling indication of the true gravity of the situation came at the end of the briefing, when [Vatican spokesman Joaquín Navarro-Valls] choked back tears as he walked away from the platform where he spoke to reporters."

Surrounded by those who had loved and cherished him for so many years, John Paul II regained consciousness several times during his final twenty-four hours, and was described by his personal physician, Dr. Renato Buzzonetti, as looking "serene and lucid." In accordance with Polish tradition, "a small, lit candle illuminated the gloom of the room where the pope was expiring." When he became aware of the crowds calling his name from the vigil below, he uttered words that Vatican officials deciphered as "I have looked for you. Now you have come to me and I thank you."

Dr. Buzzonetti ran an electrocardiogram for twenty minutes to verify Pope John Paul's death. Once this was done, the centuries-old Vatican rituals began, elements of which date back to as early as 1059, when Pope Nicholas II radically reformed the process of papal elections, in an effort to prevent further installation of puppet popes under the control of opposing imperial and noble powers, through a decree stating that cardinals alone were responsible for choosing successors to the Chair of St. Peter.

Cardinal Eduardo Martínez Somalo had been appointed camerlengo by the late pope to administer the church during the period known as the interregnum ("between the reigns," which lasts from the moment of death until a new pope is found), and he now stepped forward to call John Paul three times by his Polish baptismal name, Karol. When no answer was received, he struck a small silver hammer on John Paul's forehead as a sure indication of his death. He was then required to destroy with a hammer the Ring of the Fisherman, or Annelo Pescatorio (the papal ring cast for each pope since the thirteenth century) to symbolize the end of his reign.

And so the death of John Paul was announced to the world. The public outpouring of grief was breathtaking, with many soon referring to him by the prestigious (albeit unofficial) appendage of "the Great," previously afforded only to pope-saints Leo I (ruled A.D. 440–461), Gregory I (590–604), and Nicholas I (858–867). His body was dressed in bloodred vestments and taken to the Apostolic Palace, where members of the papal administrative offices and agencies of the Catholic Church, known as the Roman Curia, could pay their respects, before being transferred to St. Peter's Basilica the following day for the beginning of the nine official days of mourning known as the *novemdiales*, a custom dating back to the *novemdiale sacrum,* an ancient Roman rite of purification held on the ninth and final day of a period of festivity. An estimated four million pilgrims and three million residents of Rome filed past to give thanks and pray for this most beloved of men, astonishing figures when compared with the previous record of 750,000 people who visited the body of Pope Paul VI in August 1978. John Paul had left instructions that, should he not be alive to read it himself, his final address be read out by the substitute of the Secretariat of State, Archbishop Leonardo Sandri. During mass at the Feast of Divine

Mercy held at St. Peter's Square on Sunday, April 3, Sandri read John Paul's final message of peace, forgiveness, and love, which told the people, "As a gift to humanity, which sometimes seems bewildered and overwhelmed by the power of evil, selfishness, and fear, the Risen Lord offers his love that pardons, reconciles, and reopens hearts to love. It is a love that converts hearts and gives peace."

Tough act to follow.

And there was no time to waste. Interregnum tradition demanded that the funeral take place between the fourth and sixth day following a pope's death. Therefore, it was scheduled for Friday, April 8. Likewise, the conclave to elect his successor must occur no earlier than fifteen or later than twenty days after his death, so was announced to begin on April 18.

The Vatican began planning the funeral with military precision. The responsibility of presiding over events fell to Joseph Ratzinger, as dean of the College of Cardinals—who, despite having no authority over his brother cardinals, "is considered as first among equals" and who, incidentally, had also been John Paul's right-hand man for twenty-four years. Nicknamed the Pilgrim Pope on account of his globetrotting travels to 129 countries, John Paul II had traveled more miles than all the previous popes in the church's two-thousand-year history combined, ensuring that heads of state, royalty, and dignitaries from across the globe would be in attendance alongside the crowds of Catholic faithful. A more diverse group of people had gathered at few other moments throughout history, and many opposing nations were united through their mutual respect for the late pontiff. Prince Charles postponed his wedding to Camilla Parker-Bowles to be able to attend alongside the British prime minister, Tony Blair, and the archbishop of Canterbury, Rowan Williams. U.S. president George W. Bush was seen leaning over to shake the hand of staunch Iraq War critic President Jacques Chirac of France, as United Nations secretary-general Kofi Anan watched on alongside former presidents Bill Clinton and George H. W. Bush. The Israeli president, Moshe Katsav, chatted and shook hands with Syrian leader Bashar al-Assad and the president of Iran, Mohammed Khatami, although Khatami later strenuously denied the exchange. It would be the largest funeral of a pope in the history of the Catholic

Church, and an estimated two billion people worldwide tuned in to watch the live broadcast on television, with one million of those watching on large outdoor screens specially erected around the city of Rome.

The ceremony began with a private requiem mass inside St. Peter's Basilica attended by members of the College of Cardinals and the nine Patriarchs of Oriental Catholic Churches, which, though celebrating different liturgies and having their own structures of government, are in full communion with the pope. His body was laid inside a coffin made from cypress wood, a centuries-old tradition that symbolizes his humanity among men, and would later be further enclosed in two caskets of lead and elm, signifying his death and dignity respectively. Inside the coffin a sealed document officially concluding his entire life's work as pope was placed alongside "three bags, each containing one gold, silver, or copper coin for each year in Pope John Paul II's reign," before a white silk veil was placed over his face and hands. That ceremony concluded, the now-closed coffin was carried by twelve papal gentlemen—formerly known as secret chamberlains, these are laymen of noble Roman families who have served the popes for centuries as attendants of the papal household—and accompanied by the slow procession chanting hymns, who made their way into St. Peter's Square to begin the public funeral.

Many would come to believe that Cardinal Ratzinger's conduct during this three-hour-long spectacle secured him the papacy. In his homily, amid continual interjections of applause from the crowds, he spoke at length in "human, not metaphysical, terms" of John Paul's life from his childhood in Poland through to the end of his days in Rome. In his recollection of one of the pope's last public appearances, the usually unemotional and ultraformal German's voice cracked as he choked back tears. It was a magnificent and surprising performance to all who witnessed it.

As the funeral drew to a close and the motorcades and helicopters of the dignitaries began to depart, the crowds were left chanting, *"Santo subito!"* (Sainthood now!) When exhaustion finally descended across the city, people too weary to attempt the journey home lay sleeping on the streets. Talk inside the Vatican and among the world's media turned to who would succeed the pope now buried in the "bare earth" in the crypt below St. Peter's Basilica, in accordance with his wishes.

ISSUES FACING THE CARDINAL ELECTORS

With just ten days to go before the 115 cardinals who had assembled in Rome for the funeral would be drawn into conclave to choose the next pope, discreet conversations to promote favored candidates— open campaigning is strictly forbidden—could begin in earnest. This was a delicate balancing act, and the process needed to be handled carefully to avoid the dreaded Pignedoli Principle. This respected theory, conceived by George Weigel of the Ethics and Public Policy Center in Washington, D.C., is named after Cardinal Sergio Pignedoli, hotly tipped by the press to win the 1978 conclave that elected Pope John Paul II. The principle states that "a man's chances of becoming pope decrease in proportion to the number of times he is described as *papabile* [the unofficial term used to refer to cardinals who are viewed as potential future popes] in the press." Technically, all cardinals entering the conclave were eligible candidates for consideration; however, this veneer of simplicity shielded myriad theological and political outlooks that mean electing a successor to the Chair of St. Peter would be far from simple, just as it had been throughout the 729 years since the first conclave, in 1276.

Following an impasse that resulted in an interregnum of almost three years, Pope Gregory X was elected in 1271 and set about developing a format to ease the process whereby cardinals were required to remain in conclave until a decision was reached and even have their food rations reduced to just bread, water, and wine after five days or more of deadlock. Unfortunately, despite efforts to implement these changes when Gregory died, on January 10, 1276, political power plays and infighting would see four popes in as many years after his death and three further interregnums lasting more than two years, in 1292–94, 1314–16, and 1415–17. Centuries would go by until conclaves ceased to last longer than a week, with the election of Pope Pius VIII in 1831. All meetings bar one were held in Rome—which perhaps influenced the Italians' complete dominance in the role from 1523 until the election of Polish John Paul II in 1978—and had a strictly European result before Pope Francis's succession in 2013.

The warmth and affection for John Paul displayed by the millions of mourners at his funeral could almost mislead one to believe that the Catholic Church was in better shape than it had ever been. The harsh reality was that this was a church increasingly at odds with modern society, one that seemed unable to find a way to keep pace with, let alone guide, the lives of its followers around the globe. John Paul's tenure had been like no other in touching the faithful, but dwindling numbers of church attendees in country after country proved that this was not enough to sustain the church's position. Michael J. Lacey, coauthor of *Crisis of Authority in Catholic Modernity,* described the Catholic Church as suffering from "an underlying crisis of authority . . . the laity seems to be learning to deal with it to their own satisfaction by not expecting too much from Rome or from their local ordinaries. . . ." What was the church to do to combat these problems?

Problems had been further intensified by the sexual abuse crisis that rocked the church in 2002 and continues to shake it to this day. The Vatican fervently defended John Paul's record of handling abuse cases reported to the church, claiming, in 2014, that he did not understand the severity of the "cancer" because the "purity" of his mind and thoughts made this whole situation "unbelievable" to him. But the crisis loomed large in the minds of the assembling cardinals, and as respected Catholic author and journalist David Gibson describes, "the anger over the scandal went much deeper than the sexual abuse itself . . . and centered principally on the abuse of authority that had allowed such crimes to go unchecked for years, even decades. In that sense, the sexual abuse scandals were symptomatic of a larger crisis afflicting the Church, one that centered on how authority—and the power that authority conferred—was wielded in the Church of John Paul II."

Alongside these key issues, cardinals brought their own regional troubles to the table, among them "secularism in Western Europe, the rise of global Islam, the growing gap between rich and poor in the north and the south, and the proper balance in church government between the center and the periphery."

Thanks to the positive media attention that had surrounded the funeral, one could easily assume that the swell of public feeling presented the ideal opportunity for the church to shake things up and tackle its institutional failings. Internally, however, opinions were quite the opposite. It was felt that the problems facing the church in the future were so great that radical changes at this juncture could not resolve the dividing issues faced by cardinals from Western and developing nations, while at the same time continuing John Paul's legacy as an inspirational and engaging man of the people. It was too tall an order, and the majority of cardinals decided they needed a safe pair of hands and a smooth transition to deal with issues that could crush the church irreparably. The only remaining question was, Whose hands?

THE CANDIDATES

As the pressure began to mount, the Vatican took the unprecedented move of imposing a media blackout from April 8 until the opening of the conclave. Putting aside the irony of such a move, given that the process itself was secret, this was seen by many to be a frustrating interference by none other than the famed Vatican enforcer of rules and doctrine, the prefect of the Congregation for the Doctrine of the Faith, Cardinal Ratzinger. In reality, it was an attempt to even the playing field for the cardinals from non-Italian or non-English-speaking countries, especially those from Africa, South America, and Asia, who believed themselves to be at an unfair disadvantage to European and American cardinals, who had a disproportionate amount of airtime in which to outline their opinions on the issues facing the church.

The media blackout, unsurprisingly, did not prevent gossip from reaching the newspapers, but many of the cardinals remained diplomatic, insisting that there was no clear favorite in the lead-up to the conclave. In reality, there was considerable speculation about a

Breakdown of 115 cardinal electors at the 2005 conclave

Western Europe	26 (23%)	Eastern Europe	12 (10%)
Italy	20 (17%)	Africa	11 (10%)
Latin America	20 (17%)	Middle East & Asia	10 (9%)
North America	14 (12%)	Australia & New Zealand	2 (2%)

number of candidates representing both conservative and progressive ideologies. One issue that most were certain of, after the twenty-six-year papacy of John Paul, was that the new pope was unlikely to be a young man, so as to ensure a significantly shorter tenure than that of his predecessor—although few would have believed just how short it would be. As writer Paul Collins notes, "a weakened or even senile pope who is unable or unwilling to resign could confront the Church with a massive constitutional conundrum. Under present rules, no one can sack the pope." John Paul's personalization of the papacy had resulted in a reign more akin to a centralized autocracy, where little freedom of action was afforded to individual bishops or heads of religious orders; consequently, there had been a direct correlation between the pope's deteriorating health and the reduced ability of the church to act on pressing issues. It had been left in limbo, unable to act on any major decisions, "forced to mark time with important problems unaddressed as [it awaited] the demise of the Pope."

John Paul II had appointed more cardinals than any other pontiff (231) and had set the record for largest number created at any one time when he named forty-four in February 2001, a move seen by many as an effort to secure his legacy by choosing cardinals who espoused his theological views on the direction the church should take after his death. These were swiftly followed by a further thirty creations in 2003. The total number of cardinals still young enough to vote—after the age of eighty, cardinals become ineligible—at the conclave who had been chosen by John Paul himself was 113. While not all were carved in John Paul's mold as orthodox conservatives with a passion for the disenfranchised poor, this staggering figure did ensure that his shadow lingered long in the minds of many when voting began.

The nine meetings (known as consistories) in which John Paul created his 231 new cardinals occurred over a period of twenty-four years and had allowed for the evolution of many differing opinions, in the most simplistic terms, two opposing camps within the modern church.

THE CONSERVATIVES

This group of cardinals had all been appointed precisely because of their strong belief in John Paul's teachings and a papal-centric church and in the hope that they would continue his work after he was gone. They believed that "Catholicism must increasingly stand against the prevailing post-modern culture" and that "there [was] a real danger that many Catholics, including priests and theologians, [would] become completely compromised by secularism and relativism." Fundamentally, the conservative candidates were all strong believers that doctrine must not be altered to assimilate the church into a changing society.

Cardinal Joseph Ratzinger of Germany (age 78)

As John Paul II's longtime right-hand man, and considered by many to be the obvious successor, Cardinal Joseph Ratzinger was a front-runner from the start.

Of the 115 cardinals eligible to vote in the conclave, Ratzinger was one of only two whom John Paul II had not appointed himself. The two men had, however, formed a close bond when both were cardinals. As Ratzinger described it himself, "As soon as he became pope he had made up his mind to call me to Rome as Prefect of the Congregation for the Doctrine of the Faith [CDF]. He had placed a great, very cordial, and profound trust in me. As the guarantee, so to speak, that we would travel the right course in the faith." Having occupied this role since 1981, Ratzinger was John Paul's doctrinal watchdog—the press referred to him as "God's Rottweiler," his fellow clerics as the "Panzer Kardinal"—and one of the most powerful men in the Vatican. The two men shared and exercised hardline conservative beliefs, tempered by a social conscience for the poor and disadvantaged.

The official role of the CDF, founded in 1542 and perhaps better known by its original name, the Sacred Roman and Universal
Inquisition, was "to promote and defend the doctrine of the faith
and its traditions in all of the Catholic world." The world had
changed somewhat since the sixteenth-century days of heresy and
the Inquisition. The most recent Vatican Council meeting, from
1962–65 (more commonly known as Vatican II), had managed to
"[drag] the Catholic Church, part of it kicking and screaming, out
of the early nineteenth into the mid-twentieth century . . . [and
opened] the Church to the contemporary world . . . to enter into a
serious but critical dialogue with it." It soon became apparent to
many that the conclusions of the council had in fact been left wide
open to opposing interpretations. Consequently, when John Paul II
became pope, many of those who had assumed him to be a liberal
and progressive candidate were surprised at the speed with which
he reinterpreted Vatican II in a much more conservative light.

From within his department at the CDF, Ratzinger was considered to have had the last word on the enforcement of John Paul's
theological interpretation of Vatican II, as well as on disciplinary
matters within the church—including, most recently, high-profile
sexual abuse cases. Ratzinger aired his concerns for the church's
future in a speech the day before the death of John Paul, stating that
North America and Europe had "developed a culture that excludes
God from the public consciousness, either by denying him altogether
or by judging that his existence cannot be demonstrated, is uncertain and, therefore, somewhat irrelevant."

As well as his pivotal role in the CDF, Ratzinger also held the
office of dean of the College of Cardinals. When it came to the conclave, he once more was to be found presiding over official proceedings. He was ideally placed to do so, for he knew all the cardinals
by name and, moreover, spoke a reported ten languages. Although
he was previously dismissed as a quiet but divisive theologian and
scholar with a weak public presence, his successful handling of
events prior to and following the death of John Paul culminated in
a huge shift of opinion in his favor.

It was not just his commanding performance of John Paul's funeral homily that had turned the heads of many cardinals. On Good

Friday, March 25, 2005, Ratzinger had spoken in place of the ailing pope during the traditional Way of the Cross procession. When he came to the Stations of the Cross, colleagues listened in disbelief as he said, "How much filth there is in the Church, and even among those who, in the priesthood, ought to belong entirely to him." And praying to God, he said, "Lord, your church often seems like a boat about to sink, a boat taking on water on every side."

It is hard to read these words and not feel that this was a thinly veiled attack on all those involved in the sexual abuse crisis that was poisoning the reputation of the Catholic Church. What was this performance if not that of a man showing he was capable of challenging the rot within the church head-on and publicly? But did he intend to do so as another pontiff's right-hand man, or was Ratzinger in fact proposing *himself* for consideration with this startling condemnation of church failings?

The cardinal's past—to those who had studied it—would indicate otherwise. He had resisted elevation to high office on numerous occasions, preferring instead to devote himself to a quiet life of theological writing. But only the days that followed would reveal if Ratzinger did want to be pope. If he did, his complete lack of pastoral experience, and his own advancing age and poor health—he had suffered a stroke in 1991—might lead some cardinals to wonder if he was too weak and ill equipped for the task.

Cardinal Francis Arinze of Nigeria (72)
A convert to Christianity at age nine, Arinze was born into the Ibo tribe in Nigeria and became a rising star among African Catholics when he was consecrated a bishop at just thirty-three years old. The idea of a pope from a developing country would be greeted with a rapturous response from neighboring regions, but Arinze's outspoken, ultraconservative views weighed against any real chances.

Cardinal Camillo Ruini, Vicar of Rome (73)
Described as getting "high marks for administration but low marks for charisma," Ruini was another of John Paul's close allies and a familiar face in Italian media. Though he was regarded as "the most

powerful Italian cardinal," his quadruple bypass surgery in 2000 and outspoken criticisms of Italian government policies on, among other things, euthanasia, same-sex marriage, and artificial insemination, meant opinions of him were strongly divided.

THE REFORMERS

The opposing group of cardinals were mostly from pluralist societies in which traditional church teachings on such controversial issues as divorce, abortion, and homosexuality were continually up for debate among faithful and clergy alike. These men, while having been appointed by John Paul, were only now as cardinals free to express dissenting opinions on orthodox doctrine and a centralized church without fear of their career prospects being curtailed. They acknowledged and respected John Paul's many diplomatic achievements in global peace conflicts and his passion for greater social equality, but many of these cardinals "had real problems with his moral, doctrinal, reproductive and intra-mural church stances."

Cardinal Carlo Maria Martini of Italy (78)

Unlike the majority of his Italian colleagues, Cardinal Martini was an outspoken, left-of-center cardinal who had both pastoral and administrative experience. A highly respected and thoughtful Jesuit theologian, he was a surprising appointment for the notably conservative John Paul and was described by John Allen Jr. as being "the great white hope of Catholicism's liberal wing for more than two decades."

However, his chances of becoming pope had faded somewhat in recent years. No Jesuit has ever sat in the Chair of St. Peter. And there was another stumbling block: he, like John Paul before him, had been diagnosed with Parkinson's and, at seventy-eight, was one of the oldest men in contention. In 2002, John Paul had granted Martini's request to resign from his position as archbishop of Milan, and he relocated to Jerusalem to live out his retirement in scholarly peace—hardly the actions of a man who wished to take on the greatest responsibility of his life.

Cardinal Claudio Hummes of São Paulo (71)

Known for his exemplary skills as a pastor and for championing marginalized peoples, the archbishop of São Paulo "assumed mythical status in his battles with the generals of the Brazilian dictatorship" as a young bishop in the late 1970s and early 1980s. His radicalism had softened somewhat with age, and he had been invited to preach to John Paul and senior clergy at the Vatican in 2002, which many felt indicated strong approval from the late pope. As a leading voice in favor of reform, he believed that the church was too concerned with the West and should open itself up to place developing nations on an even footing. As 42 percent of the world's Catholics lived in Latin America, the election of Claudio Hummes would no doubt receive a rapturous response.

THE MODERATES

Falling somewhere in between the conservatives and the reformers, the moderates were not bound by a united vision for the future of the church, as the opposing two camps were, and as a consequence were perceived as more malleable by either side, should one of them be elected pope. Conversely, however, they had the potential to disrupt any clear conservative or progressive candidate's chances, if a losing side decided to put votes behind a moderate to try to force a stalemate.

Cardinal Dionigi Tettamanzi of Milan (71)

Aptly described as being "roly-poly, affable," and "short, stout, and quick to smile," Cardinal Tettamanzi was another socially conscious conservative who had been very close to John Paul. With a strong background in theology, he worked with the late pope on his seminal encyclical *Evangelium Vitae* (The Gospel of Life), which reaffirmed the Catholic Church's views on the sanctity of life with respect to abortion, euthanasia, birth control, and the death penalty, but according to leading Vatican commentator Sandro Magister, "now that these topics have become more crucial than ever in the United States, Europe and Italy, both inside and outside the Church, a real 'epochal question' in Ratzinger and Ruini's judgement, he doesn't talk about them anymore." Tettamanzi was a vocal campaigner for the rights of underprivileged populations. He stood in support of the antiglobalization protests at the G-8 summit protests in Genoa in 2001 and was quoted as saying, "A single African child sick with AIDS counts more than the entire universe."

All this had made him one of the odds-on favorites in the always-a-bit-myopic Italian media, but Tettamanzi did not speak English, and a poor grasp of languages would create a significant barrier for any potential new pope.

Cardinal Jorge Mario Bergoglio of Buenos Aires (68)

Another Jesuit, Cardinal Jorge Bergoglio was known as the "slum bishop" on account of his compassionate work with the poor in his native Argentina, but his politics were more conservative-liberal than liberal-conservative—he was a strong supporter of traditionalist doctrine and had opposed legal reforms on same-sex marriage, gay adoptions, and abortion. At sixty-eight, he was the youngest contender; he also stood out in that he had been made a cardinal only four years earlier, in 2001.

Bergoglio had a reputation for being a compassionate, humble, and spiritual man who rejected the luxurious trappings available to one in his position and instead chose to live alongside his parishioners in a modest apartment and to ride the buses and subways of Buenos Aires rather than using a chauffeur-driven limousine. He had first come to prominence in 1998, when he made headlines by washing and kissing the feet of HIV/AIDS sufferers at a hospital in Buenos Aires. He had also made an impression within the church when, in October 2001, John Paul II selected him as relator at the Synod of Bishops, responsible for summarizing information to the conference, replacing Archbishop of New York Edward Egan, who had stayed in the city following the terrorist attacks of September 11, 2001.

At the time of the conclave, Latin America's Catholics made up 40 percent of the church's 1.1 billion followers; it was a long shot, but the prospect of a pope from one of the developing countries was not to be dismissed easily. As a cardinal (from a developing country) is quoted in John Allen's book *The Rise of Benedict*

XVI, "If we elect a pope from Honduras or Nigeria, there would be a very dynamic and excited local church behind him, as there was with John Paul II and Poland. If we elect someone from Belgium or Holland, can you imagine the Belgians or the Dutch getting excited? He simply wouldn't have the same base of support."

Bergoglio had garnered significant high-ranking support among those who thought him capable of lowering the Vatican's fortress-like walls and opening the church up to the wider world, while at the same time maintaining an "unwavering commitment to rather traditional doctrinal views." But there were concerns as to whether he would even accept the pontificate if he won the election on account of his preference toward a humble lifestyle and the fact that Jesuits are oath-bound not to seek power.

Cardinal Angelo Sodano, Vatican Secretary of State (77)

The fourth and final Italian in contention, Cardinal Sodano had occupied many senior roles within the church before settling into his post as Vatican secretary of state in 1991. He accompanied John Paul on numerous diplomatic missions abroad, and controversially struck up a friendship with Chilean dictator Augusto Pinochet, even campaigning for his release from detention in the United Kingdom in 1999. He maintained strong ties with Latin America and was a respected theologian, but his old age and rumored poor health meant he, too, was an unlikely successor to John Paul.

THE CONCLAVE APPROACHES

During a *conclave* ("with a key"), cardinals are literally locked inside the Sistine Chapel, with Vatican Swiss Guards keeping watch outside the doors, until they come to a successful agreement on who should be the next pope. John Paul had left strict instructions about maintaining the secrecy of the gathering, so Wi-Fi is blocked throughout the Holy City for the duration of proceedings, the Sistine Chapel is closed to tourists and swept for bugging devices, and sophisticated jamming devices are fitted throughout the Apostolic Palace to prevent information from leaking out. Inside the chapel, wooden walkways are specially laid to preserve the ancient floor, and long trestle tables with deep crimson fringing are brought in to seat the cardinal electors, adding even more color to a room already adorned with five-hundred-year-old frescos on its walls and ceiling.

One could easily be forgiven for assuming that, during the election of a pope, those locked inside the chapel debate the various merits of candidates and the importance of issues facing the church, just as democracies do throughout the world. Not so. A conclave is a quiet period of solemn prayer and reflection during which cardinals look for guidance from the Holy Spirit in their election of a new pope. Cardinal Jorge Bergoglio later described "a climate of intense recollection—almost mystical—that was present at those sessions. We were all conscious of being nothing but instruments, to serve divine providence in electing a proper successor for John Paul II."

Before the beginning of the conclave, during *sede vacante* (the period when the seat of St. Peter is vacant), all cardinals met in a general congregation presided over by Cardinal Ratzinger, as dean, and in smaller groups of just four cardinals, known as particular congregations. In these meetings, they were required to act on any pressing Vatican business that could not wait until a new pope was in place, as well as review John Paul's fourteen-thousand-word apostolic directive *Universi Dominici Gregis* (The Shepherd of the Lord's Whole Flock), in which he explained updated rules for how the conclave was to be conducted, revising the previous set of changes decreed by Pope Paul VI in 1975. Cardinal Ratzinger insisted that it be read aloud, line by line.

As he had at the funeral, Ratzinger surprised his colleagues with a glittering display of authority, fairness, and diplomacy. Not only did he know every cardinal by name—a feat John Paul never quite managed—but his facility with languages meant he could address and be understood by the many cardinals who did not speak Italian, let alone Latin. But it was not just his display of memory and linguistic flair that was impressive; the cardinals felt that he was genuinely concerned with what they had to say. At several times during proceedings he is said to have "intervened to ask those who had not yet spoken to do so"; and "when he had to summarize a discussion, he always seemed fair to the various points of view that had been expressed." Some even came away from these discussions feeling he had outperformed the late, great pontiff himself, saying that "Ratzinger had heard them in a way that John Paul II did not always manage."

TENSIONS AND SMEAR TACTICS

It is fair to suggest that the conduct of the general congregation was largely collegial and that cardinals were able to put their differences aside for the greater good of the church. But arguments did, on occasion, get heated and, even worse, smear stories began to appear in the media about each of the men considered *papabile,* despite the press blackout.

The most frequent bad press focused on candidates' health, and stories of illness ranging from diabetes to depression surfaced in the papers and on TV news channels. The most aggressive form of sabotage, however, emerged three days before the conclave was scheduled to begin, when a deeply compromising emailed dossier "dropped anonymously into the inbox of senior cardinals as they gathered in Rome." The email contained details of a complaint filed by Argentinian human rights lawyer Marcelo Parrilli, accusing Cardinal Jorge Bergoglio of "complicity in the kidnapping of two Jesuit priests, whose work with the poor in a Buenos Aires shanty town was considered by Argentina's military death squads in 1976 to be subversive." Bergoglio had dismissed the priests a week prior to their disappearance, and Parrilli claimed that this dismissal had contributed to their being tortured and kept hooded and shackled during their five-month-long detention.

There was little time in which to refute these claims on any grand scale, let alone establish who had sent the email—we shall return to this chapter of Bergoglio's life later—but what was immediately clear was that his candidacy was considered to be a significant threat among certain factions of the church, and there were some prepared to take desperate measures to discredit him. Supporters of Bergoglio strenuously denied the accusations in hushed conversations down the Vatican's marble corridors and over dinners hosted by anti-Ratzinger "conclave power brokers," one of whom wryly remarked,

"Ever since the Last Supper, the church has decided its most important affairs at the dinner table." But as the congregations drew to a close and the conclave began, it was uncertain whether the campaign against Bergoglio had been successful.

"EXTRA OMNES!"

And so it was time.

At exactly 4:30 P.M. on Monday, April 18, the 115 cardinals, resplendent in their traditional crimson "choir dress," with accompanying wide white-lace sleeves, took their final steps of the procession from the Hall of Blessings—traditionally cardinals start the procession in the Cappella Paolina, but it was undergoing extensive renovations between 2002 and 2009—into the Sistine Chapel, singing the ninth-century "Litany of the Saints" as they walked. For the first time in history, this dazzling spectacle was broadcast live on television, and Catholics around the world were given a glimpse of ancient ritual as the cardinals took their assigned seats, arranged in order of seniority, and then an oath of secrecy, first collectively and then individually.

Once the last cardinal had placed his hand on the Book of the Gospels and stated that he did "promise, pledge, and swear, so help me God and these Holy Gospels which I now touch with my hand," transmissions were ceased and at 5:24 P.M. Archbishop Piero Marini, papal master of liturgical ceremonies, declared "Extra omnes!"— Everyone out! When all but the cardinal electors had departed, the Swiss Guards, on duty during the entire process, locked the doors of the Sistine Chapel from the outside, and the voting began.

THE FIRST BALLOT

Tradition states that no one but cardinal electors are permitted inside when voting is taking place. Consequently, the cardinals have to roll up those beautiful sleeves and take turns at pivotal jobs.

Nine names were drawn each morning by lot and assigned equally to the following roles:

Scrutineers These three men sit center stage at a table in front of the altar, beneath Michelangelo's imposing fresco of the Last Judgment, and count the ballots.

Infirmarii Though none was required in the 2005 conclave, three men are still assigned to collect the ballots of any cardinal electors too ill to make it to the Sistine Chapel.

Revisers Another three cardinals are required to double-check the work of the scrutineers to ensure that the tallies of names and ballots are correct. If they are, the revisers return the ballots to the scrutineers, who read each name aloud before piercing the word *Eligo* on each ballot with a needle, then preserving the papers for burning in the chapel's special stove once the count is complete.

During each round, cardinal electors were presented with a rectangular ballot paper with the words *Eligo in Summum Pontificem* (I elect as Supreme Pontiff), and required, per John Paul's directive, to write, somewhat comically, "as far as possible in handwriting that cannot be identified as his," the name of the man he would like to be pope (naturally excluding themselves). After folding the paper in half, the cardinals approached the altar, knelt to recite a prayer, and then took another oath, before placing their ballot on a gold paten, or plate, for all to see, then tipping it into a specially designed urn.

No pope has ever been elected after the first round of voting, and tallies are generally very disparate, after which numbers begin to align behind leading candidates until the final candidate is chosen. In his book *The Rule of Benedict,* David Gibson notes that it is customary for cardinals during the first ballot to "vote for a friend or to honor someone who will never be pope but who can at least know that they received a vote in a conclave"; it is even joked that they "vote for who they want on the first ballot, then they let the Holy Spirit guide them." In the eight conclaves held during the twentieth century, the greatest number of ballots held in any one papal election was fourteen (Pope Pius XI, 1922) and the fewest was three

(Pope Pius XII, 1939); the average is just under eight ballots per conclave, over an average of 3.5 days.

The number of cardinal electors had risen significantly from just sixty-four in the 1903 conclave to 111 in 1978, when John Paul II was elected. With the record-breaking 115 cardinals in 2005, the process of voting took a significant amount of time, but shortly after 8 P.M. on April 18, the forty-thousand-strong crowd gathered in St. Peter's Square was momentarily confused when a weak plume of what looked to be whitish-gray smoke began to emerge from the chimney above the Sistine Chapel. The unfortunate coincidence of the first ballot being burned at the same time as the hourly chiming of the bells of St. Peter's Basilica caused many to erupt into cheers and applause. However, what would truly have been a miracle—a pope elected on the first ballot—was quickly dispelled by the sight of a thicker trail of dark gray-black smoke.

The Vatican had been using a white smoke signal to indicate the election of a new pontiff only since 1914, but its reliable unreliability had become something of a running joke. Countless hours and a significant amount of money had recently been spent upgrading the system . . . only for it to fail again on the first try.

As many had expected, this conclave did not end on the first day. What was unexpected, however, was that in September 2005 an anonymous cardinal broke the oaths of secrecy he had sworn to God on the altar of the Sistine Chapel and published an account of the voting tally throughout the conclave in the Italian foreign affairs magazine *Limes*.

Results of the first ballot of the papal conclave, 2005

Cardinal Joseph Ratzinger	Germany	47 votes
Cardinal Jorge Mario Bergoglio	Argentina	10 votes
Cardinal Carlo Maria Martini	Italy	9 votes
Cardinal Camillo Ruini	Italy	6 votes
Cardinal Angelo Sodano	Italy	4 votes
Oscar Rodríguez Maradiaga	Honduras	3 votes
Dionigi Tettamanzi	Italy	2 votes
Other candidates		34 votes

Thanks to this anonymous cardinal's decision to break his oath, we now know that in line with the initial predictions of many going into the conclave, Ratzinger was way out in front of all the other candidates but had not yet won the race. To secure the papacy, a cardinal is required to obtain seventy-seven votes (equivalent to two-thirds of the total), so he still required a hefty thirty minds to swing in his favor.

Among Ratzinger's hotly tipped rivals, Tettamanzi performed the poorest, managing just two votes; and Martini's meager nine felt more like a token of respect—recalling Gibson's remarks regarding the first round of votes—for all his years of being *papabile*, rather than any serious move to elect a retired man with Parkinson's.

The real surprise of the first ballot was Jorge Bergoglio's count of ten. He was not considered by the secret diarist to be "a true candidate of [the] 'left,'" but in the absence of Martini, he became the one to whom liberal, anti-Ratzinger votes would now fall. Still, he needed a significant number to swing behind him if he was to catch the Panzer Kardinal, who would likely benefit from the votes of John Paul allies Ruini and Sodano in the next round.

At the end of the first day, the cardinals made their way out of the Sistine Chapel and were bundled into waiting minibuses that whisked them back to their luxury lodgings—which the Vatican had spent a modest twenty million dollars on—for dinner, deliberations, and debate, in discreet but deliberate contravention of the rules, ahead of the next day's voting. Cut off from the outside world, conversations ran long into the night and the air was thick with speculation about Bergoglio as a potential successor to John Paul.

Our secret Italian diarist suspected that "the realistic objective of the minority group that wants to support Bergoglio is to create a deadlock, which leads to the withdrawal of the Ratzinger nomination." He also was not even sure if the Argentinian would accept the papacy, having watched him place his vote beneath the looming fresco of Christ: "He had his gaze fixed on the image of Jesus, judging souls at the end of time. His face, suffering, as if pleading: 'God, please don't do this to me.'"

THE SECOND AND THIRD BALLOTS

On the morning of Tuesday, April 19, the cardinals were woken at 6:30, attended mass at 7:30, and began the second round of voting at 9:30. When the results came in, it was clear that the previous evening's discussions had been persuasive, and firm alliances were now being made.

Results of the second ballot of the papal conclave, 2005

Cardinal Joseph Ratzinger	Germany	65 votes	+ 18
Cardinal Jorge Mario Bergoglio	Argentina	35 votes	+ 25
Cardinal Angelo Sodano	Italy	4 votes	+ 0
Dionigi Tettamanzi	Italy	2 votes	+ 0
Other candidates		9 votes	− 25

Cardinal Ratzinger was still in the lead, having gained eighteen votes—six from Ruini and twelve from the other unnamed candidates—but he remained twelve votes shy of the total required to win. Sodano's four supporters were not yet ready to concede, and neither were Tettamanzi's two voters. The biggest gain of all came to Bergoglio, who received a staggering twenty-five more votes—nine from Martini, three from Maradiaga, and thirteen from new supporters—taking his total to thirty-five.

Despite this impressive leap, Ratzinger's lead was strong enough for it now to be impossible for another cardinal to win unless a large number of voters deserted him. But the anonymous cardinal's prediction about Ratzinger's opponents wishing to create a deadlock was just four votes off fruition if Bergoglio were to receive the necessary one-third plus a vote total of thirty-nine in the next round. As titillating as this prospect might be, it was highly unlikely that the cardinals would let it get that far, for fear of damaging the reputation of the church with a hung conclave.

So as not to lose momentum, it was customary to proceed immediately to another ballot before announcing the results, so the cardinals voted a third time, at 11 A.M. Ambiguously gray smoke rose from the chimney just before noon, but no bells chimed, so the crowds understood there was still no pope.

Results of the third ballot of the papal conclave, 2005

Cardinal Joseph Ratzinger	Germany	72 votes	+7
Cardinal Jorge Mario Bergoglio	Argentina	40 votes	+5
Other candidates		3 votes	−7

The results of the third ballot showed that the election was now a two-horse race. Ratzinger's increase of seven votes meant he needed only five more to secure the Chair of St. Peter, but with just three open voters remaining and Bergoglio's increase of five, it was impossible for him to do so unless some of the Argentine's supporters changed allegiance to him.

The break for lunch couldn't have come at a more decisive moment. While the world waited, the cardinals were bused back to their hotel to quietly thrash out the results at their favorite boardroom: the dinner table. Ratzinger was described as being "the picture of calm," while those around him scrabbled for stray votes to seal the deal. According to the diarist, Cardinal Martini had begun speculating that if the deadlock continued, then a change of candidates would be inevitable the following day and the process would have to start afresh. It was a prospect that few but Martini would relish.

THE FOURTH BALLOT

The time for conversations and campaigning over, the cardinals returned to the Sistine Chapel. When the afternoon's voting began, the newspapers were speculating that Ratzinger was struggling to reach a convincing majority. To the electors voting inside the chapel, however, the feeling was that the race had finally been won.

At 5:30 P.M., almost twenty-four-hours exactly since the conclave began—making it one of the fastest elections in history—the votes were tallied and read aloud. Although most cardinals, including Ratzinger himself, had been keeping score themselves, Cardinal Cormac Murphy-O'Connor recalled that when the elusive seventy-seventh vote was reached, "there was sort of a gasp all around, and then everyone clapped."

Tears of joy flowed freely among Ratzinger's supporters.

And the happiest guy in the room? Cardinal Jorge Mario Bergoglio.

Over the following days, while Benedict was settling into his new role, the cardinals who were resident outside the city began to depart Rome for their respective dioceses. Many were leaving with feelings of surprise that the conclave had ended so quickly, and many were leaving with a huge sense of relief that it had, none more so than Cardinal Bergoglio. He could not wait to return home from the unexpected chaos of the conclave to his familiar streets of Buenos Aires.

At sixty-eight, Bergoglio would be eligible for retirement in just over six years, and he had even decided where he would like to spend his final days: back at the humble priests' house he had lived in for five years when he was vicar general of the parish of Flores in Buenos Aires between 1993 and 1998. All he needed was a simple room, preferably on the bottom floor, as he didn't "want to be above anybody else."

2

FRANCIS

After the election of Pope Benedict XVI in April 2005, a biography of Cardinal Bergoglio would have been of mild interest to the world's conclave watchers. Who was this mysterious Argentinian who had almost beaten the favorite to the title of pope? But there was nothing. Diligent Catholics might have found a solitary copy of *Meditations for the Religious* (1982), *Reflections of Hope* (1992), or *Putting the Motherland on One's Shoulders* (2003) in a very well-stocked library, but these books were *by* the man, not about him. Bergoglio had never worked in Rome, so the usual Vatican gossip channels proved fruitless; nor did he come from a country with a strong voice in global Catholic debate. So who was he?

Born in the central district of Flores, Buenos Aires, on December 17, 1936, Jorge Mario Bergoglio was the eldest of the five children of Regina María Sívori (1911–1981) and Mario José Bergoglio (1908–1959). Regina was the daughter of immigrants from Genoa-Piedmont, and Mario had arrived in Argentina from Piedmont with his parents in 1929. They met at mass in 1934 and married the following year. Jorge later recalled, "My strongest childhood memory is that life shared between my parents' house and my grandparents' house. The first part of my childhood, from the age of one, I spent with my grandmother." This was Mario's mother, Nonna Rosa. Biographer Austen Ivereigh, who interviewed Francis at length following his election as pope, described her as "the single greatest childhood influence" and "a formidable woman of deep faith and political skill, with whom he spent most of his first five years."

Rosa and her husband, Giovanni, having decided to leave their home in an impoverished Italy controlled by the totalitarian government of Benito Mussolini, had originally bought tickets for the family to sail to Argentina aboard the illustrious *Principessa Mafalda* in 1927. But they were not the only family in the region fearful of the rise of fascism and planning their escape. So great was the number of hopeful émigrés that the Piedmont housing market crashed and prices plummeted, preventing the couple from selling off properties and forcing them to sit tight and wait for the situation to recover. Little did they know how lucky they were. On October 11, 1927, the once-great vessel set sail from Genoa for Buenos Aires. After nine years of ocean crossings, the crumbling ship began to sink off the coast of Brazil. It was chaos. Crew were alleged to have disembarked first in some of the only seaworthy lifeboats, leaving terrified passengers to scramble for what was left as rescue vessels watched on, fearful the ship might explode. A total of 1,252 passengers were saved, but 314 perished in the shark-infested waters.

Grateful for their miracle escape, Giovanni and Rosa eventually managed to sell their properties and arrived in Argentina fourteen months later. According to Paul Vallely's biography *Pope Francis: Untying the Knots,* "family legend has it [Rosa] came down the gangplank of the steamship *Giulio Cesare* on a sweltering morning wearing a full-length fox fur, not because she had failed to appreciate that she would be arriving in the southern hemisphere where January would be high summer, but because sewn into its lining was the entire proceeds of the sale of the family's home and café back in Piedmont." This shrewd move enabled Rosa and Giovanni to support themselves during the subsequent economic crash of 1929 and a military coup that put an end to seventy years of civilian constitutional government in 1930.

By the time Jorge was born, life in Buenos Aires was tough for both his parents and grandparents, but his grandmother Rosa's stoic nature brought richness amid the poverty. She taught him how to pray; told him stories about Jesus, the Virgin Mary, and the saints;

and imbued in him a religious tolerance. His parents had developed a more puritanical outlook. Bergoglio later recalled, "If someone close to the family divorced or separated, they could not enter your house, and they believed all Protestants were going to hell." Rosa, on the other hand, taught him "the wisdom of true religion," whereby non-Catholics doing good deeds were still loved by God. She had had firsthand experience of the toxicity of intolerance back in Italy during the 1920s and had been a vocal campaigner for Catholic Action, a European movement that fought against anticlericalism in the nineteenth and early twentieth centuries. Rosa regularly stood on soapboxes in the streets denouncing Mussolini—who was known as *mangiaprete,* or "priest-eater," in his youth—and his fascist government's harassment and curtailment of the Catholic Church.

Rosa believed strongly in education and had encouraged her son Mario to study for a degree in accountancy back in Italy. His qualifications were not recognized in Argentina, however, and he was able to secure only poorly paid work as a bookkeeper in a factory. So while Regina was tending to her youngest children and Mario was out at work, young Jorge began his own education. During the days he spent with his grandmother, he learned Italian—Rosa and Giovanni still conversed mostly in a Piedmontese dialect, while their son and daughter-in-law spoke Spanish at home—and was introduced to poetry and literature. Bergoglio later said that his grandparents "loved all of my siblings, but I had the privilege of understanding the language of their memories," and this widened his perspective to include a world outside of his own.

The Bergoglios worked hard to provide a stable and loving home for their five children, and Mario frequently took on multiple jobs to keep their heads above water. Despite their hardships, the children's memories from this time were happy ones. María Elena, Jorge's younger sister, felt they "were poor with dignity" and described her father as "always a joyful man. . . . He never got angry. And he never hit us. . . . He was so in love with Mama, and he always brought her presents." The family was also bound together by faith, and when Mario returned from work each night, he would lead them in prayer around the table. Weekends consisted of Saturday mornings at home playing cards until, at two o'clock sharp, they would gather around the phonograph and listen to their parents' beloved Italian operas; Sundays the family went to mass. After the birth of her fifth and final child, Regina was partially paralyzed for several years, but Bergoglio recalled that even then, "when we got home from school during that time, she would be sitting down peeling potatoes, with all of the ingredients ready. She told us how we should mix them together and cook them, for we had no idea what we were doing: 'Now put this in the pot, put that in the pan . . .' she would tell us. This is how we learned to cook."

Outside of the home, Jorge enjoyed football with his neighborhood friends and inherited his father's devotion to their local team, San Lorenzo, which he has carried with him to this day. In true Argentinian style, he also was fond of the tango and was said to dance it very well. Most friends from this time, however, remember him as a particularly studious boy, "always with his nose in a text." The young Bergoglio did well at primary school and seems not to have been affected by turbulent politics within Argentina and the global disasters of the Second World War. As it had during the first war, the country remained neutral and resisted American pressure to join the Allied nations but still was perceived to have strong sympathies with the Axis powers, due in part to its large German immigrant population. When the government began to look as if it might bow under the pressure of international isolation from Allied nations, a breakaway faction of the military—including the fiery nationalist Colonel Juan Domingo Perón—stepped in to remove the president.

By 1945, Perón, alongside his soon-to-be second wife, the twenty-six-year-old actress and radio presenter Eva "Evita" Duarte, was serving as vice president, secretary of war, and, perhaps most crucially, minister of labor in that government. His support for labor unions and the introduction of Argentina's first system of national insurance made him hugely popular among the marginalized poor. So popular, in fact, that after the war ended, he was arrested by colleagues who had grown fearful of the powerful support he commanded. Mass protests in the streets, however, forced them to release him. The people had spoken. Five months later, on February 24, 1946, he was elected president.

In 1949, with Regina still paralyzed, and while Rosa was caring for the two youngest Bergoglio children, Alberto and María Elena, it was decided that twelve-year-old Jorge and his other two younger siblings, Marta and Oscar, should be sent to boarding school for a year to alleviate the pressure on their mother. Don Enrico Pozzoli, the family's priest, found the boys, Jorge and Oscar, places at a Salesian-run school called Wilfrid Barón de los Santos Ángeles. The Salesians of Don Bosco were founded in 1859 by Saint John Bosco with the simple mission to "be a friend to young people who were poor, abandoned or at risk, and in doing so be a friend to Christ." In a letter dated October 20, 1990, Father Bergoglio detailed how the year spent at the school had shaped him:

> I learned to study in the school. The hours of study, in silence, created a habit of concentration, of a quite strong control of dispersion. . . . Sport was an essential aspect of life. One played well and a lot. . . . In study, as in sport, the dimension of competition had certain importance: we were taught to compete well and to compete as Christians. . . . A dimension that grew a lot in the subsequent years to the one spent in the school was my capacity to feel good: and I realized that the base was set the year of boarding school. . . . They educated my sentiment there. . . . I am not referring to "sentimentalism" but to "sentiment" as a value of the heart. Not to be afraid and to say to oneself what one is feeling.
>
> All these things configured a Catholic culture. They prepared me well for secondary school and for life. Never (in so far as I remember) was a truth negotiated. The most typical case was that of sin. The sense of sin is part of the Catholic culture . . . and what I brought home in that sense was reinforced, took shape. One could then play the rebel, the atheist . . . but imprinted deep down was the sense of sin: a truth that could not be thrown out, to make everything easier.

When this formative year came to an end, Jorge returned home for the summer before he enrolled in secondary school at the Escuala Nacional de Educación Técnica, with a view to gaining a diploma as a chemical technician. Happily reunited with his old friends from the neighborhood, it soon became apparent that one relationship in particular had begun to develop in a new and different way.

In true humble style, Jorge Mario Bergoglio fell in love with the girl next door. Well, four doors down, and it was as innocent a childhood romance as one could have asked for from a man who would many years later become pope. Amalia Damonte and Jorge Bergoglio, both the children of Piedmontese immigrants, had grown up together, and that summer, she later recalled, they "mostly played on the sidewalks or in the parks in the area" and before long "started to spend all our afternoons together." Jorge, she remembered, "always liked to joke" but was definitely a "gentleman." But there was a complication. That his impactful school year with the Salesians seems to have coincided with his first inklings that he might be considering joining the priesthood was revealed in a somewhat unconventional way. He wrote Amalia a letter in which he drew a white house with a red roof and explained that it was the house he would buy her when they were married. However, so as not to look too confident, and to let her know he had options, he clarified that "if you don't marry me, I'm going to become a priest."

Unfortunately, when Amalia's horrified parents discovered the letter, her father beat her because she "had dared to write a note to a boy." The Damontes were traditional Catholics, with what their daughter described as "good principles" that held that the children "were still too young for love." Amalia described later how she "never saw him after that—my parents kept me away from him and did everything possible to separate us."

And with that, the romance was over. And of course, Jorge Bergoglio did go on to become a priest.

When the summer was drawing to an end, Jorge began preparing for life at his new secondary school, albeit with a slightly broken heart. After his brush with love, he stepped firmly toward a life filled with greater responsibility. Mario informed his son that because the school day lasted from 2 P.M. until 8 P.M., the time had come for him to begin working: he had secured Jorge a position as a cleaner at the hosiery factory where he worked, from 7 A.M. until 1 P.M. Jorge dutifully agreed and put his priestly ambitions back on the shelf for the time being. Over the next two years he cleaned the factory every day before school; this was followed by a year helping with administrative tasks, then taking a job in a food chemistry laboratory.

In a 2010 biography entitled *El Jesuita,* Bergoglio told interviewers, "I'm so grateful to my father for making me work. The work I did was one of the best things I've done in my life. In particular, in the laboratory I got to see the good and bad of all human endeavor." It was in this role that he encountered another of the strong female role models who were to have considerable impact on his life and outlook. Her tragic death, several years later, also left a deep mark on him.

Described as "an extraordinary boss," thirty-two-year-old Esther Ballestrino de Careaga was an exceptionally bright young woman. She was born in Uruguay and spent her youth in Paraguay. After achieving a doctorate in biochemistry, she had become a founding member of Paraguay's first feminist movement, but her outspoken communist sympathies became too dangerous under the ruling military junta, and she felt forced to leave the country for the safety of Argentina in 1947.

At the laboratory, she educated Jorge in the diligence, patience, and thoroughness required in scientific experimentation, and taught him "the seriousness of hard work," as he described it, but with good humor and only a bit of gentle chiding.

Bergoglio's grief at Ballestrino's death was connected to a great many aspects of his life. She had not only taught him the foundations of good practice and science but had also educated him in politics outside of religion. Following the example set for him by the other strong woman in his life, Nonna Rosa, he accepted her views without judgment.

During the years they spent working together in the laboratory, Esther had read him passages from Communist Party texts and given him books to read on his own. He later recalled that learning about communism "through a courageous and honest person was helpful. I realized a few things, an aspect of the social, which I then found in the social doctrine of the Church." The passionate way in which Esther had spoken to him galvanized in him an interest in widening his understanding through further reading, and he described

how "there was a period where I would wait anxiously for the newspaper *La Vanguardia,* which was not allowed to be sold with the
other newspapers and was brought to us by the socialist militants."

Bergoglio's fond and happy memories of this time are marked,
however, by a brutal aftermath. Having fled one military dictatorship in Paraguay, Ballestrino had lived under three further juntas
in the thirty-two years she had been in Argentina, but it was the
fourth coup, of 1976, that would prove to be the most barbaric in
the country's history. Outspoken people began vanishing and were
soon ominously named the "Disappeared." Following the abduction and torture of her pregnant sixteen-year-old daughter and her
son-in-law, Esther joined forces with others and founded a protest
group called Mothers of the Plaza de Mayo. In spite of a ban on
public gatherings of more than three people, the women would
gather on Thursdays outside the presidential palace in the Plaza de
Mayo, Buenos Aires, to demand information about their missing
loved ones. Their pleas fell on deaf ears.

Even after her daughter was released after four months, in September 1977, Esther continued to campaign for the Mothers. Un-
beknown to them, however, the group had been infiltrated by
twenty-five-year-old Alfredo Astiz, a naval intelligence captain nicknamed the "Blond Angel of Death" on account of his fair hair and
murderous nature, who was posing as the brother of a missing young
man. On December 8, 1977, the Mothers of the Plaza de Mayo published a newspaper advertisement listing the names of their "disappeared" children, in an attempt to pressure the government for
answers. Their bravery was extraordinary, but such outspokenness
was not tolerated. That night, Astiz arranged for Ballestrino, along
with two other founding members of the Mothers and two Franciscan nuns who had been supporting them, to be abducted and taken
to the Navy School of Mechanics, which the junta was using as a
detention center. It is not known how many days the women were
savagely tortured, but on December 20, 1977, the body of Esther
Ballestrino, along with those of her two friends, washed ashore near
the beach resort of Santa Teresita, just south of Buenos Aires. They
had been bundled onto a so-called "death flight" (hands and feet
bound to ensure they could not fight or swim), drugged, and then

rolled out the rear cargo door of a plane high above the sea. Esther was fifty-nine years old.

It was nearly three decades before forensic anthropologists began exhuming the bodies of those murdered and buried in mass graves during Argentina's bloody military dictatorship, known as the Dirty War (1976–83). When DNA tests confirmed the women's identities in 2005, Esther's family requested permission from the now Cardinal Bergoglio to bury their remains in the gardens of Santa Cruz Church because, as her daughter explained to him, "it was the last place they had been as free people." It had been almost thirty years, but still he shook with emotion upon hearing the fate of his friend and mentor.

Bergoglio had last seen Esther one evening shortly before she disappeared. In an interview with Argentinian journalist Uki Goni, her daughter Ana María recounted how her mother had telephoned her old friend to ask him come to their house and administer the last rites to a dying relative. This was a strange request, given that the family was not religious. Upon arrival, Bergoglio learned that no one was dying but that the family was fearful that their phones were being bugged and the house would soon be raided. Their bookshelves were full of works on philosophy and Marxism that were tantamount to a death sentence should they be discovered, so they asked Father Bergoglio if he would smuggle them out and hold them for safekeeping. The risk of discovery was acute, but he accepted.

"THEY WERE WAITING FOR ME"

Long days of morning work and afternoon lessons meant the years at secondary school passed swiftly for Jorge Bergoglio. The studious young boy had become a fiercely intelligent young man who astonished his fellow students with his impressive aptitude for learning and ability to absorb information instantaneously. Friend and classmate Hugo Morelli recalled how his "truly enviable intelligence was honestly far above ours. He was always many steps ahead of us." But he was never arrogant, said Oscar Crespo, another of his contemporaries: "He supported us all the time if we had problems with any of the subjects; he always offered to assist."

Perhaps with the benefit of hindsight, what stood out most was Bergoglio's deep and unshakable faith, which developed in intensity during this time. One old friend described him as "militantly religious." In fact, his first moment of awaking to God came quite unexpectedly, while he was on his way to celebrate his school's Day of the Student.

It was September 21, 1953, the first day of spring. The morning was crisp and dark, even at 9 A.M. Jorge, now almost seventeen, was walking down the street past his family church, San José de Flores, when he was overwhelmed by the sudden need to go to confession. When later attempting to describe the moment in Austen Ivereigh's biography of him, Bergoglio still struggled to quantify his feelings but explained:

> I went in, I felt I had to go in—those things you feel inside and you don't know what they are. . . . I saw a priest walking, I didn't know him, he wasn't one of the parish clergy. And he sits down in one of the confessionals. . . . I don't quite know what happened next, I felt like someone grabbed me from inside and took me to the confessional. Obviously I told him my things, I confessed . . . but I don't know what happened.
>
> When I had finished my confession I asked the priest where he was from because I didn't know him and he told me: "I'm from Corrientes and I'm living here close by, in the priests' home. I come to celebrate Mass here now and then." He had cancer—leukemia—and died the following year.
>
> Right there I knew I had to be a priest; I was totally certain. Instead of going out with the others I went back home because I was overwhelmed. Afterward I carried on at school and with everything, but knowing that was where I was headed.

In this moment, Bergoglio later felt he had been caught completely off guard. Yes, he had toyed with the idea, as many devout young Catholics do at some point, but in another interview, with biographers Sergio Rubin and Francesca Ambrogetti, he explained, "It was the surprise, the astonishment of a chance encounter. I realized that they were waiting for me. That is the religious experience: the astonishment of meeting someone who has been waiting for you all along. From that moment on, for me, God is the One who *te primera*—'springs it on you.' You search for Him, but He searches for you first. You want to find Him, but He finds you first."

Although he had found what he hadn't even realized he was looking for, the magnitude of this calling drew him into a long period of what he called "passive solitude." He confided in no one until a year later. With his secondary education almost complete, and as fellow classmates were excitedly planning their careers as doctors and scientists, he finally revealed to Oscar Crespo, who worked alongside him in the laboratory, what he intended to do: "I'm going to finish secondary school with you guys, but I'm not going to be a chemist, I'm going to be a priest. But I'm not going to be a priest in a basilica. I'm going to be a Jesuit, because I'm going to want to go out to the neighborhoods, to the *villas,* to be with people."

The Society of Jesus, or Jesuits, as they are more commonly known, was founded by Ignatius of Loyola in 1534 and is currently the largest male religious order within the Catholic Church. Its members, often thought of as God's soldiers or God's marines, take solemn vows of perpetual poverty, obedience, and chastity, dedicating themselves to the propagation of the faith through preaching and ministering the word of God, and works of charity, especially through teaching the young and uninstructed, and through spiritual direction of souls. While they are renowned for their evangelism and obedience, the Jesuits' commitment to social justice has recently seen them placed firmly in the liberal wing of the Church, and they have sometimes expressed more rebellious views than their history would lead one to expect.

This desire to dedicate himself to social justice, intertwined with his strong political conscience, left Bergoglio with a tremendous amount to contemplate. He was seventeen, and his thoughts, as he explained, "were not focused only on religious matters. I also had political concerns . . . I had a political restlessness." In the latter years of Perón's second term (1951–55), Argentina been suffering from a progressive economic downturn, which Austen Ivereigh argues caused Perón to become "defensive and paranoid," eventually "descending into the authoritarian madness that commonly afflicts populist-nationalist governments in Latin America, whether of the right or left." Relations between the church and state deteriorated, and the Vatican became more forceful in its opposition to Perón by instigating a greater political involvement than ever before.

On November 10, 1954, following the creation of the Christian Democratic Party in July of that year, tensions boiled over when Perón launched a searing attack on the church's interference in labor unions and politics. A number of priests labeled subversive were subsequently arrested, and the government began implementing laws "aimed at restricting the Church and flouting its moral concerns, legalizing divorce and prostitution, banning religious education from schools, and derogating tax exemptions to religious institutions." Catholics were outraged, and Jorge Bergoglio, like Nonna Rosa before him, decided to join Catholic Action and defend the church's position in Argentine society. Following the execution of Perón's ban on religious instruction and iconography in public schools in April 1955, and the expulsion of two priests critical of his government to Rome, tensions boiled over and people took to the streets. On June 11 the traditional Corpus Christi procession became a defiant show of protest by over a quarter of a million people, including Bergoglio, silently walking behind papal and Argentine flags.

The Vatican excommunicated Perón on June 16, and government loyalists held protests in Plaza de Mayo to denounce the alleged burning of the national flag during the Corpus Christi procession five days earlier. While church and state were fighting it out publicly on the streets and in official decrees, the military launched an abortive coup attempt in which bombing raids on the square killed 364 civilians and wounded more than eight hundred. Perón survived, and his supporters retaliated by burning sixteen churches across the city. The military retreated to lick its wounds before regrouping under the leadership of the devoutly Catholic general Eduardo Lonardi, who successfully deposed Perón three months later in the Revolución Libertadora (Liberating Revolution). In the two months that followed, Perón and his supporters were forced into exile, and order was restored.

Swept up in the political turmoil of the period, Bergoglio put his ambitions of priesthood on hold, and he expressed an interest in pursuing a career in medicine, much to the delight of his parents. Regina, in particular, was thrilled at the prospect of having a doctor in the family and, following her son's graduation in 1955, cleaned out the attic to create a quiet place for him to work. Having assumed that the hours Jorge was spending up there were consumed with all things medical, she was shocked to discover textbooks primarily in Latin and all concerning theology.

Confronted with his mother's confusion—"You said you were studying medicine"—Bergoglio simply replied, "I didn't lie to you. I'm studying medicine—but medicine of the soul." But this response did nothing to alleviate her fears, and she insisted he remain at university and complete his degree before deciding on his future path. Bergoglio recalled later, "Since I saw where the conflict was heading, I went to see Fr. Pozzoli and told him everything. He examined my vocation. He told me to pray, to leave everything in the hands of God and gave me the blessing of Our Lady of Perpetual Help." He considered the advice of his priest and decided to raise the subject with his father. "I definitely knew my father was going to understand me better. His mother was a very strong religious role model for him, and he had inherited that religiousness, that fortitude, as well as the great pain that comes from being uprooted," he recalled. Bergoglio's sentiment was sincere, but it was also a tactical move. Well aware that his parents would ask their priest for guidance on the subject—for it was he who had baptized their son nineteen years earlier—he waited to declare his intentions until the day of their twentieth wedding anniversary, when the family had arranged a celebratory breakfast following the commemorative mass that Don Enrico Pozzoli was holding for them. Mario suggested, "Why don't we go ask Fr. Pozzoli?" And Bergoglio remembers, "And I, with my best straight face, said yes. I still remember the scene. It was December 12, 1955."

When the question of his desire to enter the seminary eventually arose over breakfast, Don Enrico handled it sensitively:

> Fr. Pozzoli said that yes, university was good, but things have to be taken up when God wants them taken up . . . and he

began talking about different vocations (without taking sides), and finally spoke about his own. He said how a priest had suggested he become a priest, and how in a very few years he became a subdeacon, then deacon and priest. . . . Well, by this stage my parents had already softened their heart. Of course Fr. Pozzoli did not finish up by telling them to let me go to the Seminary nor did he demand a decision . . . Simply let them see that they should soften, and they did . . . and the rest followed on. It was typical of him.

Regina, however, agreed reluctantly. She felt it was all happening too quickly and that a decision of such magnitude required much greater time and consideration. Bergoglio later admitted that his mother was "extremely upset" that her eldest child was to leave the family and considered it "a plundering." She was so distressed that she even "refused" to accompany her son when he entered the San Miguel seminary in March of the following year.

It is interesting that in all the interviews with Jorge Bergoglio throughout his life, he happily regales biographers and journalists with stories of his kind and loving grandmother Rosa, who, upon hearing of his news, exclaimed with joy, "Well, if God is calling you, blessed be." And he always speaks with deep respect and gratitude of his courageous and passionate mentor Esther: "I loved her very much." But there are no equivalent accounts of his mother. Being denied her support at this most significant moment of his life cast a shadow over what should have been a joyful announcement, especially since the resentment persisted even when he began his life at the seminary.

It was four long years before Regina visited her son, by which time he was a Jesuit novice in Córdoba, Argentina, the Spanish colonial city four hundred miles from Buenos Aires. He would not feel her true acceptance until she knelt before him and asked for his blessing following his ordination as a priest on December 13, 1969. It was fourteen years and one day since the anniversary breakfast conversation with Father Pozzoli.

ENTERING THE SOCIETY OF JESUS

Life in the Diocesan Seminary of Villa Devoto in San Miguel suited Bergoglio very well. He was affectionately nicknamed El Gringo by his friends, on account of his perceived lack of Latin looks, and described himself as "a normal guy, happy in life." Once again he excelled in class and impressed fellow students with his intelligence and aptitude for learning. Days were filled with a variety of activities ranging from study to mass to communal prayer, and leisure primarily revolving around football.

It's easy to paint a picture of a young man who had finally found his calling and was happily on his way to becoming a priest, but Bergoglio admitted in a 2010 interview with Rabbi Abraham Skorka for the book *On Heaven and Earth* that it was not always a simple choice for him. He was a young man considering a way of life that requires the disciple to relinquish all forms of physical interaction just at the time in his life when he would naturally begin to explore this: "We are so weak that there is always a temptation to be contradictory. One wants to have his cake and eat it too, he wants the good things from the consecrated life *and* from the lay life. Before entering the seminary, I was on that path."

Bergoglio was also a late starter, as it were, in joining the seminary at twenty-one, and admitted that at times his resolve was greatly tested:

> When I was a seminarian, I was enchanted by a young woman at my uncle's wedding. I was surprised by her beauty, the clarity of her intellect . . . and, well, I kicked the idea around for a while. When I returned to the seminary after the wedding, I could not pray during the entire week because when I prepared to pray, the woman appeared in my mind. I had to go back to thinking about what I was doing. I was still free because I was only a seminarian, I could have gone back home and said *see you later.* I had to think about my choice again. I chose once again—or allowed myself to be chosen for—the religious path. It would be abnormal for these types of things not to happen.
>
> When they do happen, one has to rediscover his place.

Once he began his second year, however, Bergoglio had made his decision, explaining that "when one cultivates the choice for the religious life, he finds strength in that direction." Buoyed by the conviction that he had chosen the right path, he also followed through on the promise he'd made to Oscar Crespo at the laboratory four years earlier and decided to apply to join the Society of Jesus. Later, when asked why he became a Jesuit priest, Bergoglio explained: "To tell the truth, I didn't know which path to take. What was clear to me was my religious vocation. . . . I ultimately entered the Society of Jesus because I was attracted to its position on, to put it in military terms, the front lines of the Church, grounded in obedience and discipline. It was also due to its focus on missionary works."

In August 1957, before he had applied to join the Jesuits, he was struck down by an infection. Delirious with fever and struggling to breathe, he was rushed to the hospital. Doctors diagnosed him with severe pneumonia and immediately operated to remove three pulmonary cysts and excise the upper section of his right lung. Two of the seminarians who had accompanied him to the hospital donated blood in person-to-person transfusions. The superior of the seminary, Fr. Humberto Bellone, stayed with him throughout and later recalled, "When he first got ill, he was in such a bad way that I thought he was going to die."

Thankfully, the surgery was a success. After spending several days in an oxygen tent, Bergoglio had a chest tube inserted—bear in mind, this was in 1957—and "every day, saline was pumped through his body to clean out his pleura and scar tissue." It was agony. Family and friends visited him daily, offering the usual bedside reassurances about how he would recover in no time and how wonderful it would be when he got home, but nothing permeated the pain until Sister Dolores, the nun who had prepared him for his First Communion, "said something that truly stuck with me and made me feel at peace: 'You are imitating Christ.'"

Those words gave him a whole new perspective on pain, life, and faith. Years later he explained that "pain is not a virtue in itself, but you can be virtuous in the way you bear it. Our life's vocation is fulfillment and happiness, and pain is a limitation in that search. . . . Any attempt to cope with pain will bring partial results, if it is not based in transcendence. It is a gift to understand and fully live through pain. Even more: to live life fulfilled is a gift."

Blessed by these "gifts" and his newly developed strength of resolve, Jorge Mario Bergoglio entered the Society of Jesus on March 11, 1958.

Traditionally, it takes fifteen years to become a Jesuit. Bergoglio completed the process in thirteen: "Two years' novitiate, a year's juniorate (university-level humanities), three years' philosophy, three years' school teaching, three years' theology, and a year's tertianship." As a member of an order famed for its missionary zeal and global presence, and that requires its candidates to move around during the course of their studies, Bergoglio was exceptional inasmuch as he never particularly enjoyed traveling. A self-described "homebody," he confessed, "I love my home. I love Buenos Aires. . . . After a while [abroad], I always wanted to come back." Apart from his juniorate, which he studied in Chile, and his tertianship, which was completed in Spain, he spent the rest of his training, or "formation," in the Argentine cities of Córdoba, Santa Fe, and Buenos Aires.

Bergoglio was deemed ready to take the Jesuit vows of poverty, chastity, and obedience on March 12, 1960. He then transferred to Casa Loyola, the Jesuit teaching institute just outside the Chilean capital of Santiago, where he spent a year completing his juniorate. The structure was less rigid than it was during his two years as a novitiate, and the Casa Loyola estate was opulent, surrounded by large ancient orchards, farmland, vineyards, and kitchen gardens. But the young candidates' lives remained simple and monastic in style, in accordance with their vows. The bedrooms were sparse, newspapers and the radio were prohibited, and hot-water showers were available only twice a week. Classical music, however, was encouraged, and the rich landscape provided endless opportunities to relax in the fresh mountain air. Bergoglio, still not wholly recovered from his lung operation, was unable to participate in sports, or go hiking or camping, but he was especially fond of swimming in the surrounding rivers and lakes during the brief periods of recreational time afforded to him.

The days were largely well structured. After rising at 6 A.M., candidates would spend an hour in meditative prayer, followed by mass at seven thirty, breakfast at eight, and then housework until lessons began at nine. Predominantly focused around an intense study of the humanities, classes would last until 1 P.M., when candidates would break for a lunch—customarily, all meals were taken in silence and candidates would serve their own food and wash their own dishes. Class would resume at 2:30 P.M. and last until 8 P.M. Bergoglio's reputation as a quiet, intellectual, and thoughtful young man remained unchanged, but for him the greatest fulfillment came on the weekends, when he and his fellow candidates traveled to neighboring villages to teach and help the poor. Having cited his desire to "go out to the neighborhoods, to the *villas*, to be with people" when first discussing his vocation with Oscar Crespo, Bergoglio was deeply moved by the poverty of the Chilean people. In a letter to his eleven-year-old sister, María Elena, on May 5, 1960, he wrote:

> The boys and girls are very poor, some even come to school without shoes on their feet, and very often they have nothing to eat and in the winter they feel the harshness of the cold. You don't know what that's like because you've never wanted for food and when you're cold you just get close to the stove. But while you're happy, there are many children who are crying. When you sit at the table there are many who don't have more than a piece of bread to eat, and when it rains and it's cold many of them are living in tin shacks and they have nothing to cover themselves with.

Poverty of this kind was shocking to the twenty-three-year-old Bergoglio, who had never traveled farther than the streets of Buenos Aires, and only increased his desire to dedicate his life to social justice.

After completing the yearlong juniorate, he returned to Argentina in March 1961 and began his studies in philosophy at the prestigious Jesuit Colegio Máximo de San José in San Miguel, a city in the northwest of Buenos Aires Province. In his absence, the three-year reign of the democratically elected left-wing government of Arturo Frondizi had shown signs of cracking. The continued suppression of

Peronism, coupled with the kidnapping in Argentina of the Nazi fugitive Adolf Eichmann in May 1960, had led to an emergence of far-right guerilla groups with links to other exiled Nazis, who began a campaign of anti-Semitic violence and bombing across the country.

For Bergoglio, however, the political turmoil was little match for the personal upheaval he was about to encounter. On September 24, 1961, his father, Mario Bergoglio, was watching his beloved San Lorenzo play football at the stadium in Flores with his youngest son, Alberto, when he suffered a heart attack and died. He was just fifty-one. Despite all his training, Jorge Bergoglio found himself completely at a loss as to how to deal with grief and death. In a letter he wrote to Fr. Cayetano Bruno twenty-nine years later, he described a moment of great shame that had haunted him throughout his life: "Fr. Pozzoli came to the funeral parlour and wanted to take a photo of dad with the five children. . . . I was ashamed, and with all the superior pride of a young man I saw that it did not happen. I think Fr. Pozzoli saw my stance but he said nothing."

The awkwardness of that occasion was compounded by another tragedy less than a month later, when Father Pozzoli himself died. Bergoglio had now lost his spiritual father as well. This was the man who had baptized him, who had listened to his confessions, and who had supported and facilitated his desire to become a priest. Again, Bergoglio felt himself unequal to the moment. When Bergoglio heard that Pozzoli was gravely ill in the hospital, he visited but found him sleeping:

> I did not want to wake him (I felt bad deep down, and did not know what I would say to him). I left the room and stopped to talk with a priest who was there. After a moment, another priest came out of the room and told me that Fr. Pozzoli was awake, that they told him about my visit, and he asked if I was still there to come. I told them to tell him I had gone. I don't know what came over me, if I was timid or . . . I was 25 years old and already in 1st year philosophy . . . but I can assure you . . . that if I could have this moment back again, I would do so. How often I have felt deep sorrow and pain for this "lie"

of mine to Fr. Pozzoli at the time of his death. There are moments in life (perhaps a few) when one would like to be able to relive them and act in a different way.

CHANGING THE CHURCH

The strength Bergoglio had discovered during his own illness was a great help when guilt and shame bore down on him. These losses were devastating, but he managed to continue and complete his studies in philosophy by the end of 1963. Just as the world was experiencing a marked shift in societal attitudes, so, too, was the Catholic Church. The previous year, Pope John XXIII (1958–1963) had convened the Second Ecumenical Council of the Vatican (Vatican II) to discuss the future of the church in the modern world. Described by historian John W. O'Malley, S.J., as "the most important religious event of the twentieth century," it signified the growing divide between those wishing for reform and those staunchly opposed to it in any form. For young seminarians hoping to make a difference in the world, such as Bergoglio, this was an immensely exciting time.

For four council sessions over three years, more than twenty-eight hundred bishops from around the world descended on Rome. The Argentine contingent constituted the tenth-largest group. The Catholic Church in Argentina had remained loyal to the Vatican's teachings and had fought hard against any attempts to separate church and state that would have diluted its position in society. Bergoglio and his fellow classmates were, according to friend Fernando Montes, firmly "on the side of those who wanted a more open Church, not a Church of resistance to the world." This view, combined with their philosophical explorations, dominated their discussions during the council's three-year deliberations.

In 1964, twenty-eight-year-old Bergoglio applied to Father Pedro Arrupe, the first Jesuit provincial for Japan, who had been living in Hiroshima when the atomic bomb was dropped in August 1945, to complete the regent phase of his formation at a Japanese mission. He was turned down on account of his lung condition and was instead sent to the Colegio de la Inmaculada Concepción in Santa Fe

to teach literature, art, and psychology. It was an incongruous place-
ment after his outreach work in Chile: this was an esteemed and
expensive boarding school for the children of wealthy families who
wished for their offspring to follow in the footsteps of its many
illustrious alumni.

But Bergoglio's scientific background proved no hindrance to his
teaching of the arts, and the rigorous routines of Jesuit institutions
suited his methodical nature. In his first year at the college, he taught
the boys about Spanish literature, and in the following year turned
his attention to Argentine works. With particular focus on *gauche-
sco* literature, he introduced the class to one of his favorite poems,
Martín Fierro, the 1872 epic by José Hernández (a saga likened by
many to *Don Quixote* and *The Divine Comedy*) and even arranged
for the legendary author Jorge Luis Borges to visit and lecture on
the significance of this movement in literature. Students were en-
thralled by the varied and engaging education he offered, and as
Germán de Carolis, a former pupil, recalled, "[Bergoglio] was serious as far as personality went but youthful and with a sense of hu-
mour. He had authority, earned respect, and was popular with the
students. His knowledge of the subjects he taught was immense, and
his literature lessons captivated us. You could tell that he liked teaching and that he was totally convinced of his priestly vocation. It was
impossible to doubt it."

On December 8, 1965, the bells of St. Peter's Basilica signaled
an end to the Second Vatican Council and the dawn of a new era of
change within the Catholic Church. During the three years of intense debate, the world, too, had changed: seventeen coups had
overthrown governments in developing nations across the globe;
Cold War tensions had eased, somewhat, following the Cuban mis-
sile crisis of 1962; the fierce battle for civil rights and social progress
in America gave rise to Martin Luther King Jr.'s legendary "I Have
a Dream" speech in 1963, and to the assassinations of President
John F. Kennedy (1963) and Malcolm X (1965); and by the close of
1965, the war in Vietnam had rapidly escalated following the deployment of more than two hundred thousand U.S. ground troops.

Society, as a whole, was desperately calling for change, and in a
series of sixteen published documents, the Vatican answered those

calls by lowering the drawbridge and opening up the church not just to its followers but to the world and other religions. It was a watershed moment, this attempt to humanize the church.

Mass was to become more inclusive, doing away with archaic Latin liturgy in favor of allowing people to worship in their native languages. Anti-Semitic references were removed from Catholic writings, and the previously fierce condemnation of atheism was softened, and discrimination was condemned in any form "against men or harassment of them because of their race, color, condition of life, or religion." While papal infallibility was by no means abolished, collegiality was also emphasized, which meant that bishops, including those from developing countries, would from now on have a greater role in decision making, therefore diluting the previously formidable powers of the Roman Curia. Most significantly for Bergoglio and other Latin American Catholics, however, was the focus on social justice and peace. These were at the forefront of a desire, as expressed by Pope John XXIII at the opening of the council, to return the institution as a whole to being a "Church of the poor."

It was a clear message of reform, but problems arose when progressives and conservatives, who had been wrestling it out for three years, chose to interpret the council's findings in markedly different ways. The most notable radical interpretation of Vatican II occurred in Latin America, where returning bishops began reassessing the ways in which they could help the continent's poor and marginalized peoples. In Argentina, priests who dispatched themselves to so-called *villas miserias* (literally, "misery villages") to fight poverty and protect the rights of the poor in slum shantytowns, joined together to form the Movement of Priests for the Third World (Movimiento de Sacerdotes para el Tercer Mundo, or MSTM).

Through their support of the poor and the rights of workers, the movement developed a greater association with trade unions, which were predominantly Peronist and socialist in their political leanings, but it was still disorganized, and its message remained unclear until a landmark 1968 publication by Rubem Alves, a Brazilian theologian, entitled "Towards a Theology of Liberation," united the MSTM's struggles with those of other movements from across the continent under one banner: liberation theology.

While not endorsing MSTM by name, the Latin American Catholic Bishops' Conference (Consejo Episcopal Latinoamericano, or CELAM) supported many of the theories put forward by the movement when it met in Medellín, Colombia, in 1968 to discuss the continent's interpretation of Vatican II. But at a time when revolution and rioting were erupting around the world and the threat of communism still loomed large in the minds of Western democracies, liberation theology's Marxist undertones were perceived as dangerous to the institution of the church as a whole. Consequently, the conclusions reached in Medellín warned firmly against Marxist and liberationist systems that stood in opposition to the dignity of the human person, and quoting the words of Pope Paul VI, they denounced violent revolutions that "engender new injustices, introduce new inequities and bring new disasters. The evil situation that exists, and it surely is evil, may not be dealt with in such a way that an even worse situation results."

Despite its unifying intentions, the Second Vatican Council's reforms had not been able to bridge the divide between grassroots priests and the senior echelons of the church. According to Paul Vallely, prior to the meeting at CELAM, "1,500 priests from the Movement of Priests for the Third World signed a letter to Paul VI condemning 'violence of the upper class' and 'the violence of the state' as the first violence. In the face of this, they argued, the violence of the poor was an understandable response." Argentine bishops, having experienced another military coup in 1966, and acknowledging that many in the church were "seduced by Marxism," issued their own interpretation of CELAM in the 1969 Declaration of San Miguel, which concurred in its condemnation of Marxism, social protest, and challenges to authority but promoted the idea that people should be active agents of their own history, stating that "the activity of the Church should not only be oriented toward the people but also primarily derive *from* the people."

The declaration had such a profound influence on the soon-to-be priest that throughout his spiritual life, Bergoglio would continue to refer back to it, as he did in this 2010 testimony, and eventually use it to form the basis of his entire papal outlook:

The option for the poor comes from the first centuries of Christianity. It's the Gospel itself. If you were to read one of the sermons of the first fathers of the Church, from the second or third centuries, about how you should treat the poor, you'd say it was Maoist or Trotskyist. The Church has always had the honour of this preferential option for the poor. It has always considered the poor to be the treasure of the Church. . . . At the Second Vatican Council the Church was redefined as the People of God and this idea really took off at the Second Conference of the Latin-American bishops in Medellín.

A VOCATION FULFILLED

On December 13, 1969, five days before his thirty-third birthday, and watched by his mother, grandmother Rosa, and siblings, Bergoglio stepped forward in the chapel of Colegio Máximo and was ordained by Archbishop Ramón José Castellano.

The year marked the start of that bloody period of violence in Argentina that would escalate into the brutally oppressive and murderous civil conflict known as the Dirty War (1976–83). The instability that followed the 1966 revolution resulted in civil unrest and mass protests, known as the Rosariazo and Cordobazo uprisings, between May and September 1969. Fourteen students and protesters were killed by police, prompting a surge in left-wing guerilla groups that would eventually succeed in returning Juan Perón to power after twenty years in exile.

As the lines between religion, politics, and violence became increasingly blurred—and with 10 percent of Argentina's clergy officially endorsing Peronism and liberation theology and many more sympathetic—Bergoglio found the country much changed when he returned after completing his tertianship at the Universidad de Alcalá de Henares in Spain. On March 11, 1973, the country headed to the polls for the first time in ten years and democratically elected as president former dentist, and the official representative in Argentina of the exiled Juan Perón, Dr. Héctor José Cámpora, much to the chagrin of the military junta.

While talk of Perón's return was exciting the electorate, Jorge Mario Bergoglio was uttering rather different words: his final Jesuit vows. On April 22, 1973, he was invited to publicly promise obedience to the sovereign pontiff before privately taking his simple vows in a side chapel of the church at the Colegio Máximo de San José in San Miguel, Argentina. The next five vows Bergoglio promised were: first, never to change the Jesuit Constitutions concerning poverty, except to make them "more strict"; second, never to "strive or have ambition" for any high office in the church; third, never to strive or have ambition for any high office in the Jesuits; fourth, to "communicate the name" of any person found striving for either office to the Society of Jesus; fifth, and finally, to promise to listen to the superior general of the Society of Jesus should he ever be made a bishop.

Although they were unaware of the greatness that lay ahead, Jorge Bergoglio's superiors had been impressed throughout his formation. Even before he had taken his final vows, they began to fast-track him toward leadership within the order, appointing him master of novices when he returned from studying in Spain, followed by a short stint as rector of Colegio Máximo. Even so, it was still a surprise to many when, on July 31, 1973, he was made provincial superior, head of all the Jesuits in Argentina. At thirty-six, he was the youngest person ever to be appointed to the position—a promotion that he himself later described as "crazy" given his age.

Having succeeded the man who had appointed him master of novices, Father Ricardo O'Farrell, Bergoglio assumed the role of provincial superior at a time of great crisis among the Jesuits. Under O'Farrell, the number of men joining and remaining in the order had plummeted, and those who had stayed reflected the familiar churchwide divisions between reformist and conservative opinions. O'Farrell's natural successor, Father Luis Escribano, had died in a car crash, so Bergoglio was seen by his new boss, the head of the Society of Jesus, Superior General Father Pedro Arrupe, as the only man who could potentially satisfy the warring factions. He was faced with the near-impossible challenge of combining the roles of peacemaker, recruiter, and politician.

THE PRODIGAL SON RETURNS

It was not only the Jesuits and the wider church that were struggling for unified peace and agreement. Argentina was once again in crisis.

Despite the euphoria that followed the democratic election in March 1973, underlying tensions had not abated. In the eighteen years since Perón had fled to Franco-ruled Spain, his followers had splintered into left- and right-wing opposition groups, both laying claim to his message. When it was announced that Juan Perón and his third wife, María Estela (known as Isabel), would at last return, hopes were high that he could once more unite the country and put an end to the bloodshed. On June 20, an estimated 3.5 million people gathered at an airport in Buenos Aires to welcome the seventy-seven-year-old, but armed members of the right-wing death-squad the Alianza Anticomunista Argentina (known as Triple A) opened fire on the crowd, killing thirteen and wounding 365.

The Ezeiza Massacre marked the start of one of the most violent periods in Argentine history. The streets of Buenos Aires rapidly became the front line of the conflict between the military and leftist and rightist guerilla factions battling it out for power. After the resignation of Cámpora in July 1973, Perón was reelected president and took office on October 12, with Isabel serving as vice president. But he failed to unite the country. Right-wing groups had free rein of the city as the military set about eliminating the left-wing opposition, driving the guerilla groups further underground.

Almost no sooner had he returned to the country than Perón died from a heart attack, on July 1, 1974, and forty-three-year-old Isabel was sworn in as president. She was completely unprepared for the task, and her presidency was a disaster from start to finish. Perón's personal secretary and, horrifyingly, minister of social welfare, José López Rega, acted as her adviser–cum–puppet master, using his position to enable Triple A, the death squad he founded, to carry out, in collaboration with the military, the state-sponsored murders of close to three hundred people, including Father Carlos Mugica, a liberation theologian.

Now one year into his six-year term as superior, Bergoglio was desperately trying to convince Argentine Jesuits not to get drawn into the conflict and to put aside "sterile inter-ecclesiastical contradictions" in favor of a "true apostolic strategy." But politics had infiltrated the Jesuits. How could it not have? Their work as missionaries brought them face-to-face with the poverty of innocent civilians caught in the crossfire of corruption and violence; as far as they were concerned, they were following the teachings of Vatican II. However, almost ten years on, its message was still producing widely differing interpretations. The superior general, Father Arrupe, also believed he was following the council's guidelines to support the separation of church and state when he tasked Bergoglio with depoliticizing Jesuits by carrying out "a sweeping purge of left-wing students and radical teachers, among them several Jesuits who had taken control of the Jesuit University of Salvador, in Buenos Aires."

The move made Bergoglio deeply unpopular with many Jesuits, primarily because the replacement teachers and directors belonged to an anti-Marxist militant Catholic group loyal to Peronism called Guardia de Hierro (Iron Guard). Bergoglio had known them in the early 1970s, when he was a novice master and rector of Colegio Máximo, but despite his assurance that these men would run the university in accordance with Jesuit principles, his stance was viewed as a political betrayal, for which many would never forgive him. His intent was to realign the Jesuits with Ignatius's teachings and the conclusions of the conference of CELAM, but his actions throughout his tenure as superior were perceived as quite the opposite, and for many years he was labeled a staunch conservative.

THE COUP TO END ALL COUPS

The disastrous tenure of Isabel Perón came to an end on March 24, 1976, when a military junta, led by General Jorge Videla, Admiral Emilio Massera, and Commander Orlando Ramón Agosti, assumed control of Argentina.

With the country's economy in ruins, many welcomed the intervention of the military, which, as Jimmy Burns notes in his biography *Francis: Pope of Good Promise,* was comparatively "bloodless, serene and quickly executed, with a majority of the population breathing a sigh of relief with the end of the Peronist government."

Although rumors quickly began circulating of the many "disappeared," it was years before the general population understood the true and horrifying extent of the carnage caused by the Dirty War conducted by the military dictatorship between March 24, 1976, and October 30, 1983.

It is estimated that thirty thousand Argentines were "disappeared" during this time.

Many of their bodies were dumped in unmarked graves, never to be recovered, leaving families with an unending quest for information and justice. Most were young people, aged between sixteen and thirty. Their murders constituted what Argentines have described as "the killing of a generation." These harrowing figures do not include the 3 percent of captured women who were pregnant when kidnapped and gave birth in the death camps before they were murdered, leaving an estimated 270 babies unaccounted for.

An overwhelming sense of guilt and shame followed, not least for the Catholic Church. In declassified U.S. State Department documents published by the National Security Archives on the thirtieth anniversary of the military coup, the U.S. embassy officer in charge of human rights, F. Allen "Tex" Harris, filed a report on December 27, 1978, following an "informal meeting" with Nunciature First Secretary Kevin Mullan, in which he stated that "a senior army official had informed the [Catholic] Nuncio that the armed services had been forced to 'take care of' 15,000 persons in its anti-subversion campaign."

The shocking proof that the church, more than most, was acutely aware of the extent to which the junta was disposing of its critics was compounded by testimonies given during the 1984 National Commission on the Disappearance of Persons, in which several victims alleged that "priests of the church cooperated with the military to the point of inviting prisoners to confess everything in order to serve their nation. Numerous survivors tell of fruitless searches for their loved ones, in which officers of the church refused help but passed on information given in confidence [to the junta]. When the Mothers of the Plaza de Mayo sought support and a place to meet, the churches in the centre of the city were unable or unwilling to accommodate them."

Furthermore, leading figures within the church such as the cardinal primate of Buenos Aires, Juan Carlos Aramburu, never turned down the junta's invitations for public functions. Between 1976 and 1981 the bishops issued only four pastoral letters condemning the torture and abuse of human rights, but at the same time seemed to acquiesce to the military's determination to act in any way that it deemed proportionate to maintaining society. At no point did the church take a public stand against the junta, even when its own priests began being murdered. In total, during the Dirty War twenty priests and members of religious orders were killed, eighty-four were "disappeared," and seventy-seven were exiled.

All things combined, the church found herself too internally divided to agree on an appropriate response. So, too, it would seem, was Jorge Bergoglio.

Superior General Arrupe had set him two key tasks. First and foremost, he must protect the Jesuits; his second task was to aid civilians caught in the conflict. As Austen Ivereigh notes, "The two objectives were, obviously, in tension with each other: if it had been known that their provincial was abetting subversives sought by the state, all Jesuits would have been suspect." Ivereigh argues that "it was a high-wire act, but Bergoglio pulled it off. Not one Argentine Jesuit lost his life in the dirty war, and he managed to save dozens of people."

In later years, as pope, when Francis would regularly state, "I am a sinner," making clear that he is someone who has sinned in profound ways, it is obviously his actions and inactions during the black days of the Dirty War to which he is mostly referring: days of life-and-death decisions for the Jesuit leader, of judgment calls that might send one of his flock into exile or another—to his horror and despite his protests—to the torture chamber. Such images must live in him still, such as when he strategically celebrated mass in the home of General Videla, hoping to speak with the tyrant about two captured

Jesuits, but still placing a Holy Communion wafer on the outthrust tongue of the very man implicated in ordering Esther Ballestrino into a sea-transport plane, legs and hands bound for her final terrible ride. The conscience does not easily sleep with such facts, so it is natural that these days should haunt him, bear down on him, demanding atonement and a full reckoning while also teaching him much of lasting value about the true nature of sin, and how sin must be confronted and dealt with if it is to be turned finally to the good.

A TIME OF UNCERTAINTY

By the time the junta finally fell in 1983, following a humiliating defeat in the Falklands War against Great Britain in 1982, Bergoglio was two years into another stint serving as rector of the Colegio Máximo in San Miguel, having resigned his role as Jesuit superior in 1979. The position suited him well, for he was always commended on his ability to inspire candidates training in Jesuit formation.

Bergoglio busied himself with building new churches; hosting international conferences at the university; reforming the syllabus of education; and even building a Jesuit-run community farm on a spare twenty-five-acre plot on the grounds of the college, which helped to feed the poor families of the parish. One student recalled just how busy he was: "He went from giving spiritual direction to speaking on the phone with a bishop to washing clothes in the laundry before going to the kitchen and the pigsty and then back to the classroom. He was involved in every detail with us." But Bergoglio began to grow restless.

At this point John Paul II, now four years into his papacy, decided it was time for a shake-up of the Jesuits, including in Argentina. When a new superior general was appointed to lead the order in 1983, he was approached by powerful Argentine Jesuits who lobbied "against the rector [Bergoglio] and his followers, arguing that Bergoglio's model of formation was backward and out of step with the Society of Jesus in Latin America." The campaigning worked, and in 1986 a more conservative candidate, Father Víctor Zorzín, was appointed as head of the Argentine Jesuits.

Weary at the thought of political infighting, in May 1986 Bergoglio requested permission from Zorzín to take a sabbatical in Germany to complete his doctorate in theology. There are some who believe he was ordered to leave by his superior, which, when considering this was a man who hated travel, perhaps holds some truth—especially when, after just seven months, fifty-year-old Bergoglio abandoned his studies and returned to Argentina. He has never spoken in any detail about the reasons for this change of course, saying only, "I remember that when I was in Frankfurt, working on my thesis, I'd take strolls in the evenings to the cemetery. You could see the airport from there. One time I bumped into a friend who asked me what I was doing, and I replied, 'Waving to the planes. I'm waving to the planes bound for Argentina.'"

It is a revealing comment. Bergoglio clearly longed for home and was pained by the knowledge there was no place for him there. Unexpectedly, he found an answer to his dilemma painted on the wood-paneled wall of a small church in Bavaria. Gazing down at him was *Mary Untier of Knots,* an eighteenth-century depiction of the Virgin Mary as she unties the knots in a piece of thread passed to her by one of the many angels that surround her. She is bathed in a Heavenly glow, with the Christ child in her arms and her foot crushing a serpent. It spoke to Bergoglio at a time when he himself had many knots to untie and seems to have given him the confidence to return to Argentina by the end of 1986, accompanied by pocketfuls of prayer cards depicting *Mary Untier of Knots.*

He was not welcomed home with open arms. Nonetheless, he still had some friends in the society and, through their support, was appointed in March 1987 to the advisory position of procurator general, much to the annoyance of more conservative Jesuits. Unfortunately for Bergoglio, the ill feeling against him continued, and those determined to be rid of him finally succeeded. In April 1990, they removed him from his teaching post and two months later exiled him to Córdoba.

RETURN FROM THE WILDERNESS

The exile forced upon Bergoglio gave rise to an intense period of spiritual reflection as he listened daily to the confessions of parishioners and immersed himself in the daily life of a parish priest. It was a humbling existence that came to an end two years later with the offer of a new and very different position within the church.

On May 20, 1992, Jorge Mario Bergoglio, confessor, teacher, and outcast Jesuit, was ordained an auxiliary bishop to the archbishop of Buenos Aires, Antonio Quarracino, to whom he would act, alongside four other auxiliaries, in an assistant capacity—the role is most commonly requested to support either an ailing archbishop or one whose diocese has a large population. Having developed a relationship with Quarracino at a series of spiritual retreats when he was provincial superior, Bergoglio had so impressed the archbishop with his "spirituality and his cleverness" that upon hearing of his "penance in Córdoba [Quarracino] decided to rescue him" by personally requesting approval for his appointment to the role of auxiliary from Pope John Paul II himself.

Bergoglio was stunned. Recalling the moment in an interview many years later, he said, "My mind went blank. As I said before, my mind always goes blank after a shock, good or bad. And my initial reaction is also always wrong." He had never considered the possibility of becoming a bishop, partly on account of his Jesuit vows but also due to his recent fall from grace within the society. But the years spent in Córdoba had been formative, and it was clear from his first day in high office that he was not about to let the trappings of power go to his head. He politely refused the more exclusive bishops' accommodation in favor of a simple apartment in his home parish of Flores, where he was to be based. He also declined the offer of a driver and a priest, acting as personal secretary, to help him with administrative matters, preferring instead to answer his own telephone, keep his own diary, and take the bus wherever he needed to go.

When a Jesuit becomes a bishop, he is automatically released from his vows and is no longer accountable to the superior general of the society. Despite this change in his circumstances, Bergoglio remained true to his commitment to a life of poverty, chastity, and obedience, as he would do throughout the rest of his career in the church.

Perhaps the most pleasing part of his new role was that it allowed him to return once more to working with the people of the *villas miserias*. It had been a source of great disappointment when, during the struggle for authority within the Jesuits, those opposed to his efforts had removed the community outreach work that Bergoglio had so treasured. Now his dedication, loyalty, and undeniable talents made a deep impression on the archbishop, who began accelerating Bergoglio's rise through the ranks over a very short period of time. In December 1993 he was made vicar general in charge of the archdiocese, and then, in May 1997, Quarracino invited his auxiliary bishop to lunch.

As Bergoglio recalled, "At mid-morning on May 27, 1997, Calabresi [papal nuncio to Argentina] called and asked me to lunch with him. We were drinking coffee, and I was all set to thank him for the meal and take my leave when I noticed that a cake and a bottle of champagne had been brought in. I thought it must be his birthday, and I was just about to offer my best wishes. But the surprise came when I asked him about it. 'No, it's not my birthday,' he replied, grinning broadly. 'It so happens that you are the new coadjutor bishop of Buenos Aires.'" At seventy-three, Cardinal Quarracino's health was failing. He was keen to ensure that were he to die in office, Bergoglio, as coadjutor, would automatically succeed him as archbishop and assume responsibility for Argentina's principal diocese and the 3.5 million Catholics living in central Buenos Aires. Quarracino had been right to put his house in order, for a little over eight months later, on February 28, 1998, he died from complications resulting from an intestinal blockage. In his place, Jorge Mario Bergoglio, now sixty-one years old, was appointed archbishop of Buenos Aires.

FROM BLACK TO RED

The dizzying speed of Bergoglio's eclipse as leader of the Argentine Jesuits followed by his near-stratospheric rise from priest to archbishop must surely have left not just his mind blank but his head spinning. In just six years, he had gone from a kind of exile to become the leader of the Catholic Church in Argentina. He was barely afforded much time to process the change—three days, in fact, during which he withdrew from the maelstrom of funeral preparations for his predecessor and official inductions to a silent retreat, where he could grieve the loss of his friend and contemplate the path down which he must now tread.

After he returned, Bergoglio remained as resolved as ever to eschew the decadence and ostentation that came hand in hand with the upper echelons of the Catholic Church, committing himself instead to a life of humility and simplicity, helping the poor just as Saint Ignatius of Loyola had directed more than five hundred years earlier.

Bergoglio's way of doing things was somewhat puzzling for the staff attempting to follow the traditional protocol of transition for a new archbishop. When the diocesan tailors returned their quote for his official clothing, Bergoglio balked at the price and proposed that they save the money and simply alter Quarracino's cassocks to fit his slenderer frame. As before, he declined the official archbishop's residence, located near the Presidential Palace, in the exclusive suburb of Olivos, preferring to live in a spartan single bedroom in the curia building next to the cathedral in the Plaza de Mayo. Gone was the need for limousines and chauffeurs as Bergoglio continued to walk the streets and ride the subway and buses of Buenos Aires. Nor were the grand offices of the archbishop required; all he wanted was a simple room to work in, with space for his books and a couple of chairs for guests.

His unique style was a revelation. The public and the media largely embraced and celebrated this new, more pastoral approach to governance. The politicians—in particular President Carlos Menem, who, having been elected in 1989, was entering his last year in office and was keen to garner support from the church to amend the constitution to allow him to serve a third term—had reservations. Bergoglio made it clear he was not afraid to speak plainly and critically of the government's failings and of its need to address the issues facing society as a whole. By 1998, Argentina was teetering on the brink of another great depression, the effects of which had already been felt in the poorest and most marginalized communities, where Bergoglio spent much of his time.

During previous periods of instability, the church's message had been overshadowed by infighting and partisan politics—for which Bergoglio held himself accountable. Throughout his time as archbishop, he displayed an ardent determination to rise above such temptations and to preserve the sacred and fundamental pastoral message he had learned as a young priest. Inclusivity was key, and Bergoglio drew heavily on his Jesuit training when implementing changes in the diocese.

A little over a month after his appointment as archbishop, Bergoglio delegated the traditional mass of Maundy Thursday in Holy Week, during which the archbishop would wash the feet of twelve men, representing the twelve apostles, in the city's cathedral, to his auxiliary bishop so that he could celebrate his own mass at the Muñiz Hospital for Infectious Diseases. Here, in a ceremony marking Jesus's Last Supper with his disciples, Bergoglio washed and kissed the feet of twelve patients suffering from AIDS. Father Andrés Tello, the hospital chaplain, recalled, "When he arrived, I explained that while the Gospel speaks of twelve male apostles, here in the hospital we had men, women, transvestites. He told me: 'Whom you choose, I will wash their feet.' The Mass was very emotional, everyone was crying, he gave communion to everyone. . . . He always talked about existential peripheries. He wanted to go to a place of great pain and the hospital is that." Throughout his fifteen years as archbishop it became a tradition that every Maundy Thursday Bergoglio would wash and kiss the feet of the marginalized in hospitals, prisons, rehab centers, slums, and nursing homes across Buenos Aires.

Bergoglio's reforms were not limited to the day-to-day pastoral affairs and the church's preferential focus on the poor. When he inherited the diocese, it became clear that it was not just the country's finances that were in chaos. Quarracino's death revealed inappropriately close ties between the church, its donors, and the government, which resulted in a complex mess of loans, shoddy accounts, and back-channel bribes. In an attempt to untangle the knots, Bergoglio engaged an external accountancy firm to conduct a thorough audit, which revealed that the archdiocese "regularly ignored both canon law and the Argentine bishops' own guidelines for monitoring and authorizing payments." A complete overhaul of practices was instigated by the new archbishop, but not before the diocese was raided by police in connection with a questionable ten-million-dollar loan. The scandal was later resolved and according to Ivereigh, "the auditor's report commissioned by Bergoglio was so thorough that it left no questions hanging, and the archbishop's reputation was, if anything, enhanced by his handling of the affair."

While domestic in nature, Bergoglio's actions during his three-year tenure as archbishop of Buenos Aires garnered a chorus of praise that not only was heard throughout Argentina but also traveled all the way to the Vatican. So it was that on February 21, 2001, Bergoglio stepped forward before Pope John Paul II and knelt at his feet. Gone was his simple black priest's attire; he was now dressed in the scarlet choir dress reserved only for cardinals—hand-me-downs from the late Quarracino, naturally. That was the day he was one of forty-two new cardinal appointees. The frail eighty-year-old John Paul, who was still yet to officially acknowledge that he had been suffering from Parkinson's disease for the last ten years, squinted in the bright winter sunshine as he leaned down and placed the red biretta on Bergoglio's head before saying, "[This is] scarlet as a sign of the dignity of the cardinalate, signifying your readiness to act with courage, even to the shedding of your blood, for the increase of the Christian faith, for the peace and tranquility of the people of God and for the freedom and growth of the Holy Roman Church."

After the pope kissed his newly appointed cardinal on each cheek and Bergoglio kissed the papal hand in return, John Paul smiled and in a warm, fatherly gesture, patted the slightly stunned-looking Argentinian twice on the shoulder. "You can breathe now!" seems to have been the inference. The crowds cheered and clapped for Cardinal Bergoglio, but unlike with other new cardinals, there was no special eruption of joy for him. Upon hearing that excited people had been planning trips to Rome to attend the celebrations, Bergoglio requested that they save the money they would have spent on the journey and, instead, donate it to the poor.

When the open-air ceremony in St. Peter's Square ended, Bergoglio walked through the streets to his accommodation, soaking up the vibrant atmosphere of the city. Back at the humble priests' lodgings, where he would continue to stay whenever he visited Rome, he packed his small, battered suitcase, changed back into his familiar black priest's outfit—it was a remarkable achievement for the Vatican to get him out of it for a whole day—collected his passport, and returned home to Buenos Aires . . . in economy class, of course.

FIRST STEPS ON THE ROAD TO ROME

Despite his best efforts, life for the sixty-three-year-old cardinal had inevitably to change now that curial responsibilities had elbowed their way into his annual schedule. In the first year alone, he visited Rome a further two times: once in May for the largest "extraordinary consistory" in the church's history—a meeting considered by many to be a preconclave opportunity for possible successors, from among John Paul's 115 cardinals, to display their credentials—to discuss what the pope described as "practical suggestions for the Church's mission of evangelization at the dawn of the new millennium"; then again in October, when, at the last minute, Bergoglio was appointed relator general to the Synod of Bishops—literally responsible for relating the objectives of the meeting and summarizing the speeches to the bishops to aid them when drafting proposals and conclusions of the conference, which were then presented to the pope, who was also in attendance—in place of Cardinal Edward Egan, Archbishop of New York, who was presiding over an interfaith memorial service in the recently devastated city following the terrorist attacks on September 11.

The appointment of a relatively unknown figure to this role was testament to John Paul's faith in Bergoglio and thrust him to the heights of the church hierarchy. No longer able to wear what Austen Ivereigh described as "his customary cloak of invisibility," which enabled him to move around Rome unnoticed, he would have known that a significant amount rode on his performance during the synod and the subsequent postspeech press conference held at the Vatican. And even though his thoughts were distracted by the economic and political tumult currently engulfing his own country—the government was about to be ousted, the entire banking system was on the brink of collapse, and the International Monetary Fund was about to withdraw funds to refinance the national debt—he delivered a speech of such commanding distinction that people at once began considering him as a possible contender for the Chair of St. Peter; he also revealed some flashes of his future when he said:

> Nowadays the war of the powerful against the weak has opened a gap between rich and the poor. The poor are legion. Before an unjust economic system with very strong structural mismatches, the situation of the marginalised is worse. Today there is hunger. The poor, the young and the refugees are victims of this "new civilization." . . . The Bishop must never tire of preaching the social doctrine which comes from the Gospel and which the Church has made explicit since the times of the First Fathers.

In November 2002, seasoned Vatican journalist Sandro Magister wrote an article entitled "Bergoglio in Pole Position" in which he described the Argentinian's recent ascent:

> Midway through November, his colleagues wanted to elect him president of the Argentine bishops' conference. He refused. But if there had been a conclave, it would have been difficult for him to refuse the election to the papacy, because he's the one the cardinals would vote for resoundingly, if they were called together to choose immediately the successor to John Paul II. . . .
>
> At the last synod of bishops in the fall of 2001 . . . Bergoglio managed the meeting so well that, at the time for electing the twelve members of the secretary's council, his brother bishops chose him with the highest vote possible. . . . Someone in the Vatican had the idea to call him to direct an important dicastery. "Please, I would die in the Curia," he implored. They spared him.
>
> Since that time, the thought of having him return to Rome as the successor of Peter has begun to spread with growing intensity. The Latin-American cardinals are increasingly focused upon him, as is Joseph Cardinal Ratzinger.

On his return to Buenos Aires, however, he was faced with heart-breaking evidence on every street corner of how low his beloved country had sunk.

Following a run on the banks by desperate citizens fearful of losing what little money they had, the government froze all accounts in an attempt to hold off a complete collapse of the banking system. Cities across the country descended into violence and looting on December 21 and 22, 2001. In the Plaza de Mayo, President Fernando de la Rúa looked out of the windows of the Presidential Palace at a dense fog of tear gas before turning his back and fleeing in a helicopter. From the other side of the square Bergoglio, too, was watching as police responded with brutal force against the protesters, some of whom were setting fire to banks and government buildings. It was a devastating scene.

Thirty-nine people died, and hundreds more were injured. And it took another two years of economic decline before Argentina began to recover. During this time, Bergoglio continued to give pastoral support to the ever-increasing numbers of destitute and marginalized citizens. As interim president of Argentina Eduardo Duhalde said, Bergoglio "assumed a key role in the so-called Argentine Dialogue [Board]. . . . I believe history will consider it as one of our greatest collective epics. But there were providential figures in that rescue, giant personalities who, while modestly avoiding occupying the center of the scene, were decisive so that we would not fall into social dissolution, which at the time was a real and close risk. That man, Jorge Bergoglio, was one of them."

In April 2003 the country had regained some semblance of stability, and new elections were called. The problem, however, was the scarcity of candidates willing to take on the poisoned chalice that was the Argentine presidency. Duhalde would have run but had agreed not to when assuming the role of interim president. The only other options were former president Carlos Menem, seeking his third term, or an unknown candidate named Néstor Kirchner. When Menem withdrew in the days leading up to the election, Kirchner ran unopposed, and his left-wing government was elected by default, with just 22 percent of the vote.

Kirchner and his glamorous First Lady, Senator Cristina Fernández de Kirchner, had been loyal supporters of Peronism from the time they met as students in the early 1970s, and after the 2003 election they quickly took charge of Argentine politics. From 2003 to 2015 they would rule in successive two-term governments marred by allegations of embezzlement and corruption. (Cristina Fernández de Kirchner was indicted and charged with high treason in December 2017 and again in March 2018 for obstructing investigations into Iranian involvement in the 1994 bombing of a Jewish center.) Néstor Kirchner had no interest in religion or in fostering good relations with the church, and he made these feelings abundantly clear to Bergoglio from the moment he took office. Bergoglio was equally averse to the new president and was frequently critical of the government's empty rhetoric, lack of values, and individualist outlook. On December 30, 2004, a large fire broke out in a nightclub in the working-class suburb of Once, Buenos Aires. Revelers ran for the exits only to discover that they were trapped, as most of the emergency doors had been padlocked shut to prevent people from sneaking in without paying. Bergoglio rushed to the scene, where he found hundreds of bodies laid out on the sidewalk. Desperate friends of the casualties looked on while paramedics performed CPR. He comforted as many as he could, praying over the dead and wounded, and accompanied families to the hospital.

One hundred ninety-four people were killed and a further 1,492 were injured. President Kirchner declared a three-day-long period of national mourning, but grief soon turned to anger when it was revealed that the club's fire safety license had expired more than a month earlier and had not been renewed by the fire department. The club had no detection or alarm system, only one working fire extinguisher out of fifteen, and had allowed three thousand people into a 1,031-capacity venue. Bergoglio maintained a loyal support for the victims in the months and years that followed, issuing a damning indictment of the corruption that had led to the tragedy and ordering a mass for the victims to be celebrated on December 30 each year, when the bells of the cathedral would ring 194 times to remember those who had perished.

Meanwhile, the pope wrote to Bergoglio expressing his sadness and asking the cardinal to pass on his condolences to the victims.

This was most likely their last communication, for at 9:37 P.M. local time on April 2, 2005, John Paul II died.

THE THRESHOLD OF THE VATICAN

We know how the events of the conclave played out, but with a better understanding of the formative events and experiences that had shaped him to this point, the actions of this man perhaps make better sense.

He was a Jesuit through and through, and had never desired or sought power. In fact, on numerous occasions he had either flat-out refused it or taken a great deal of persuading to accept it. The mystery cardinal diarist whose account of the 2005 conclave is so revealing described Bergoglio's look of pain as he stepped up to the altar to cast his ballot, as if begging God to spare him; and another "authoritative source" revealed how Bergoglio was "almost in tears" when he implored his supporters to give up the fight for the good of the church and to vote for Cardinal Ratzinger. As the diarist noted:

> [Bergoglio was] safe on the doctrinal plane, open on the social level, impatient on the pastoral level toward the stiffness shown by some collaborators of [John Paul II] on issues of sexual ethics. Characteristics that, in the absence of a true candidate of [the] "left," alternative to the Ratzinger line, will make Bergoglio the man of reference for the entire group of the most reluctant cardinals to vote for the dean of the Sacred College [Ratzinger]. A group whose thinking core is made up of Karl Lehmann, president of the German Bishops' Conference, and Godfried Danneels, archbishop of Brussels, with a significant group of U.S. and Latin American cardinals, as well as some of the Roman curia.

There is speculation that Bergoglio's "tears" were actually the result of frustration on account of this group—a collection of reformist cardinals known in Vatican circles as the St. Gallen group—using him as an anti-Ratzinger pawn, when he had no desire whatsoever to become pope. Austen Ivereigh believes that "what upset Bergoglio was that he was the focal point of a fracturing, one destined to polarize, as in the 1970s, into ideological blocs. It upset him at a purely psychological level, in the sense that overcoming this divide had been a major part of his life's work."

Whatever his emotions, Bergoglio was certainly relieved to return to Argentina. His brush with power made him thankful for the freedom his grounded and humble life as archbishop of Buenos Aires afforded him. Now aged sixty-eight, he had just seven years until he was eligible for retirement, and he wished to live them out peacefully among the poor and needy in the city. Peace, however, was perhaps wishful thinking. The impressive support Bergoglio had received during the conclave and the great power his continent commanded had not gone unnoticed by Benedict, who later stated as pope, "I am convinced that here [Latin America] is decided, at least in part—and in a fundamental part—the future of the Catholic Church; for me it has always been evident." The church, therefore, still had plans for him, and in October 2005 he was elected to join the council of the Synod of Bishops; followed by yet another election as the leader of all Argentinian bishops in December of the same year.

The endorsements he received from those within the church were not mirrored by the Argentine government, and Bergoglio and Kirchner's relationship continued with its pattern of tit-for-tat critical statements laden with oblique subtexts about each other's failings. So antagonistic was their relationship that Kirchner was reported to have referred to Bergoglio as "the true leader of the opposition," but there were times, it seems, when the cardinal was so incensed by the president that he played right into his hands.

In December 2004, Bergoglio published an open letter condemning a Ministry of Culture–sponsored exhibition by the award-winning Argentine artist León Ferrari, among whose works were several pieces depicting Benedict XVI, most notably a green glass bottle filled with condoms and with a picture of the pope stuck to the front. Of particular offense was a piece entitled *La Civilización Occidental y Cristiana* ("Western Christian Civilization"), featuring a cheap souvenir figure of the crucified Christ pinned to a U.S.

fighter jet, originally made in 1965 as a statement against the Vietnam War. In his letter, Cardinal Bergoglio said he was "very hurt by the blasphemy" and complained that the event was "supported by the money that the Christian people and people of good will bring with their taxes." He closed the letter by appealing to the people to "make an act of reparation and a request for forgiveness" by observing a "day of fasting and prayer, a day of penance in which, as a Catholic community, we ask the Lord to forgive our sins and our sins from the city."

The attack, it would seem, was a misjudged act of artistic intolerance on the cardinal's part, and after Ferrari responded, reportedly stating, "The difference between me and Bergoglio is that he thinks that people who don't think like him should be punished, condemned, while I think not even he should be punished." Bergoglio said no more on the issue.

Relations did not improve when Néstor Kirchner's two-term limit came to an end in 2007 and his wife, Cristina, replaced him as president. Bergoglio had begun to suspect that his office was being bugged by the Argentine security services and took to playing classical music at full volume to disrupt any recording devices when discussing issues to do with the government. It is highly probable, therefore, that music was blaring out of the archbishop's office in the months leading up to July 2010, when a vote was scheduled to take place to legalize same-sex marriage.

Bergoglio had attacked Néstor Kirchner publicly in 2006, condemning an attempt to legalize abortion in cases of rape and other clearly extenuating circumstances. Now he took an even stronger stance on the proposed changes to the institution of marriage. In a private letter to four monasteries in Buenos Aires, Bergoglio described same-sex marriage as "the Devil's envy, through which sin entered the world, which artfully seeks to destroy the image of God: man and woman who are mandated to grow, multiply and dominate the earth. Let's not be naïve: it is not a simple political struggle; it is the destructive pretension against God's plan."

The bill was amended to give same-sex couples the freedom to adopt children, and this hardened opposition among those previously on the fence, but when Bergoglio's letter was leaked to the media it played right into the hands of Kirchner, who declared, "It's worrisome to hear phrases such as 'war of God' and 'projects of the devil,' which are things that send us back to medieval times and the Inquisition." When the bill passed, many jubilant supporters in the Senate were reportedly happier about beating Bergoglio than they were about increasing people's human rights.

Although he had lost the battle and, possibly, the opinion many had of him as a tolerant pastor, Bergoglio had toed the Vatican doctrinal line and proved himself capable of publicly defending the faith. In the world outside Rome, Bergoglio was—and would remain until his election as pope—an unknown figure. Back home in Argentina, his commitment to the poor and to social justice would never be eclipsed in the minds of those living in the *villas miserias*, but he had begun to alienate himself from the population living above the poverty line. Austen Ivereigh quotes an unnamed senior priest who had "spent many years working to connect the business world with the Church's social teachings" as saying that Bergoglio "showed no interest at all in the middle-class world of Catholics—not the world of business, or banking, or the arts or university."

Ivereigh draws an interesting comparison between Bergoglio's devotion to the poor and his perceived dismissal of the middle classes with the parable of the Prodigal Son from the Gospels, in which a father welcomes home with great festivity his errant youngest son, who has been away squandering his inheritance on prostitutes, much to the chagrin of his elder brother, who has remained at home toiling in the fields. The parable seeks to illustrate that those who have sinned are always welcomed back by God if they confess. However, the poor, on the whole, had not sinned and were victims of circumstances beyond their control, and therefore it feels more that Bergoglio's conscious decision to favor those in need over those who perhaps attended mass more frequently and lived better lives is more akin to the Good Samaritan, who, when he saw someone in need, "had compassion on him, and went to him, and bound up his wounds."

As criticism also came from left-wing circles, who accused him of collusion with the junta during the war, there was essentially no way Bergoglio could satisfy all parties, so he "made the decision, from the start, to focus on these peripheries [*villas miserias*], choosing to spend some time every weekend in the new barrios" and so "evangeliz[e] the city from its margins."

PREPARATIONS FOR
AN IMPORTANT BIRTHDAY

A little over a year after his very public defeat by the Kirchner government, Jorge Bergoglio was growing weary. Having resigned his post as president of the Argentine bishops when his six-year tenure came to an end in September 2011, he had just one thing on his mind: his seventy-fifth birthday, on December 17.

Giddy at the thought of being released from high office, he began to make plans for how he would spend his retirement. He selected the bedroom he wanted at the clerical retirement home in the Flores neighborhood he had grown up in. He began to mull over completing the thesis he had abandoned during the period of despondency in Frankfurt and contacted the publishers of his previous theological writings to discuss which of his other works might be of interest.

When his birthday came, Bergoglio mailed his official letter of resignation to Pope Benedict XVI. As Ivereigh describes, resignation letters "are offered *nunc pro tunc* ('now for later'), for the pope to act on at some point in the future, unless health or some other imperative requires an immediate acceptance. But he [Bergoglio] could expect his successor to be announced perhaps late in 2012 and installed in early 2013." All he had to do was wait.

At the height of the Vatileaks scandal, in which a string of documents exposed high-level corruption, blackmail, and homosexuality within the Vatican, Bergoglio was summoned to Rome to attend a consistory in February 2012, at which a tired and frail Benedict appointed twenty-two new cardinals. But he returned to Argentina without an answer to his letter, and as 2012 drew to a close he began to feel that something might be amiss. Rather than let his concerns get the better of him, he continued working, putting his house in order by giving away to friends some of his vast collection of books and sorting through documents in his office.

Bergoglio was therefore completely ready for his retirement when once more he traveled to the Vatican, this time for the consistory for the canonization of the martyrs of Otrano—the elevation to saint-hood of 813 Italians who were killed in 1480 by Ottoman soldiers for refusing to convert to Islam—on February 11, 2013. He told friends, "I want to leave as little as possible behind me when I take my leave from this world."

Little did he know the enormity of the news that awaited him in Rome.

3

CONCLAVE

Eight years earlier, when the choice of the new pope by the conclave was announced, the pontiff-elect, Pope Benedict, was described by Cardinal Joachim Meisner of Cologne as looking "a little forlorn."

Traditionally, it is the responsibility of the dean of the College of Cardinals to ask the new pope if he accepts his role, but as the dean was Ratzinger himself, it fell to the vice dean, Cardinal Sodano. While those in the room waited, Cardinal Murphy-O'Connor remembered in particular "the silence that reigned. He looked very solemn, and not only lucid, but calm." When his answer of acceptance finally came—in Latin, of course—Joseph Ratzinger officially became the 265th pope. And when asked which name he wished to take, he did not pause for consideration. He had his answer ready. He would be known as Benedict XVI. Why "Benedict"? During his first general audience, on April 27, 2005, he stated that St. Benedict was "a courageous and authentic prophet of peace" and "a fundamental reference point for European unity and a powerful reminder of the indispensable Christian roots of his culture and civilization."

Each of the cardinals congratulated Benedict and kissed his hand.

It is both fascinating and tragic to realize that, of the two leading candidates in the 2005 conclave, both are on record as saying they didn't want to be pope. Benedict, upon his election, said it was like a guillotine had fallen on him. Francis said that anyone who wanted to lead the Catholic Church didn't care very much for themselves: "I didn't want to be pope."

But then, who ever *does* want to be pope? It's a cross. It's too onerous. It ends only in death. There is a reason the small room Benedict was next whisked into is called the Sala delle Lacrime, the Room of Tears. Within those walls, countless popes have dissolved in tears under the weight of the responsibility that would be their end. Pope John XXIII famously said that no one tells the new pope whether they are tears of joy or of sorrow. He has to find out for himself.

But new popes must quickly put personal tears aside. Even in the minutes after their election they become the face of the Catholic Church. As Benedict later described it himself:

> Actually, at that moment one is first of all occupied by very practical, external things. One has to see how to deal with the robes and such. Moreover, I knew that very soon I would have to say a few words out on the balcony, and I began to think about what I could say. Besides, even at that moment when it hit me, all I was able to say to the Lord was simply: "What are you doing with me? Now the responsibility is yours. You must lead me! I can't do it. If you wanted me, then you must also help me!" In this sense, I stood, let us say, in an urgent dialogue relationship with the Lord: if he does the one thing he must also do the other.

"HABEMUS PAPAM"

As Benedict was choosing from the three white papal cassocks hand-made by the Gammarelli family, papal tailors since 1903, seasoned Vatican correspondent John Thavis remembers sitting in the heaving press office, having "just finished prewriting two stories: one saying Cardinal Ratzinger was the new pope and the other, much shorter, saying Italian Cardinal Dionigi Tettamanzi had been elected," when the first hint of smoke emerged from the Sistine Chapel chimney at 5:40 P.M.

Thavis and his colleagues knew that any smoke that emerged this early in the day must mean that Ratzinger had reached a two-thirds majority in the first ballot of the afternoon, since the cardinals could not have gone through two ballots within such a short space of time. But as the crowds in St. Peter's Square and the press corps alike strained to ascertain the color, the smoke continued to pour out of the chimney for twenty minutes without an accompanying chorus of bells. Once again, the elaborate smoke system had failed. Inside the Vatican, it was a chaotic scene, with Swiss Guards and members of the curia dashing about to alert the bell ringers that a pope had been elected, as heightened security measures meant that the phones were down around the chapel.

Even more confusion followed when the hourly chimes rang out at 6 P.M. After the previous evening's debacle, the crowds in the square were completely flummoxed as to whether to celebrate.

Finally, when the bells of St. Peter's, and thereafter nearly three hundred other churches in Rome, finally began to ring, at around 6:10 P.M., there could be no more doubt in the minds of the gathered faithful: they had a new pope. But back in the Room of Tears, Benedict, too, was encountering his own episode of farce. Despite having tailored the last nine popes, the illustrious Gammarellis' tried-and-tested method—of making three ivory satin wool cassocks with silk cuffs in sizes small, medium, and large and then making a few small tweaks on the day to fit whoever had been elected pontiff— was failing. At a reasonable five feet seven inches, Benedict could hardly be described as tiny, but none of the prepared robes or shoes fit him. Still, eager to get out on the balcony and greet his people, he instructed the tailors to pin the cassock as best they could— and, for good measure, decided to keep his black sweater on underneath, due to the cold he had been suffering from during the conclave.

At 6:43 P.M. local time, Pope Benedict XVI was announced to the world with that iconic phrase first used to announce the election of Pope Martin V in 1417, *"Habemus papam!"* (We have a pope!) Stepping out onto the balcony, the newly elected bishop of Rome smiled broadly, raised both hands in the air toward God, and then clasped them together in thanks to the crowds. Following a brief speech and prayers, Benedict returned to the hotel with his fellow cardinals for a modest celebratory dinner of traditional

German thick bean soup, dried beef salad, and champagne, followed by some Latin hymns.

On that day in 2005 when the small, quietly spoken, snowy-haired figure stepped out onto the world's most famous balcony to raise his aged hands to the crowd of thousands in St. Peter's Square and the millions around the world watching on television, there was not the usual rush (as attends the surprise elevation of a previously obscure cardinal) to learn something about the man suddenly thrust into the leadership of 1.1 billion faithful, because so much, good and bad, was already known about him, not only by Catholics but by the world at large. Throughout his years as prefect of the Congregation for the Doctrine of the Faith, he had, sometimes cruelly and sometimes gently, accumulated a great many nicknames, not just God's Rottweiler and Panzer Kardinal, but also Cardinal No and Papa-Ratzi. As these names suggest, opinions on Cardinal Ratzinger were polarized. Some perceived him as an "aggressive German of lordly air, an ascetic who carries the cross like a sword," while others saw him as quite the opposite: as a virtuous, simple, Fanta-drinking Bavarian scholar who had devoted his entire life to the observance of divine laws and the humble veneration of sublime and unchanging truths.

Which version was to be believed, and who exactly was the man behind this double-edged reputation?

A CHILDHOOD BY THE RIVER

Born on April 16, 1927, in the small Bavarian town of Marktl am Inn, near the border with Austria, Joseph Aloisius Ratzinger was the youngest of Joseph and Maria Ratzinger's three children. The day he was born was Holy Saturday, and the devoutly Catholic family would always remember the "deep snow and teeth-clattering cold that reigned" that day. His birth on the eve of Easter meant that Joseph was baptized immediately, much to the disappointment of his elder brother, Georg, and sister, Maria, who were not permitted to attend the ceremony for fear of their catching cold.

Joseph Ratzinger Sr. was a provincial policeman, and he and his family were frequently posted to various small rural towns, though they always remained within "the triangle formed on two sides by the Inn and Salzach rivers." This was the picturesque backdrop to what Ratzinger, in his *Milestones: Memoirs 1927–1977*, portrays as a bucolic childhood spent immersed in nature, scrambling up hills and tramping down valleys, or visiting the numerous churches packed into this Catholic heartland of Germany. His early life held "many beautiful memories of friendship and neighborly aid, memories of small family celebrations and of church life," but in his memoirs he does not shy away from the great hardships faced by the family during a time of deep economic depression.

Following the end of the First World War, in 1918, the Treaty of Versailles curtailed any military strength that the German nation had left and, crucially, crippled it financially. The treaty was explicit in laying all the blame for the conflict, in black and white, at Germany's door.

Aside from requiring that it accept guilt, the Allies prohibited Germany from negotiating any terms of the treaty. The German people took to the streets to voice their anger and humiliation at the loss of 10 percent of the nation's territories, all of its overseas colonies, 15 percent of its population, and vast swathes of its iron and coal industries. Germany was also ordered, in 1921, to pay reparations to the eye-watering tune of 132 billion gold marks (thirty-one billion dollars). Hyperinflation ensued, and when the country inevitably defaulted on its payments, in 1923, an attempt was made by the Allied governments to stabilize the economy. But the damage had already been done, and Ratzinger's early years were overshadowed by the sense of a country on its knees: "unemployment was rife; war reparations weighed heavily on the German economy; battles among the political parties set people against one another."

It was during this deeply turbulent period of economic depression that another shadow was beginning to stretch over Germany: the rise to power of Adolf Hitler.

THE ADVANCING CLOUDS OF WAR

Ratzinger's memories of the early 1930s are those of a child, but he writes of a growing awareness of "shrill campaign posters," of constant elections and heated public meetings during which his father would, time and again, have to "take a position against the violence of the Nazis." Joseph Ratzinger Sr.'s open criticism of the Brownshirts eventually became untenable, and in December 1932 he requested a transfer to the "well-to-do agricultural village" of Aschau am Inn.

But there was no escaping. Just over a month later, on January 30, 1933, following two elections that failed to produce a majority government, Adolf Hitler was sworn in as chancellor of Germany.

Ratzinger himself has no memory of this historic moment, but his brother, Georg, and sister, Maria, recounted how on that fateful rainy day their school was ordered to "perform a march through the village that, of course, soon turned into a tramp through the slush that could hardly have fired anyone's enthusiasm." If only this had been the case everywhere. Hitler's ascendency unleashed an overwhelming sense of nationalism, and formerly closeted Nazis were suddenly confident in expressing their political sentiments publicly. The Hitler Youth and League of German Girls soon swept into every village, and Georg and Maria, much to their parents' horror, were "obliged to participate in their activities."

What Ratzinger later remembered from those first four years under Hitler's rule was the insidious campaign against religion, "the practice of spying and informing on priests who behaved as 'enemies of the Reich.'" Schools in Bavaria were often closely linked to the church, so new teachers loyal to the party were soon installed, and the curriculum was changed in line with their ideology. Yet again Joseph Senior did what he could to stand against the tide of persecution and would "warn and aid priests he knew were in danger." But he was fighting a losing battle.

Internationally, Hitler began to set his sights on reclaiming territories stripped from Germany by the Treaty of Versailles; at home, he encouraged the people to reconnect with what Ratzinger in his memoir describes as their "great Germanic culture." Long-forgotten midsummer ceremonies celebrating the "sacredness of nature" were reintroduced, with maypoles erected on village greens. The aesthetic power of such scenes could not have been lost on the former art student who now ruled as chancellor, but it was not just propaganda that motivated these initiatives. In giving the people new rituals to celebrate, Hitler believed that he could remove the power that Judeo-Christianity had held over people through "alien notions such as sin and redemption." In eradicating religion from society, he would clear the way for his ideology. In this he partially succeeded, though one glimmer of hope Ratzinger remembered was that Hitler's "rhetorical formulas" were actually *too* subtle for the brawny young local men, who were purely focused on being the fastest to climb the maypole and retrieve the prized Bavarian sausages that adorned the top.

As Joseph Senior approached his sixtieth birthday, and mandatory retirement, in 1937, the family relocated once more. This time it was not to another set of borrowed police station–house quarters, but to a home of their own.

The Ratzingers had four years earlier purchased an eighteenth-century farmhouse surrounded by beautiful meadows and fruit trees, on the edge of a sprawling pine forest at the foot of the mountains, just outside the small southern Bavarian town of Traunstein, located west of the Austrian border. It was from here that the children could escape into the hills and woods while their parents threw themselves into renovating the tumbledown house into something quite magical—a place the young Joseph considered the family's "true home."

As well as nature, his life began to be shaped increasingly by the church. He followed in his brother Georg's footsteps and became an altar boy, although the future pope noted in his memoirs that he "could not compete with [Georg] in either zeal or diligence." In Bavarian society at this time, Ratzinger writes that for both the devoutly religious and those bound merely by social conventions, "no one could conceive of dying without the Church or of experiencing the great events of life without her. Life then would have simply fallen into the void, would have lost the solid ground that supported it and gave it meaning." He delighted in the structure, or "rhythm," as he described it, with which the church bookmarked the year, and there was always some celebration to look forward to. Joseph Senior and Maria encouraged their children's understanding of the liturgy through picture books for Sundays and major feast days when they were very young, moving them on to the complete missal for the celebration of mass on each day of the year by the time the family reached Traunstein.

Ratzinger later stated, in a 1997 interview with Peter Seewald, that "there was no lightning-like moment of illumination when I realized I was meant to become a priest. On the contrary there was a long process of maturation." Yet he recalls in his memoirs that it was at this time in his life when he "started down the road of liturgy, and this became a continuous process of growth into a grand reality transcending all particular individuals and generations, a reality that became an occasion for me of ever-new amazement and discovery." When comparing the Germanic reserve with which he recounts his vocational journey to the priesthood to that of his Argentine successor, we can trace their future conflicting styles all the way back to these moments in childhood. They are the open versus the closed. Just as the lightning-bolt moment experienced by Bergoglio mirrors his later life as a "Bishop of the Slums" who kissed the feet of AIDS sufferers, so too does the calling experienced by our shy and retiring theologian Joseph Ratzinger, a self-described "perfectly ordinary Christian" who simply felt that "God had a plan for each person," himself included.

The idyll of their new home could not last. Already searchlights were being erected to scan the night skies for enemy aircraft, and a secret ammunitions factory was being built nearby, sheltered from view by trees in the neighboring woods. Young Ratzinger found to his dismay that his new school, despite its remoteness, was also capitulating to the pressure of Hitler's regime. His beloved Latin lessons were cut back, and Greek was removed altogether; old songs now included lines of Nazi propaganda; and religious education was prohibited in favor of sports and outdoor pursuits.

On March 12, 1938, German troops marched into Hitler's homeland and annexed Austria. As Ratzinger puts it, "no one could ignore the movement of troops," but as a devoutly Catholic family living in a border village, the "Greater Germany" created by the Anschluss (annexation) presented them with a startling new freedom of movement. The Ratzingers were now able to make pilgrimages to Salzburg and its many "glorious churches"; they were delighted that ticket prices for the city's renowned music festival were greatly reduced because the approaching war deterred other tourists from visiting. There is a refreshing candor in his memoir in the way Ratzinger reflects on the moral dilemmas faced by German families such as his: they feared what Hitler's aggression would bring but also sometimes benefited from it in small ways.

The benefits were short-lived. Almost immediately after the Anschluss, the pace and vigor of Hitler's international campaign surged. In the absence of any challenge to his aggression, he was further appeased by British prime minister Neville Chamberlain at the now-infamous Munich Conference, and successfully reclaimed the former German territory of the Sudetenland from Czechoslovakia in September 1938. Shortly after Chamberlain triumphantly waved his piece of white paper to the world, declaring he had secured "peace in our time," Hitler's true intentions were revealed when, on November 9–10—Kristallnacht (the Night of Broken Glass)—his paramilitary forces and their supporters across Germany destroyed some seventy-five hundred Jewish businesses, burned a thousand synagogues, murdered ninety-one Jews, and arrested more than thirty thousand Jewish men aged between sixteen and sixty and sent them to the new concentration camps at Dachau, Buchenwald, and Sachsenhausen.

The events caused international outrage. *The Times* of London wrote, "No foreign propagandist bent upon blackening Germany before the world could outdo the tale of burnings and beatings, of blackguardly assaults on defenseless and innocent people, which disgraced that country yesterday." Yet, in his memoirs, Joseph Ratzinger makes no mention of Kristallnacht or the ongoing Nazi persecution of Jews, though there is no doubt whatsoever that he would have encountered it on a daily basis. For years.

In the early 1930s, in his own village of Traunstein, signs were erected over Jewish businesses to advise residents: "Do not buy from the Jew. He sells you, farmers, out of house and home." Ratzinger alludes time and again in his memoir to his family's anti-Nazi stance, and they were likely no more guilty of complicity with the regime than the other "good Germans" who turned the other cheek during these years of atrocities. But as John Allen writes in his biography of the future pontiff, "Ratzinger's reading of the war omits what many people would consider its main lesson, namely, the dangers of blind obedience . . . many Germans failed to question, to dissent, and where necessary to fight back."

With the country in turmoil and war approaching, in the early months of 1939 it was decided that Joseph Ratzinger would enter the minor seminary of Studienseminar St. Michael, having been "urged" by his pastor to do so "in order to be initiated systematically into the spiritual life" and begin his journey toward the priesthood. As the boarding school did not offer academic teaching as well as theological training, its members remained integrated students of the local Traunstein *gymnasium* and made up around one-third of the school's population. According to Georg Ratzinger, who had already been at the seminary for four years when his younger brother joined, "it was not that unusual at all for several boys in a family to become priests and the daughters, nuns."

Ratzinger recalls following in the footsteps of his older brother "with joy and great expectations." But the quiet and reserved Joseph, who had "built a childhood world of [his] own," soon discovered that he was not cut out for boarding school life—he was the youngest seminarian, aged just twelve—with sixty other boys and "had to learn how to fit into the group, how to come out of [his] solitary ways and start building a community with others by giving and receiving." With the outbreak of war following the German invasion of Poland, on September 1, 1939, Joseph and Georg were temporarily sent home to live with their parents, so that the boarding school could be turned into a military hospital. New living quarters for the seminary were soon found, this time in a much preferable forest location, which enabled the young scholars to return to pastimes like making dams and hiking the surrounding mountains.

Ratzinger himself admits that the scenario seems absurdly idyllic, but the fact was that, for many children, "the war appeared to be almost unreal" during this period known as the Phony War. When, eventually, the stalemate was broken and the lightning German invasion of Holland, Belgium, and France, known as the Blitzkrieg, came on May 10, 1940, Ratzinger acknowledges the surprising surge of patriotic emotions, even from those opposed to nationalism, when the powers that punished Germany after the First World War were "brought to their knees in a short time" at the beginning of the Second. The elation was not shared by Joseph Senior, who "with unfailing clairvoyance saw that a victory of Hitler's would not be a victory for Germany but rather a victory of the Antichrist that would surely usher in apocalyptic times for all believers, and not only for them."

Joseph Senior stood his ground in opposition to the Nazis and prevented his children from being forced into the Hitler Youth for as long as legally possible, in spite of a decree by the Bavarian Ministry of Education and Religious Affairs in 1938 that stated that tuition discounts would be available only to children registered as members. He would rather that the family struggle on his meager policeman's pension than acquiesce to the demands of such a tyrant, but when membership in the Hitler Youth was made mandatory for all boys aged fourteen and older, in 1939, as a precursor to conscription, fifteen-year-old Georg was unable to escape enrollment.

After Hitler launched Operation Barbarossa and marched 4.5 million German troops into the Soviet Union, in June 1941, the need for reinforcements became urgent, and Joseph, too, was reluctantly signed up, but he followed his father's example and refused to attend the meetings. Fortuitously, this came to the attention of his mathematics teacher, who, despite his own allegiance to the party, suggested that the boy "just go once and get the document," but so fervent was young Joseph's refusal that the teacher took pity on him, saying, "I understand, I'll take care of it," and agreed to sign him in for meetings regardless of his attendance so that he could receive a tuition discount.

Georg had no such benefactor when he turned seventeen, the legal age for conscription, and was drafted into the army. He was posted to the Sudetenland in the summer of 1942, much to the distress of his parents, and especially of fourteen-year-old Joseph, who idolized his brother. For the seminarians left behind, their days were spent watching the "huge transports [that] now began to roll in, in some cases bringing home horribly wounded soldiers," and scanning the local newspaper for the names of schoolmates who had been killed in action.

It was not long before Joseph Ratzinger, too, received his deployment papers. A year earlier than expected, in 1943, when he was just sixteen years old, he was drafted, along with the other boys from his class born between 1926 and 1927, and posted to several batteries around Munich to serve as student reserves in the antiaircraft defense force—first protecting a Bavarian Motor Works (BMW) factory that manufactured precious airplane engines. Ratzinger remembers that his time in the army "brought many an unpleasantness, particularly for so nonmilitary a person as myself." The students were still permitted to travel into the smoldering city three times a week to attend lessons but were horrified by the increasing devastation as the bombing of Munich intensified.

By the summer of 1944, rumors of an Allied invasion of France raised hopes that the chaos of war might soon come to an end, but it would take a further year from the D-Day landings of June 6 before Germany finally surrendered. In the meantime, Ratzinger had reached military age, so in September he was transferred to a labor detail on the border between Austria, Czechoslovakia, and Hungary, which were then German-occupied territories. The base was run by "fanatical ideologues who tyrannized [them] without respite." Desperate SS officers hauled the students out of bed during the night and attempted to coerce the drowsy young men to become "voluntary" recruits for the weapons branch. Ratzinger and his schoolmates avoided this death sentence only by declaring that they intended to become Catholic priests. The soldiers ordered them out "with mockery and abuse," and the students returned to their duties of trench-digging the following morning.

Despite having signed a nonaggression pact with Stalin, Hitler had decided to send 4.5 million troops to invade the Soviet Union in June 1941. According to German army major Hubert Menzel, the Nazis believed that "in two years' time, that is . . . [the] beginning of 1943, the English would be ready, the Americans would be ready, the Russians would be ready too, and then we would have to deal with all three of them at the same time," so they decided to remove Russia from the equation in advance of any potentially deadly alliance with the Allies.

The astonishing arrogance displayed by Germany in assuming

the campaign against Russia would be short meant its forces were entirely unprepared for the resilience, skillful military tactics, and sheer volume of men Stalin's Red Army was able to throw at the invasion, not to mention the fearsome Russian winter, nicknamed "General Winter" on account of the help it provided to the Soviet military. By September 1944, Hitler was now fighting a war of attrition, and the ever-encroaching Soviet front drew closer to Ratzinger and his comrades, who could now "hear the din of artillery in the distance." After two months of toil, German efforts to strengthen the southwestern rampart were deemed futile, and the men were dispersed to infantry regiments around Bavaria.

When the news of the Allied invasion of Germany and Hitler's suicide reached his barracks six months later, in May 1945, Ratzinger seized the opportunity to abandon his post in Munich and return home. The city was still heavily patrolled by officers "who had orders to shoot deserters on the spot," but when he encountered two of them on a quiet road leading out of Munich, "they, too, had had their fill of war and did not want to become murderers." They saw he was wearing a sling on his arm from an injury and allowed him to proceed on his way: "Comrade, you are wounded. Move on!"

Joseph and Maria were thrilled to have their youngest son return, but it was not long before American forces arrived in the village and he was forced to leave, this time as a POW. Ratzinger remembers that he had to "put back on the uniform I had already abandoned, had to raise my hands and join the steadily growing throng of war prisoners whom they were lining up on our meadow." After three days of marching, he was interned in a POW camp alongside fifty thousand fellow German soldiers. Here they slept outside, "without a clock, without a calendar, without newspapers," snatching from rumors what pieces of information they could about events in the world outside. The captivity was relatively brief, and on June 19, 1945, he was released and made his way home once more. He was followed a month later by Georg, and the pair returned to their studies in the seminary by autumn 1945.

Ratzinger's memoirs have drawn sharp criticism for their "unsettling selectiveness" and their distinct lack of introspection regarding the atrocities committed by Hitler against the Jewish people and "the moral failings of German Catholics specifically." His biographer John Allen concurs that *Milestones* leads us to believe that while war and persecution were raging, Ratzinger "was reading great literature, playing Mozart, joining his family on trips to Salzburg, and poring over Latin conjugations." Dachau was just sixty-two miles from Ratzinger's hometown and only ten miles from Munich, yet his only mention of a concentration camp in which over 41,500 people died and over two hundred thousand were incarcerated is a lament for the kindly rector who taught him at the seminary after the war and who had spent five years there. When the Red Army was closing in on Germany's eastern front, the SS began to evacuate the camp and drove more than seven thousand prisoners west, on the chillingly termed "death marches." After years of torture and starvation, many did not survive the marches, and it is recorded that thirty-six people collapsed and died in and around the village of Traunstein. The Holocaust was on everybody's doorstep.

It is commonly said that "those who cannot remember the past are condemned to repeat it." As David Gibson observes in his book *The Rule of Benedict:*

> What the Nazi experience seems to have bred in Joseph Ratzinger, or the preexisting trait it reinforced in him, was a kind of distancing, a pattern of removing himself from unpleasantness, isolating the pure ideal—of the faith, the church, the family, the nation—from the inevitable corruptions of the world. This approach fosters a sense of remoteness in his remembrances, a detachment that may strike many as cold. In fact, it is problematic when a churchman who places such a high priority on personal rectitude and individual holiness appears unreflective about his own history.

There is an undeniable parallel between Benedict's attempts to reduce the cognitive dissonance of his own experiences under Hitler's rule by painting an idyllic picture of a childhood almost entirely uninterrupted by the savageries of the Second World War and his apparent unwillingness to confront the horrific reality of widespread sexual abuse within the Catholic Church during his time as pope.

THE STUDENT BECOMES A PRIEST

When Ratzinger resumed his studies at the seminary, he saw it as an opportunity not just for himself, but also for the nation to find its way out of the ruins of war and rebuild a "better Germany; and . . . a better world." In *Milestones* he writes that "despite many human failings, the Church was the alternative to the destructive ideology of the brown(*shirt*) rulers; in the inferno that had swallowed up the powerful, she had stood firm with a force coming to her from eternity." Ratzinger here chooses to sidestep the Vatican's documented preference, under Pius XII, for the church-allied Third Reich over the specter of godless communism from Russia, instead focusing on its postwar record, more worthy of his idealized praise.

Though books were scarce, Ratzinger threw himself into his theological studies for the next two years. Then, in the summer of 1947, he was accepted into a prestigious theology institute at the University of Munich, with a view to becoming "more fully familiar with the intellectual debates of our time by working at the university, so as some day to be able to dedicate myself completely to theology as a profession."

Here Ratzinger immersed himself in philosophy and literature, and spent hours listening to the university's many inspirational thinkers: "I looked forward with burning expectation to the lectures of our renowned teachers." There was a palpable feeling among the young seminarians that they were a new generation of Catholics capable of "radical change," who "had the courage to ask new questions and a spirituality that was doing away with what was dusty and obsolete." The university had been severely damaged during the bombing raids on Munich, and large parts still "lay in ruins," but Ratzinger's department "had found temporary quarters in the former royal hunting lodge at Fürstenried." Its magnificent gardens were the ideal environment for deep contemplation of the enormous commitment he was about to make.

During his time at the university, Ratzinger developed a confidence in his own interpretation of scripture and of great theological thinkers such as Saints Augustine and Bonaventure, and the three years passed quickly. After his final examination, at the end of summer 1950, he began to prepare himself for ordination. On a "radiant summer day" in June 1951, Ratzinger, alongside Georg and forty other candidates, stepped forward to commit themselves to God. In *Milestones,* he recalled, "We should not be superstitious; but, at that moment when the elderly archbishop laid his hands on me, a little bird—perhaps a lark—flew up from the high altar in the cathedral and trilled a little joyful song. And I could not but see in this a reassurance from on high, as if I heard the words 'this is good, you are on the right way.'"

The next four weeks "were like an unending feast" of new experiences for Ratzinger. After saying his first mass for a packed congregation in his home parish, he "learned firsthand how earnestly people wait for a priest, how much they long for the blessing that flows from the power of the sacrament." After the years of academia, the new Father Joseph was taken aback by the demands of his new role:

> I had to give sixteen hours of religious instruction at five different levels, which obviously required much preparation. Every Sunday I had to celebrate at least two Masses and give two different sermons. Every morning I sat in the confessional from six to seven, and on Saturday afternoons for four hours. Every week there were several burials in the various cemeteries of the city. I was totally responsible for youth ministry, and to this I had to add extracurricular obligations like baptisms, weddings, and so on.

This was challenging work, and it exposed his lack of "practical training." And as he spent more time with the younger members of his parish, he was dismayed to find just "how far removed the world of the life and thinking of many children was from the realities of faith and how little our religious instruction coincided with the actual lives and thinking of our families." This was an issue he continued to regard as one of the greatest threats faced by the Catholic Church.

It is perhaps unsurprising, therefore, that after just over a year as a parish priest, Ratzinger was delighted to learn that his place in the doctoral degree program was confirmed to start on October 1, 1952, and he could return to his beloved theological studies. He did feel some conflict about abandoning the task he had found most taxing: "I suffered a great deal, especially in the first year, from the loss of all the human contacts and experiences afforded me by the pastoral ministry. In fact, I even began to think I would have done better to remain in parish work." But these concerns were all allayed when his proud parents watched him step onto the stage and collect his doctoral degree in July 1953.

Ratzinger had devoted a large proportion of his doctorate to studying St. Augustine, as opposed to St. Thomas Aquinas, a decision described by biographer John Allen as "a minor act of rebellion" on account of Pope Leo XIII's 1879 encyclical that declared Aquinas was "rightly and deservedly esteemed the special bulwark and glory of the Catholic faith" and should be considered the single most important philosopher of the church. This encyclical had legitimized the movement known as neo-scholasticism, which sought to resist modernity by restoring the church to the doctrinal teachings of Aquinas and suggested that "anyone who departed from their point of view was flirting with heresy." Throughout his life, Ratzinger has remained what he described as a "decided Augustinian," but in 1953, this was a surprisingly progressive move and one perhaps influenced by what Allen describes as "the intellectual ferment" felt by many in the church in the years leading up to the Second Vatican Council in 1962.

A SHINING NEW THEOLOGICAL STAR

After his graduation, Ratzinger began working on his postdoctoral dissertation at the seminary and accepted a teaching position in Freising that came with cathedral housing. This enabled him to move his brother, sister, and aging parents from the family home—now becoming a burden—to live with him in the town. Both his father and mother would remain living with him until their deaths, in 1958 and 1963 respectively.

His thesis on the works of St. Bonaventure and the concept of revelation, however, proved to be surprisingly problematic for a student who had always excelled academically, and after he submitted the finished document at the end of 1955 it was met with wildly conflicting opinions from two of his professors. According to Ratzinger, Professor Gottlieb Söhngen, who had originally suggested the theme, "accepted it enthusiastically and even quoted from it frequently in his lectures," but Professor Michael Schmaus felt it displayed "dangerous modernism" and "a forthrightness not advisable in a beginner," and rejected it "because it did not meet the pertinent scholarly standards." Upon reflection, Ratzinger believed he had offended Schmaus by not requesting his guidance on a subject well known to be the professor's specialty, and had further insulted him with conclusions that drew heavily on "new breakthroughs" from French scholars who had picked up where Schmaus's own works had stalled before the war. Unfortunately, as Schmaus was the more powerful professor, his ruling stood, and numerous revisions were required before the thesis was eventually accepted, in February 1957.

A year later, Ratzinger was finally appointed as lecturer at the University of Munich and professor of fundamental theology and dogma in Freising. This was at a time when, as David Gibson notes, "theologians were like pop stars . . . selling out auditoriums for their talks, and books of complex theology had the popularity of paperback thrillers and were featured on the cover of *Time*." It was perhaps inevitable, then, that as this young upstart with reformist zeal was making waves in theological circles, his appointments were met with what Ratzinger described as "some sniper shots from certain disgruntled quarters." These only furthered his reputation as one to watch, and he proceeded to accept positions at universities in Bonn, Münster, and Tübingen over the next eight years. But, as Allen remarks, this was the climb of a career theologian and not someone seeking to be a cardinal: "Ambitious young clerics typically will go to Rome for seminary, where it is important to make contacts early on as well as to achieve a reputation as 'safe' in terms of doctrine and personal habits."

It was during these teaching years that Ratzinger caught the eye of the cardinal archbishop of Cologne, Josef Frings, who appointed him his personal *peritus* (theological expert). Frings was progressive and, having been chairman of the Conference of German Bishops since 1945, was already considered a "legend in European church circles" on theological matters for his speeches and essays. When, in July 1959, Pope John XXIII announced Vatican II, Frings requested that Ratzinger accompany him. In declining health and nearly blind, Frings came to depend on his thirty-five-year-old aide, who, in turn, was greatly inspired by a cardinal who many felt was "positioned to be one of the most influential voices in the council even before it began."

Many in the church felt hopeful that the three-year council deliberations would signal real change, and Ratzinger, at this stage in his evolution, was certainly among them.

In their simplest form, the two opposing sides at Vatican II were referred to as *aggiornamento,* progressive "people who wanted to 'modernize' the church and bring her into dialogue with the culture," and *ressourcement,* conservatives who wished "to recover elements of tradition that had been lost." As Frings's right-hand man, there is no doubt, Ratzinger was arguing firmly in favor of the *aggiornamento* camp; his personal commentary written at the time of Vatican II supports this interpretation of his views. And yet, in less than twenty years, a relatively short time in theological circles, he began to pursue an aggressive campaign of enforcement against the very ideals he argued for during the council.

And so the question remains, intriguing both scholars and critics alike: What exactly happened to cause such a shift in opinion in Joseph Ratzinger?

FAREWELL TO THE IDEALS OF YOUTH

Ratzinger's own recollections of his theological stance are somewhat contradictory. In a 1993 interview with *Time* magazine, he maintained that his beliefs had been consistent and unwavering: "I see no break in my views as a theologian [over the years]." Yet in *Milestones* he recalls that in 1966 he was "deeply troubled by the change in ecclesial climate that was becoming ever more evident," to the extent that his colleague Cardinal Julius Döpfner "expressed surprise at the 'conservative streak' he thought he detected" in the previously liberal scholar.

The beginning of this shift from the liberal "Ratzinger I" toward the conservative "Ratzinger II" manifested itself around the time of his acceptance of a newly created Second Chair in Dogma at the University of Tübingen in the summer of 1966. The waves of social unrest that had been building since the late 1950s and early 1960s finally erupted into worldwide protests in 1968. These protests, often student led, differed in agenda from country to country. In the United States, against a background of fierce opposition to the Vietnam War, the assassination of Martin Luther King Jr. sparked violent clashes between civil rights activists and police; in Czechoslovakia, resistance to Soviet repression gave rise to the short-lived Prague Spring; and in France and other parts of Europe there were general strikes and vast student demonstrations. In Germany, anger on the part of the young that their country and homes were still dominated by leaders and parents with a Nazi past was combined with a rejection of new laws about to be passed that would allow the government to limit civil rights in the case of an emergency. Even in the small city of Tübingen, Ratzinger recalled, "At almost a moment's notice, there was a change in the ideological 'paradigm' by which the students and a part of the teachers thought. . . . Almost overnight the existentialist model collapsed and was replaced by the Marxist."

Ratzinger, passionately anti-Marx, now found himself isolated on the left-leaning campus, even among members of his own theological faculty. Having long fought against the reduction of the human struggle to economic or political factors alone, he was horrified by what he saw:

The destruction of theology that was now occurring . . . was incomparably more radical precisely because it took biblical hope as its basis but inverted it by keeping the religious ardor but eliminating God and replacing him with the political activity of man. Hope remains, but the party takes the place of God, and, along with the party, a totalitarianism that practices an atheistic sort of adoration ready to sacrifice all humanness to its false god. I myself have seen the frightful face of this atheistic piety unveiled, its psychological terror, the abandon with which every moral consideration could be thrown overboard as a bourgeois residue when the ideological goal was at stake.

It is difficult to read this without feeling that Ratzinger's fears are connected to his experiences living under Nazi rule. As Allen notes, "This was deeply troubling for Ratzinger, who felt he had already lived through one ruinous attempt at the ideological manipulation of the Christian faith in Nazi Germany, and therefore felt himself obliged to resist another." Despite this, it is still surprising that he gives little credence to the stark differences between Hitler's manipulation of society and the popular uprisings expressed by citizens, a large majority of whom was opposing political oppression, not the church itself.

When interviewed in 1997, Ratzinger reflected that he "knew what was at stake: anyone who wanted to remain a progressive in this context had to give up his integrity." But as Gibson notes in *The Rule of Benedict*, "if the principles of the progressive movement were valid at one time, their misuse by some adherents or outside forces should not automatically invalidate them." Surely someone as theologically confident and morally principled as Ratzinger, a man who "remains true to his ideals and prides himself on resisting the momentum of the crowd," would have the strength to stand against what he considered to be a mob?

The exact moment of decision remains a mystery. The dean of Ratzinger's department at Tübingen, eminent Swiss liberal theologian and onetime friend of the future pope Hans Küng, later wrote in his memoirs, "Time and again people puzzle over how so gifted, friendly, open a theologian as Joseph Ratzinger can undergo such a change: from progressive Tübingen theologian to Roman Grand Inquisitor." Ideological differences would eventually drive an irreparable wedge between the pair. Küng went on to become one of Ratzinger's most formidable critics, and in return, Ratzinger played an instrumental behind-the-scenes role in rallying German bishops "in support of John Paul II's decision to strip Küng of his right to call himself a Catholic theologian."

When a position became available in 1969 at the newly created

University of Regensburg, in his beloved Catholic stronghold of Bavaria, Ratzinger, exhausted by the many "controversies experienced during academic meetings" since the "Marxist revolution kindled the whole university with its fervor," decided to accept. In *Milestones* he laments how only "a few years before, one could still have expected the theological faculties to represent a bulwark against the Marxist temptation. Now the opposite was the case: they became its real ideological centre." His brother, Georg, was also working in the city as director of the prestigious Regensburg Cathedral choir, and the opportunity to develop his own "theology further in a less agitated environment" was too good to pass up. As he had no desire to remain the lone figure "always forced into the contra position," the role of Second Chair in Dogma at a new university meant he could help shape the institution from the inside, alongside like-minded colleagues. With this decision to withdraw to the safety of an ideologically united institution, Ratzinger was making a concrete move away from his liberal past into the conservative future that awaited him.

While this was a shocking disappointment for some former colleagues, there were others for whom the move was not altogether unsurprising. Father Ralph M. Wiltgen wrote an account of Vatican II in 1967, in which he remarked, "Father Ratzinger, the personal theologian of Cardinal Frings . . . had seemed to give an almost unquestioning support to the views of his former teacher during the council. But as it was drawing to a close, he admitted that he disagreed on various points, and said he would begin to assert himself more after the council was over."

And assert himself he did.

Ratzinger describes his years at Regensburg as "a time of fruitful theological work." He reveled in the pure, uninterrupted time he was now able to devote to his writings. His prolific output during this period drew increasing attention from senior echelons of the church, and his reputation as a "conservative standard-bearer" was swiftly affirmed. Distancing himself yet further from his former colleagues in Tübingen, in 1972 he resigned his seat on the board of the progressive journal *Concilium* and joined forces with a group of distinguished conservative theologians to launch the rival journal *Communio*. As Allen remarks, it is a "telling indicator" of the church under John Paul II that all the founding members of *Communio* were elevated to senior positions during his papacy, while those from the more progressive *Concilium* received no such honors.

Joseph Ratzinger was bound for the top.

THE THEOLOGIAN BECOMES A CARDINAL

By July 1976, forty-nine-year-old Joseph Ratzinger was considered by many to be at the pinnacle of his academic career. But when news was announced of the sudden death of the archbishop of Munich, Cardinal Julius Döpfner—who had expressed surprise at Ratzinger's emerging conservative streak ten years earlier—everything changed in an instant.

Shocked at the news—Döpfner was only sixty-two—Ratzinger dismissed the quickly circulating rumors that tipped him as Döpfner's natural successor. In his 1997 memoir he wrote:

> I did not take them very seriously, because my limitations with regard to health were as well-known as my inability in matters of governance and administration. I knew I was called to the scholar's life and never considered anything else. Academic offices—I was now dean again and vice-president of the university—remained within the realm of functions that a professor must assume and were very far from the responsibilities of a bishop.

These were prescient words: eight years after he wrote that passage, during the 2005 conclave, Ratzinger would again be confronted by doubts about the serious "limitations" of his capacity to fulfill the responsibilities of the office presented to him. Furthermore, those who were opposed to his candidacy for the papacy would also refer to his "inability in matters of governance and administration," claiming he was a theologian and not a pope, and that his lack of pastoral experience would be detrimental to the Catholic Church as a whole.

It was Plato who said, "Only those who do not seek power are qualified to hold it." When Döpfner died, it wasn't just that Ratzinger was *not* seeking power, but that he would very soon make every effort to reject it. When analyzing his career in detail, clear patterns of behavior begin to emerge. Throughout his service to the church, it is in the exact moments that many would see as prodigious opportunities that Ratzinger seems to have felt quite the opposite.

Believing he had put an end to discussions regarding his succession, Ratzinger was surprised when the apostolic nuncio visited him in Regensburg "under some pretext" and, after dispensing with general pleasantries, pressed a letter detailing his appointment as archbishop of Munich and Freising into his hands. Permitted by the nuncio to consult his confessor, Ratzinger spoke with Professor Alfons Auer, whom he describes as having "a very realistic knowledge of my limitations, both theological and human." Having fully expected that Auer would advise him to decline, he found it more than a little surprising, therefore, when "without much reflection," Auer told the forty-nine-year-old Joseph that he "must accept." Still deeply unsure, Ratzinger returned to meet the nuncio and once more plead his reservations, but described how, "in the end, with him as my witness, I hesitantly wrote my acceptance on the stationery of the hotel where he was staying."

Ratzinger's anxious hand-wringing in 1976 grew, over his first four years as archbishop of Munich, into confidence in asserting what he felt his true calling to be—or, inversely, a certainty of what he was *not* meant to do. The responsibilities of his office were demanding, especially when he was "said to have had rocky relations with the priests in his archdiocese." Perhaps the challenges were compounded by the breakneck speed with which he was thrust into high office: he was appointed archbishop on March 25, 1977, consecrated on May 28, and as the new leader of a major metropolitan archdiocese, he was whisked off to Rome less than a month later, handed a red silk hat, and elevated to the College of Cardinals on June 27.

In the last pages of his memoirs Ratzinger admits that "the weeks before the consecration were difficult. Interiorly I was still very unsure, and in addition I had the huge burden of work that was nearly crushing me. And so it was in rather poor health that I approached the day of consecration." There is no mention of his feelings during that momentous visit to Rome, but one could not fault him for having a sense of trepidation.

Newly appointed Cardinal Ratzinger was afforded little time to dwell on these concerns, for a little over a year later, on August 6, 1978, Pope Paul VI died, and he was summoned to Rome to attend his first conclave.

Remarkably, as a "young and intelligent conservative" who was not Italian, Ratzinger made several lists of potential papal candidates, but what held more significance for him—for it's a safe bet that those lists would have terrified the life out of him—was his first meeting with another candidate, Cardinal Karol Wojtyla of Kraków.

The pair were already acquainted, having exchanged books since 1974, but this meeting enabled them to connect personally through the "deep orthodoxy" that the "young . . . and intelligent conservatives" both shared. Neither man ultimately emerged as a real contender. Ratzinger was considered to be carrying "too much baggage as a theologian who had so publicly changed his mind about Vatican II," and Wojtyla, despite receiving four votes in the second ballot, was "much less well known, a minor figure at Vatican II who lived in a closed-off society under the Communists in Poland." Instead, after two days of voting, the conclave elected Cardinal Albino Luciani, who had been considered even less *papabile* than Ratzinger and Wojtyla, and was viewed by many as a "simple, pastoral, direct and non-intellectual" alternative to the fifteen-year reign of Paul VI, which many had felt to be too heavily concerned with the bureaucracy of reforming the Roman Curia in favor of a more collegial church, in line with the conclusions reached at the end of the Second Vatican Council.

When the postconclave dust had settled after the election of the new Pope John Paul I, Ratzinger was dispatched as a papal representative at a Marian (relating to the Virgin Mary) congress in Ecuador in September 1978. Here he "cautioned against Marxist ideologies and the theology of liberation" and "pressures from the forces of the left."

John Paul I was known to the public as "the smiling pope," but he began his papacy with a sense of foreboding. Following the final ballot count that confirmed his majority, he shocked fellow cardinals with his answer to the traditional question "Do you accept?" by replying, "May God forgive you for what you have done in my regard" before adding, *"Accepto."* He felt himself ill equipped and unworthy of the Chair of Saint Peter, and admitted to the crowds during his first address, "I am still overwhelmed at the thought of this tremendous ministry for which I have been chosen: as Peter, I seem to have stepped out on treacherous waters. I am battered by a strong wind. So I turn towards Christ saying: 'Lord, save me.'" A few days later, when a church historian commented pedantically that his name should surely just be John Paul, rather than John Paul I, he replied ominously: "My name is John Paul the first. I will be here only a short time. The second is coming."

In the early hours of September 29, 1978, just thirty-three days into his papacy, John Paul I was found dead in his bed, with his reading light still on and an open book beside him. Vatican doctors estimated he had died of a heart attack around eleven o'clock the previous evening.

We will never know if the fears John Paul expressed were simply an acknowledgment of his shortcomings or whether he knew in a deeper sense that he was unwell. Whatever the truth, and despite the absurd conspiracy theories that flowed, many commentators felt that he was fundamentally cast adrift by the Vatican, who did little to look out for his well-being when he was clearly completely overwhelmed, both mentally and physically, by the demands of the papacy. Despite his somewhat reluctant start and his brief time in office, his attitudes had swiftly impressed people as a genuine chance for reform. His simple pastoral approach saw him renounce the traditional majestic plural, preferring to refer to himself by the singular *I* (although the Vatican continued to use *We* on all documentation); refuse a coronation in favor of a simple mass; and request that staff refrain from kneeling in his presence. He also set out his plans to tackle the murky world of the Vatican Bank, took bold steps toward reversing Paul VI's controversial encyclical on birth control, and expressed a strong desire to return the church to the poor.

But that dream was over before it began. The cardinals returned to Rome for the funeral and yet another conclave. After several rounds of balloting in which the previous two favorites, Italian cardinals Giuseppe Siri and Giovanni Benelli, were running neck and neck, the mood inside the Sistine Chapel shifted and Wojtyla began to gain ground. Several commentators at the time believed that this was no coincidence, but rather was due to a good deal of background campaigning from Joseph Ratzinger. Having just lost a pope at only sixty-five years of age, the cardinals must have seen the strong appeal of an even younger successor, and after eight ballots and three days, Wojtyla emerged victorious. He took the name John Paul II as a mark of respect for his predecessor.

Having identified Ratzinger as someone who shared his beliefs, and perhaps grateful for his support during the conclave, John Paul II wasted no time in drawing him into his inner circle, offering him the role of prefect of the Congregation for Catholic Education, a senior role within the curia responsible for the three major educational sectors: seminaries and religious formation institutes; institutes of higher education such as universities; and all religious schools. Ratzinger refused, explaining that it was too early to abandon his post in Munich, but the pair continued to work closely during the 1980 Synod of Bishops on "The Role of the Christian Family in the Modern World," in which Ratzinger excelled in his role as relator. Aside from an embarrassing visit by the new pope to Bavaria in which one of Ratzinger's young acolytes gave a somewhat scathing speech about the church's archaic views on women, sexuality, and relationships, the association between John Paul II and Ratzinger continued to strengthen.

Undeterred by his cardinal's earlier refusal, John Paul had a deep respect for Ratzinger's theological expertise and was determined to have him in Rome. The perfect opportunity presented itself when the most senior curial position, outside of the pope's own, became vacant. John Paul immediately offered Ratzinger the role of prefect of the Sacred Congregation for the Doctrine of the Faith (CDF), which he dutifully accepted on November 25, 1981, tasked to promote and defend the doctrine of the faith and its traditions in all of the Catholic world.

DEFENDER OF THE FAITH

While heresy-hunting was no longer its primary function, the CDF's Holy Inquisitorial origins were well known to all. Ratzinger had already demonstrated himself capable of getting his hands dirty at John Paul's behest, having successfully stripped his former friends and colleagues Hans Küng and Johann Baptist Metz of their theological authority within the German Catholic Church in 1979. Both men were widely respected, and many considered their treatment a scandal, occurring, as it did, largely behind a veil of secrecy and without due process, but the new pope considered them to be dangerous political radicals who posed a real threat to the church. So they had to go.

In his handling of these two cases, Ratzinger had displayed an unerring capacity to do what he deemed necessary to protect the faith. He proved there "would be no hesitation, no muddled half-moves, when the time came to act, and there would be no reversals when the inevitable outcry of protest rolled in." This, combined with his chief concern that "attempts to emphasize the social and political dimension of Christianity, or to challenge Roman authority, were not to be tolerated," confirmed to John Paul that he had chosen the right man for the job.

Ratzinger spent just shy of twenty-four years in a role that people loved to hate. Such feelings had resulted, in part, from the CDF's fearsome reputation as a rigid enforcer of doctrine but also on account of historic resentment of its Supreme and Sacred status, titles that were removed in rebranding efforts of 1965 and 1985, respectively. Yet it was not just the position that drew murmurs of dissent. Many felt betrayed by a theologian once seen as a progressive liberal hope. As Allen notes, "When someone moves from exploring the boundaries to enforcing them, as Ratzinger has, it naturally arouses suspicion. . . . The questions arise: Did he sell out? Did he earn his success by betraying his earlier convictions?"

Ratzinger's first major battle once again brought him face-to-face with his old foe Marxism. He looked to Latin America to tackle the rise of liberation theology, a movement founded in the late 1960s "that sought to align the Roman Catholic Church with progressive movements for social change"—a movement that, at this same time, was stirring the imagination of one Jorge Bergoglio. Pope John Paul, with his deep-rooted support for social justice, was less threatened by this school of thought than Ratzinger but did not contest his cardinal's proposed course of action. The movement's leaders were ordered to appear before the CDF in Rome, where sanctions on their teachings were outlined in detail, and a report was published in August 1984 attacking the movement as a "perversion of the Christian message as God entrusted it to His church." In support of Ratzinger's efforts, John Paul made a conscious effort to appoint only hard-line bishops in Latin America who would be loyal to Vatican teachings.

It was not just Latin America that harbored rebellious theologians. Ratzinger soon turned his gaze to North America, and in particular to an outspoken critic of Pope Paul VI's controversial 1968 encyclical on contraception, *Humanae vitae.* At a time when John Paul II was reaffirming papal infallibility, Fr. Charles Curran's argument that the encyclical was in fact "noninfallible," and therefore open to interpretation for those Catholics wishing to use birth control, was unwelcome. Again, Ratzinger called his target to appear before him in Rome, in March 1986, but was dissatisfied with Curran's testimony and stripped him of his right to teach Catholic theology. Consequently, Curran was fired from his teaching post at the Catholic University of America, in Washington, D.C. As Collins notes, "choosing a leading figure in a theological movement seemed to be the CDF prefect's methodology—that you frighten the disciples by picking off the leader."

A long line of dismissals followed these first two major cases, and numerous priests and bishops were reined in, removed from their posts, or excommunicated for their views. Ratzinger's "willingness to polarize, to draw lines in the sand," combined with his hard-line approach to differing theological schools of thought, drew significant criticism, not least because "the man who once complained that the Holy Office was insufficiently tolerant of different theological schools has shown too little tolerance himself." His time in office represents a period of doctrinal rigidity within the church, when theological dissent, and even dialogue, was drastically curtailed. The effects of this were felt most notably in developing countries, which had not only some of the world's highest populations of Catholics per capita but also fragile political systems, within which local priests and bishops were attempting to interpret the Vatican's teaching in the best way possible to engage and enrich their predominantly poor communities. The fact that they were presented with a Vatican almost as hard-line as many of their ruling communist or fascist governments made their jobs all the more difficult.

But for all the criticism of Ratzinger's relentless methods, there was a strong level of support among conservative Catholics, who gratefully welcomed him as a tireless defender of the faith, steering the church away from harm. Ratzinger's own defense was that his responsibility as prefect of the CDF was to protect the teachings of the church on behalf of "those who can't fight back intellectually." If that brought him up against "intellectual assaults" by theologians, then so be it. His supporters also made great efforts to rebut allegations that his aggressive methods were a direct reflection of his personality: far from it, they said and still say. The descriptions of Ratzinger as a good listener, calm, kind, and serene, seem incongruous in light of his reputation as an enforcer. But as David Gibson remarks, "The paradox of the ivory tower is that the scholarly academics are among the most combative people, fiercely promoting their ideas and principles, but their dirty work is usually done at a bloodless distance, in journals or from the parapet of the conference lectern." It is only natural, therefore, that those defending issues of faith are, bloodlessly, elevated to a position of righteousness.

When reviewing Ratzinger's record at the CDF, Gibson believes that he "too easily ignored the fact that he was dealing with fellow human beings, with other Christians, and not just with ideas. Abstracting people into their positions can make personal confrontations more palatable, especially for someone with Ratzinger's mix of zeal and timidity." This viewpoint was all too apparent within the context of issues that affected a billion Catholics on a daily basis, such as divorce, contraception, homosexuality, and sexual abuse by priests. These are universal experiences in the modern world, and it is in pluralist societies such as western Europe and the United States that so many people have turned away from the church, in part because of its reluctance to engage in any form of debate. As Paul Collins, a former priest who fell afoul of the CDF and John Paul II's papacy, remarks in his book *God's New Man:*

> There is an emerging assumption among some very senior church leaders that the contemporary western world is so far gone in individualism, permissiveness and consumerism that it is totally impervious to church teaching . . . churchmen, such as Ratzinger, have virtually abandoned the secularized masses to their fate, to nurture elitist enclaves which will carry the true faith through to future, more "receptive" generations.

Throughout John Paul's papacy, both he and Ratzinger made concerted efforts to centralize the Catholic Church by drawing power back to the curia, most notably by, in direct contradiction of Vatican II, reducing the authority of bishops. It was no longer, for instance, possible for a bishop to allow Catholic social services to counsel a woman considering an abortion; Rome, and Cardinal No, had spoken. And when wine is turned into blood, during mass, the priest's words were changed from "this is the cup of my blood . . . shed for you and *for all people,* so that sins will be forgiven" to merely "shed *for many,*" arguably excluding in one stroke all but Christians from Christ's forgiveness.

Pope Paul VI's intentions when he assumed control of the council, following the death of Pope John XXIII, between 1963 and 1965 had been to move away from papal infallibility and promote a more collegial approach to governance through a newly created body known as the Synod of Bishops. Granting them authority to address local issues via a democratic voting system, he declared that "because of our esteem and regard for all the Catholic bishops," he wished to provide them with abundant "means for greater and more effective participation in our concern for the universal Church." As Allen explains, "The theory of collegiality holds that the bishops are jointly the successors of the original Twelve Apostles who followed Jesus, and thus they form a 'college.' As such, they together enjoy supreme authority for the church. This authority does not exceed the pope's, but neither is it subsumed into the pope's." Having initially supported this move in his essays following the council, Ratzinger once more shocked his former colleagues with a drastic U-turn on the validity of the synod almost as soon as he was appointed prefect of the CDF. Eventually, this resulted in John Paul's 1998 decree, *Apostolos suos*, which reduced the synod to a position of complete impotence and "asserted that bishops' conferences have no right to teach authoritatively."

As well as reducing the power and standing of the bishops, John Paul went even further to ensure his papacy was watertight against dissent by appointing a number of ill-qualified bishops who were willing to toe the party line. When reflecting upon his reign, academics are in agreement that this was his greatest failing. Paul Collins writes that, significantly, "the biggest problem was the appointment of a large number of mediocre bishops who lacked any real leadership skill or genuine pastoral sensitivity," and that this resulted in large numbers of "conformist 'yes men' utterly loyal to Rome rather than to their dioceses."

The consequences of John Paul's appointments were exposed when the allegations of sexual abuse by members of the clergy exploded in the press, and many dioceses were found incapable of handling the crisis. The loss of confidence in the church from those affected by the abuse was only furthered by the Vatican's interpretation of the scandal as a campaign against the church by Western media. Rather than excommunicating and bringing to justice those accused after an open investigation, the Vatican refused to divulge information to aid criminal investigations, blocked several internal inquiries, and in countless cases moved priests accused of abuse to new parishes or quietly reinstated those who had been forced by bishops to stand down from their positions.

Prominent cases under the tenure of Pope John Paul II and Cardinal Ratzinger include: Cardinal Hans Hermann Gröer of Vienna, accused of abusing more than two thousand boys over several decades, victims having since come forward stating that they were offered payments by the church in exchange for their silence; Father Marcial Maciel Degollado, founder of the Legionaries of Christ, first accused of the sexual abuse of children in his congregation in 1976, with allegations stemming back to as early as 1943 and new victims coming forward to report stories of abuse as late as the mid-1990s; and Bishops Joseph Keith Symons and Anthony J. O'Connell of Palm Beach, Florida, the first confessing to the sexual abuse of five boys within his congregation, while his replacement, O'Connell, who was installed in 1999, tasked with healing the community, resigned three years later after admitting he had abused a seminary student in the 1970s, revealing that the victim was paid a legal settlement of $125,000 by the church in 1996, three years before O'Connell was appointed to Palm Beach by Pope John Paul. Archbishops were not unrepresented in this gallery of evil. Archbishop Juliusz Paetz of Ponzań, Poland, was accused of the abuse of teenage seminarians in his diocese by ignoring letters from victims and their advocates, and was permitted to resign without investigation; Cardinal Bernard Law of Boston, exposed by the *Boston Globe* in 2001, resigned for ignoring evidence of decades of sexual abuse by numerous priests in his archdiocese, moving them from parish to parish rather than removing them from the church, and was thereafter rewarded by John Paul II, who appointed him archpriest of the Basilica di Santa Maria Maggiore—Law even gave an address during the 2005 conclave.

John Paul's succession to the papacy coincided with a time of great decline within the Catholic Church, with attendance falling dramatically in Western countries (offset only by increases in Africa and Asia) and men abandoning the priesthood (laicization) in record numbers. During his fifteen-year reign, Pope Paul VI granted more than thirty-two thousand requests for laicization, and his successor was determined to put a stop to this practice and remind priests that the vows they had taken were a sacred lifelong commitment and near unbreakable, except in cases of illness or infirmity. John Paul immediately froze all pending applications when he took office and in 1980 began a complete overhaul of canon law. The resultant 1983 Code of Canon Law now stipulated that applications would be considered only if they came directly from priests over the age of forty and would be granted only to those who had already entered into a marriage or had children, and to those who claimed they entered the priesthood not of their own free will.

Most crucial, however, was the removal of provisions previously afforded to diocesan bishops through which they could request the laicization of priests within their ministries, with or without the priest's consent, for example, in the cases of sexual abuse. As Nicholas P. Cafardi, professor and specialist in canon law, points out, "It is truly ironic that, just as the clergy child sexual abuse crisis began to mushroom in the mid-1980s, the bishops in the United States (and throughout the world, for that matter) lost . . . highly effective ways to deal with priests who had sexually abused children."

Many Catholic commentators have asked the awful question: Did the declining numbers of priests have any influence on John Paul II's reluctance to remove abusive clergy? Speculation aside, the perceived persistent secrecy and lack of resolution surrounding the Vatican's handling of the sexual abuse crisis meant many followers began turning their backs on a church they felt was completely disconnected from the modern world, and this consequently became *the* legacy of the papacy of John Paul II.

This has resulted in Cardinal Ratzinger's twenty-four-year tenure at the CDF being tainted by association. But exactly what responsibility should be borne by Ratzinger for such a catastrophic mismanagement of a global scandal?

A RELUCTANT ENFORCER?

When attempting to delve into the psyche of Joseph Ratzinger, it is difficult to penetrate the fortress of privacy surrounding his own true feelings. There is evidence, however, that makes one confident that his time as prefect of the CDF did not fill him with great happiness.

After ten arduous years of enforcement, in 1991 Ratzinger suffered a cerebral stroke that affected his left field of vision. Having always had concerns regarding his own health, the sixty-four-year-old cardinal now asked John Paul to release him from his duties as prefect and allow him to return to Germany to resume his writings. His request was denied.

A year later, in 1992, Ratzinger was again hospitalized and required stitches after his head was cut open on a radiator when he blacked out in his rooms. Rather than allowing him to step down, John Paul "rewarded" him with yet more responsibility, elevating him to the prestigious rank of cardinal bishop—there are only ever six selected from within the College of Cardinals and these are the only cardinals eligible to become either dean or vice dean of the college—in 1993 and assigning him the Suburbicarian Diocese of Velletri-Segni, located just outside Rome.

Five years after making his first request, Ratzinger once more asked the pope for dispensation to resign his post and return to Germany. He was again met with refusal and, two years later, another promotion, this time to vice dean of the College of Cardinals, a vice president–like role assisting the dean. In 2001, after another five-year interval, seventy-five-year-old Ratzinger made a last appeal to the now-ailing pontiff. Again his request was refused by John Paul, who, perhaps sensing the end was nigh, wanted his most loyal of servants with him in those last years. Ratzinger was "rewarded" for his service in 2002, when he was elected as dean of the College of Cardinals.

The Catholic Church reveres its martyrs and the exemplary suffering they have borne for their beliefs. Ratzinger proved no different when probed about his reluctance to accept high office and his numerous attempts to resign. Instead of complaining that he had never wanted such responsibility in the first place and would rather have been tucked up in Bavaria leading a life of quiet scholarship, he always brushed off such suggestions (with the exception of his "falling guillotine" comment) and insisted that he follows where God leads him. And it is precisely this air of unquestioning obedience, combined with his involvement in the abuse scandal and controversial output as prefect of the CDF—for example, he described homosexuality as a "strong tendency ordered toward an intrinsic moral evil" and once called Buddhism an "auto-erotic spirituality" that seeks "transcendence without imposing concrete religious obligations"—that has led to the predominant characterization of him as a relentless and aggressive inquisitor.

When considering all the facts and speculation, two things are clear. One is that Ratzinger truly wished to return home to Germany and live out the end of his days writing in solitude; the other is that his reputation upon the conclusion of his twenty-four years as chief inquisitor was far from favorable, and of this he would have been acutely aware. It is perhaps unsurprising, therefore, that after his election as pope, in 2005—at a time when the church was facing one of its greatest crises—the inner conflicts he had already faced did not dissipate when the trust of God and his peers was placed in him to lead the church. They would only intensify under the pressure, continuing to haunt him and driving him down a path no one could have ever expected.

4

THE RELUCTANT
POPE

At the age of seventy-eight, it was clear to both Pope Benedict XVI and the cardinals who would now serve under him that his papacy would not be a lengthy one. But it might be a safe one, providing continuity.

After twenty-six years of John Paul II's theatrics, his outreach, his travel, travel, travel, the church needed to rest, regroup, and take stock. Ratzinger would be housekeeper in chief: steady, predictable, and able to reassert, protect, and strengthen ancient doctrine. In short, he would make sure that overdue reforms remained overdue.

In the days following his election, the new pope candidly—to a fault, some might say—admitted that as the tally of votes had increased in his favor and he understood that the "guillotine was coming closer and was meant for me," he had prayed to God to spare him this burden. He had felt that "up until now my life's work was done and that the years ahead of me would be more restful," and that there were many candidates who were "younger, better, stronger, and have more élan" than he. His prayers went unanswered.

Now, when the new but very old pope found himself in the spotlight, his impulse was to retreat. As David Gibson notes, "Five days after his stunning election as pope, on the Sunday morning when Joseph Ratzinger was supposed to be introducing himself to the world as Benedict XVI, the new pontiff was instead confounding everyone around him by doing everything possible to disappear into the background." In stark contrast to his publicity-savvy predecessor, Benedict attempted to hold his inaugural mass inside St. Peter's Basilica, because, as he explained to the master of ceremonies in charge of the event, "there the architecture better directs the attention toward Christ, instead of the pope." He was advised against such a move, not least because it would exclude the vast crowds expected to arrive in Vatican City on April 24.

When denied the privacy he craved, John Paul's successor fell back on what he knew best: tradition. During his inaugural address on April 25, Benedict spoke of the strength he needed from the church and her followers, asking them to "pray for me, that I may not flee for fear of the wolves" as he embarked on a task which "truly exceeds all human capacity." The mass proceeded with formal Gregorian chants, classic polyphony, and Bach's Toccata and Fugue in D Minor. The contrast with the folksier and more familiar feel of the past twenty-six years was seen as a confirmation of how Vatican II would continue to be interpreted under his rule and as a strong "advertisement for *ressourcement* by returning to traditions from more than a millennium ago."

It was not just musical traditions that were revived. The bookish Cardinal Ratzinger had been transformed overnight into the sartorially opulent Pope Benedict XVI, presenting himself in only the best that the papal wardrobe could provide. The internet was ablaze when the newly nicknamed "Prada Pope" stepped out in a pair of natty red leather loafers and an ermine-trimmed red velvet cape known as a *mozzetta* that had not been worn by a pope since Paul VI, in the 1970s. During his first papal Christmas, he donned yet more red velvet with ermine trim in the form of a *camauro*—a hat, not dissimilar to that of Father Christmas, popular with popes in the twelfth century—prompting headlines such as "SANTA POPE" WOOS VATICAN CROWDS and POPE DELIGHTS CROWDS WITH SANTA LOOK. Gone were the days of walking the streets of Rome in the traditional cardinal's cassock: Was it possible he might have even begun to enjoy his new role?

While his evident passion for fashion was unexpected, Pope Benedict's inaugural address merely revealed much of what was already known about his appetite for glorious liturgy. He held back key details when outlining his intentions as leader of a church in crisis and stated only that his "real program of governance is not to do my own will, not to pursue my own ideas, but to listen, together with the whole Church, to the word and the will of the Lord." These sentiments may have served him well in his role as prefect for the Congregation for the Doctrine of the Faith, when he was shielded from any real challenges thanks to his symbiotic relationship with John Paul II, but the office he inherited in 2005 had been wholly redefined by his predecessor and he had become more Bishop of the World than Bishop of Rome. With the pope, rather than Jesus Christ, now seen as *the* face of the church, Benedict's stating that he wished to revert to traditional church principles during his homily suggested that he was attempting to manage the expectations of the faithful . . . and the media.

BENEDICT AND THE "DICTATORSHIP OF RELATIVISM"

The greatest threat to Catholicism perceived by Pope Benedict was from what he called in his last speech before election a "dictatorship of relativism." *The Stanford Encyclopedia of Philosophy* defines *relativism* as a philosophical concept in which "the truth or justification of moral judgments is not absolute, but relative to the moral standard of some person or group of persons." It is understandably anathema to the Catholic Church's adherence to absolutism, in which there is only one truth. Benedict believed that the faithful should strive to live by the unwavering moral standards of the church and its teachings, not that the church should update its views on such controversial moral issues as contraception, marriage, and homosexuality to sustain its position in the modern world.

This belief that truth, in the Christian sense, was under threat—by what Benedict described in 1999 as "the dissolution of law through the spirit of utopia . . . [where] the real and ultimate source of law becomes the idea of the new society: which is moral, of juridical importance and useful to the advent of the future world"—was, on the other hand, considered by many to be positive progress toward greater freedom and human rights. But the new pope remained fearful that if the "dictatorship of relativism" were allowed to remain, people would forget the concept of sin and become detached from the morals of God:

> The majority determines what must be regarded as true and just. In other words, law is exposed to the whim of the majority, and depends on the awareness of the values of the society at any given moment, which in turn is determined by a multiplicity of factors.

The same fears that had plagued Ratzinger since the Marxist uprisings of 1968, when he was second chair in dogma at Tübingen, and throughout his time at the CDF now beset him as pope. And he would tackle them in his own way. Where John Paul had embraced celebrity culture, photo opportunities, far-reaching worldwide travel, and mass outdoor events of worship, Benedict was of the view that, as Gibson notes, "every aspect of modern, postconciliar culture, from pornography to rock music, was . . . a symptom of the crisis." He even went as far as to publicly support theological criticism of the Harry Potter books (despite having never read them himself), saying they were "subtle seductions, which act unnoticed and by this deeply distort Christianity in the soul, before it can grow properly."

But the wheels of societal change were well in motion, and Benedict's traditional outlook, combined with his detachment from the everyday lives of millions of people he was now tasked with leading, risked alienating an already dwindling population of Catholics in the twenty-first century.

It is fair to say that Pope Benedict's papacy got off to a rocky start and never really recovered its footing. As one journalist noted, he frequently appeared to be "as gaffe-prone as his secular counterpart in Rome, Silvio Berlusconi, as he lurched from one public relations disaster to another." In November 2005, just seven months into his new role, Benedict released his first major instruction as pope. In it, he described acts of homosexuality as "grave sins," "intrinsically immoral," and "contrary to the natural law," as well as reiterating that it was "necessary to state clearly that the Church, while profoundly respecting the persons in question, cannot admit to the seminary or to holy orders those who practice homosexuality, present deep-seated homosexual tendencies or support the so-called 'gay culture.'" The global media picked up on these descriptions of homosexuality as evidence of the church's willingness to link the ongoing sexual abuse scandals to priests with homosexual tendencies. And while this was an unsurprising position, given what we know about Benedict and the church's views on the subject, it was hardly in line with his statement in his first general audience speech: "I would like to place my ministry at the service of reconciliation and harmony between persons and peoples."

INTERFAITH CONTROVERSIES

Pope Benedict fared equally poorly when it came to diplomatic relations with the Islamic world. In a September 2006 speech entitled "Faith, Reason and the University—Memories and Reflections," which he delivered at the University of Regensburg in Bavaria, where he had been a professor, he compared the "structures of faith contained in the Bible and in the Qur'an." He sparked outrage by quoting the Byzantine emperor Manuel Palaeologus, who, in a dialogue with a Persian scholar, dated to 1394 and 1402, had written, "Show me just what Mohammed brought that was new, and there you will find things only evil and inhuman, such as his command to spread by the sword the faith he preached." The pope *later* claimed to have referenced the quotation with the sole intention of drawing out "the essential relationship between faith and reason." But the damage had already been done.

As Paul Badde, a member of the Vatican press corps who was traveling with Benedict on the papal plane, recalled, "It would have taken a Shakespeare to capture the cosmic drama that came crashing down on him upon his return to Rome with the delayed reaction to a few of his many words, at a watershed of his pontificate." The speech drew fierce criticism from Islamic leaders, who demanded an immediate personal apology; violent protests erupted across the globe, and attacks on Christians soon followed. In Iraq, effigies of Pope Benedict were burned, two Christians were murdered, and the Vatican was threatened with a suicide attack by an insurgent group; in Somalia, a sixty-five-year-old Italian nun was murdered in an apparent reprisal attack; firebombs were thrown at churches in the West Bank and Gaza Strip; and a fatwa against the pope was issued by the political wing of the Pakistani militant group Lashkar-e-Taiba.

Four days later the Vatican issued a statement defending the pope's use of Manuel's words within the wider context of his speech and insisting that Benedict "sincerely regrets that certain passages of his address could have sounded offensive to the sensitivities of the Muslim faithful and should have been interpreted in a manner that in no way corresponds to his intentions." Support for the pope came from Western politicians, including German chancellor Angela Merkel, American secretary of state Condoleezza Rice, and Australian prime minister John Howard, but did little to dampen the flames.

It is hardly surprising that the Catholic Church and various other Christian leaders rallied around the pope, denouncing the hysteria surrounding the speech as absurd. What was surprising was a statement made by the very man who was runner-up in the previous year's conclave: Cardinal Jorge Bergoglio. A spokesman for the cardinal told *Newsweek Argentina* of Bergoglio's "unhappiness" with the pontiff's speech, declaring that "Pope Benedict's statement doesn't reflect my own opinions. . . . These statements will serve to destroy in 20 seconds the careful construction of a relationship with Islam that Pope John Paul II built over the last twenty years."

The Vatican was furious at this flagrant act of insubordination during the first major crisis of Benedict's pontificate and demanded the removal of Bergoglio's spokesman of eight years, Fr. Guillermo Marcó. Marcó dutifully resigned and explained that he had not, in fact, been speaking on behalf of the cardinal but as president of the Institute for Interreligious Dialogue, thereby sparing his boss the Vatican's further wrath.

By November 2006, the post-speech furor had calmed somewhat, so rather than cancel his planned trip to Turkey, the pope decided to use the opportunity to try his hand once more at diplomacy, on what he termed a "mission of dialogue, brotherhood and reconciliation" designed to promote better relations with the Eastern Orthodox Church. It was seen as a deeply symbolic gesture when Benedict became only the second pontiff (after John Paul II) to visit an Islamic place of worship, silently praying alongside senior Muslim clerics at Istanbul's Blue Mosque.

Protests were minimal, and the trip was largely considered to be a success. Benedict chose his language more carefully than he had at Regensburg: he praised the "remarkable flowering of Islamic civilization in the most diverse fields," and hoped that Christians and Muslims would "come to know one another better, strengthening the bonds of affection between us in our common wish to live together in harmony, peace and mutual trust."

If a collective sigh of relief was breathed in the corridors of the Vatican as the pope boarded his plane back to Rome, it did not last long. No sooner had he built bridges between Catholics and Muslims than he began dismantling those with Judaism.

Benedict's much-talked-about childhood under Hitler's shadow should have meant that he, more than anyone, was acutely sensitive to Jewish-Catholic relations. He did indeed make some solid efforts in the early days of his papacy to strengthen ties between the two faiths by visiting synagogues in Cologne, New York, and Rome; and he condemned "the genocide of the Jews [as] atrocious crimes that show all of the evil that was contained in the Nazi ideology." But this period of goodwill was relatively short-lived.

Pope Benedict's detachment from subjects he found difficult, evident in his memoir, *Milestones,* outraged some members of the Jewish community. During a visit to Auschwitz in May 2006, he failed to mention anything to do with collective German or Catholic guilt over the Holocaust and made no reference to anti-Semitism. A little over a year later, in July 2007, the pope—bowing to traditionalist pressures, many believed—decided to give widespread permission for the celebration of the Latin-spoken Tridentine Mass. Largely in abeyance since 1970, it featured a Good Friday prayer that called for Jews to acknowledge Jesus Christ and referred to "the blindness of that people; that acknowledging the light of thy Truth, which is Christ, they may be delivered from their darkness."

Benedict justified his decision in a letter to bishops, stating, "What earlier generations held as sacred, remains sacred and great for us too, and it cannot be all of a sudden entirely forbidden or even considered harmful." Jewish leaders around the world were quick to condemn the move, and in a statement issued by the Jewish-American advocacy group the Anti-Defamation League, spokesman Abraham H. Foxman called it a "body blow to Catholic-Jewish relations." He said, "We are extremely disappointed and deeply offended that nearly 40 years after the Vatican rightly removed insulting anti-Jewish language from the Good Friday Mass, it would now permit Catholics to utter such hurtful and insulting words by praying for Jews to be converted. . . . It's the wrong decision at the wrong time."

Benedict's attempt six months later, in February 2008, to resolve the crisis by modifying the missal and removing reference to "blindness" left many unsatisfied, because it still called for God to "enlighten [Jewish people's] hearts" and for them to recognize Jesus Christ as their savior.

The entire affair could have been avoided had Benedict sought greater and more balanced advice before pursuing a potentially damaging course of action. The Tridentine Mass was known to be controversial. In fact, it was considered so provocative that the council of Vatican II had toned down the language of the Good Friday prayer and replaced it with "Let us pray for the Jewish people, the first to hear the word of God, that they may continue to grow in the love of his name and in faithfulness to his covenant." Yet Benedict, a learned theologian, seemed completely unprepared for the outrage its reintroduction sparked.

All this leads to speculation over whether the pope was arrogant, incompetent, suffering from a failure of foresight, or just indifferent. Was Benedict so self-confident on theological matters that he led without consultation? Was he simply blind to the consequences of his actions? Or, rather, did he just hope for the best and fail to consider anything but a positive response? One thing was certain: the pope was incapable of learning from his mistakes. Less than a year after the unsatisfactory revision of the Good Friday prayer, his very ability to lead the Catholic Church was called into question when he decided to lift the twenty-year-long excommunication of four members of the ultratraditionalist group the Priestly Society of Saint Pius X, one of whom was a known Holocaust denier.

Cambridge University–educated bishop Richard Williamson was

an insidious and unrepentant fundamentalist of the worst order; he referred to Jews as "enemies of Christ bent on world domination" and had articulated various theories disputing the reality of the Holocaust since the 1980s. Days before the pope announced his decision to lift the excommunications, Swedish television aired an interview with Williamson in which he stated his belief that the historical evidence was "hugely against six million [Jews] having been deliberately gassed in gas chambers as a deliberate policy of Adolf Hitler. . . . I believe there were no gas chambers. . . . I think that two hundred thousand to three hundred thousand Jews perished in Nazi concentration camps but none of them by gas chambers."

Intent on his words causing as much offense as possible, Williamson had even calculatingly traveled to Regensburg to give his interview on German soil, with full knowledge of that country's laws against Holocaust denial. The church, however, proceeded with the reinstatement, stating, "The Vatican has acted in relation to the excommunication and its removal for the four bishops, an action that has nothing to do with the highly criticisable statements of an individual."

The outcry was deafening. Benedict's decision was described by an anonymous senior Vatican source as "the biggest catastrophe for the Roman Catholic church in modern times." Placing such great importance on healing internal schisms with an ultratraditionalist faction of the church that would bring 150,000 Catholics back into the fold seemed unfathomable when set against the damage it would do to interfaith relations globally. Benedict's legitimizing of Williamson was described as "shameful" by Rabbi David Rose of the American Jewish Committee: by "welcoming an open Holocaust denier into the Catholic Church without any recantation on his part, the Vatican has made a mockery of John Paul II's moving and impressive repudiation and condemnation of anti-Semitism."

In Germany, the Central Council of Jews severed ties with the Catholic Church in protest at the lifting of the excommunications, and Chancellor Angela Merkel, who had always maintained a strict policy of not commenting on internal church matters, took the unprecedented step of making a statement on the crisis: "If a decision of the Vatican gives rise to the impression that the Holocaust may be denied, this cannot be left to stand. . . . The pope and the Vatican should clarify unambiguously that there can be no denial and that there must be positive relations with the Jewish community overall. These clarifications have, in my opinion, not yet been sufficient."

These words carried so much weight that the following day, February 5, 2009, the Vatican made its own statement, claiming that Pope Benedict had not been aware of Bishop Williamson's views when he lifted the excommunication and that Williamson had been ordered to publicly withdraw his comments before being readmitted to the church. (He refused and was promptly removed from his seminary.) But this excuse only exacerbated uncertainty about the pope's competence. How could he not have been aware? And if he genuinely hadn't been aware, why had his advisers not informed him?

In a letter of apology to bishops a month later, Benedict effectively admitted his own incompetence, writing, "I have been told that consulting the information available on the internet would have made it possible to perceive the problem early on." But he also defended the concept of welcoming the priests back into the fold: "Should not we, as good educators, also be capable of overlooking various faults and making every effort to open up broader vistas? . . . I do not think that they [Williamson and the others] would have chosen the priesthood if, alongside various distorted and unhealthy elements, they did not have a love for Christ. . . . Can we simply exclude them, as representatives of a radical fringe, from our pursuit of reconciliation and unity?"

The picture of Pope Benedict that we are left with is not of a commanding leader steering his then 1.18 billion followers through a time of crisis, but of a frail and confused old man drowning in shallow waters while those closest to him watched. At eighty-one, and after a lifetime of prayer and study inside his theological ivory tower, he was completely unprepared for the fact that the decisions he made as pope had real consequences for real people. His failure to grasp the severity of this and previous crises made it clear just how detached from the world the pope really was, left many within the church questioning whether they had elected the wrong man, and caused many outside its walls serious concern about the impact these failings were having on society.

Such fears were published in black and white in November 2010, when secret cables released by WikiLeaks revealed a damning report sent by the U.S. embassy in the Vatican to the secretary of state in Washington, dated February 20, 2009, and entitled "The Holy See: A Failure to Communicate":

Summary: Together with other flaps, the recent global controversy over the lifted excommunication of a Holocaust denying bishop . . . exposed a major disconnect between Pope Benedict XVI's stated intentions and the way in which his message is received by the wider world. There are many causes for this communication gap: the challenge of governing a hierarchical yet decentralized organization, leadership weaknesses at the top, and an undervaluing of (and ignorance about) 21st century communications. These factors have led to muddled, reactive messaging that reduces the volume of moral megaphone the Vatican uses to advance its objectives.

The report went on to outline in detail the failures, perceived by the embassy and their confidential high-ranking Vatican sources, of a small number of "decision-makers advising the Pope," who were "all men, generally in their seventies" with a distinct lack of "generational or geographical diversity," all of which meant they "do not understand modern media and new information technologies." The pope's right-hand man and "highest ranking official," Secretary of State Tarcisio Bertone, who was "tasked with managing the Curia," came in for the worst criticism and was labeled a "yes man" by critics who held him responsible for the curia's disorganized state. Sources labeled "strictly protect" by the embassy also revealed concerns over the "Italio-centric nature of the Pope's closest advisors," who favored "old-fashioned, inwardly focused communications written in 'coded' language that no-one outside their tight circles can decipher." Among Benedict's staff, there was only one senior member, Archbishop James Harvey, from an Anglophone country, and the source felt this "meant few had exposure to the American—or, indeed, global—rough and tumble of media communications." Furthermore, Benedict had surrounded himself with such a small pool that advisers outside the inner circle lacked "the confidence to bring him bad news."

Amid such chaos and with such a secretive institute as the church, it was impossible to ascertain not only who was responsible for the failings but also whether there were any credible candidates available to begin to tackle the problems faced and, in doing so, save Benedict from further disaster.

THE FINAL THREE YEARS OF TURBULENCE

The final three years of Benedict's papacy afforded him little respite from scandal. The rigidity of his traditionalist views consistently put him at odds with a society more vocal and critical of the church's conduct than any pope had experienced. He prefaced visits to Spain, the United Kingdom, and Ireland with statements condemning these countries' "aggressive secularism" with respect to campaigns over gay and abortion rights, which he believed contrary to "natural law." Moralizing such as this was met with particular hostility in Britain and Ireland, for at the same time as he was criticizing people's demands for greater freedoms, he was also calling a meeting of all Irish bishops to address the scandal of sexual abuse of children by clergy.

Years of abuse in Ireland had left many questioning the Vatican's desire or ability to deal with the crisis. Cardinal Sean Brady, the most senior figure in the Irish church, had admitted to attending a meeting in 1975 in which victims were forced to sign an oath of silence about the abuse they had suffered at the hands of a pedophile priest. Pope Benedict, distressed by what he heard during his meeting with the bishops, attempted to calm tensions by issuing an open letter in March 2010 to the Catholics of Ireland, in which he said he had been "deeply disturbed" by such revelations and shared "in the dismay and sense of betrayal that so many of you have experienced." The letter is long and heartfelt, but while the pope stated that he was "truly sorry" for the victims' grievous suffering, he clearly laid the blame at a domestic level.

This letter signaled a turning point in the Vatican's approach to dealing with the sexual abuse by its clergy. Benedict's handling of the crisis must be considered mediocre at best, but he should perhaps be given credit for becoming the first pope to expel pedophile priests from the church, removing 384 worldwide between 2011 and 2012.

There was further turmoil for the church in September 2010, when the head of the Vatican Bank, Ettore Gotti Tedeschi, was placed under formal investigation on suspicion of violating Italian money-laundering laws, and a Vatican bank account containing twenty-three million euros was frozen after the bank failed to disclose details regarding the transferring of funds. (No charges resulted.) As a sovereign state, the Vatican had long been criticized for its lack of transparency and cooperation in its financial dealings. Now parallels were being drawn with the Vatican's failure to report abuse within the church to the civil authorities, and questions were being asked about whether anyone was capable of holding it to account in financial matters.

The sense of a new impending crisis landed more quickly with Benedict this time, and he wasted no time in creating a new Vatican agency to act as financial watchdog and ensure the Vatican complied with EU and global financial standards. The move was well received and seen as a sign that the secretive state was taking seriously allegations of corruption and money laundering.

Unfortunately for Benedict, it was a case of too little, too late. In January 2012, the Vatican was once again overwhelmed by scandal. In the preceding month, reports had surfaced that Benedict, now eighty-four years old, was looking tired, thin, and weak. So when the so-called Vatileaks story, later described by John Allen as "Puccini meets Watergate," broke on Italian television, he was in no fit state to deal with its consequences. The leaked documents revealed alleged financial corruption, infighting, homosexual exploits of priests, and nepotism within the Holy See. They were believed to have been exposed not by a conscientious whistle-blower hoping for reform, but rather by those with "personal and political axes" to grind. In response, Benedict assembled a crack team of cardinals— led by Cardinal Julián Herranz, a member of the archly conservative Opus Dei—to investigate the source of the leaks. A month later, in true whodunit style, the police arrested none other than the pope's butler, Paolo Gabriele.

After investigators raided the butler's Vatican apartment, Gabriele was duly charged with illegally possessing confidential documents. But leaks continued to appear, leading many to conclude that the web of conspirators reached far wider than just one man—perhaps as many as twenty might be implicated, although no one else was ever charged.

Suspicions about the involvement of more senior members of the curia prompted accusations of a cover-up following the conviction and sentencing of Gabriele to eighteen months in jail and the suspended sentence of a Vatican IT expert for aiding and abetting him. In reality, Gabriele, although a member of the pope's inner circle, was a man with no real power who had leaked documents written in languages he did not speak. Speculation that he had made a deal and agreed to be the fall guy to save the church from further embarrassment was seemingly confirmed in December 2012, when Pope Benedict visited his former butler in prison and pardoned him for his involvement in the scandal, enabling him to retain his pension, accommodation, and employment within the Vatican.

As Allen noted at the time, "One of the ironies of the Vatileaks saga is that it's the fact of the leaks, not really their content, that seems to be doing the Vatican the most harm." The Vatican wanted the story to go away, and to go away quickly. Gabriele's conviction was the simplest way of publicly achieving this. Behind closed doors, however, Benedict was harboring a far greater concern than he had let on, and so ordered Cardinal Herranz to continue his investigations—this time, in the strictest secrecy.

On December 17, 2012, Herranz delivered a three-hundred-page, two-volume, leather-bound report known as the "red dossier" to Pope Benedict. It in, he detailed the discovery of a network of gay clergy within the Vatican who would regularly meet for illicit liaisons, often with male prostitutes, at various locations in and around Rome. The report also stated that some of the persons involved were being blackmailed by outsiders over their secret homosexual activities. The Italian newspaper *La Repubblica* later alleged that this was the day when Pope Benedict XVI made the decision that would send shock waves around the world and leave 1.2 billion Catholics grasping for answers.

5

THE RESIGNATION
OF A POPE

Waves of thunder rumbled across the sky, the rain came down hard, and the heavy darkness that hung over the Vatican was punctuated by a flash of lightning that tore across the sky and struck the spire of St. Peter's Basilica. Was it a sign from God? Or perhaps the culmination of some kind of kinetic energy that had amassed across the world in the preceding hours? The symbolism was not lost on anyone, for earlier that same day, February 11, 2013, news of another bolt of lightning had struck straight into the heart of the Catholic Church. Pope Benedict XVI had resigned.

The College of Cardinals and members of the curia had assembled in Rome the previous day for a meeting to discuss some forthcoming canonizations, but there had been a surprise addition to the agenda. Before the other business got under way, Pope Benedict delivered a short statement (in Latin, of course):

Dear Brothers,
I have convoked you to this Consistory, not only for the three canonizations, but also to communicate to you a decision of great importance for the life of the Church. After having repeatedly examined my conscience before God, I have come to the certainty that my strengths, due to an advanced age, are no longer suited to an adequate exercise of the Petrine ministry. I am well aware that this ministry, due to its essential spiritual nature, must be carried out not only with words and

deeds, but no less with prayer and suffering. However, in today's world, subject to so many rapid changes and shaken by questions of deep relevance for the life of the faith, in order to govern the barque of Saint Peter and proclaim the Gospel, both strength of mind and body are necessary, strength which, in the last few months, has deteriorated in me to the extent that I have had to recognize my incapacity to adequately fulfill the ministry entrusted to me. For this reason, and well aware of the seriousness of this act, with full freedom I declare that I renounce the ministry of Bishop of Rome, Successor of Saint Peter, entrusted to me by the Cardinals on 19 April 2005, in such a way, that as from 28 February 2013, at 20:00 hours, the See of Rome, the See of Saint Peter, will be vacant and a Conclave to elect the new Supreme Pontiff will have to be convoked by those whose competence it is.

One eyewitness at the meeting, Mexican prelate Monsignor Oscar Sanchez Barba, recalled, "The cardinals were just looking at one another. Then the pope got to his feet, gave his benediction and left. It was so simple; the simplest thing imaginable. Extraordinary. Nobody expected it. Then we all left in silence. There was absolute silence . . . and sadness."

No one was prepared for this, and no one truly could prepare for the reaction, but the Vatican did know news of the resignation could not be contained, and so released Benedict's statement to the media the following day. Rolling coverage gave minute-by-minute updates; commentators were rushed into news stations to speculate over events during his papacy that might have caused the most conventional man in the Catholic Church to do the most unconventional thing in its modern history. Bookmakers rushed to issue odds for bets on who might succeed him.

The Vatican's spokesman, Rev. Federico Lombardi, admitted during the subsequent press conference, "The pope took us by surprise. It was a public holiday in the Vatican, so we've had to prepare for this important situation quickly. . . . You will no doubt have many questions, but I believe we need a few days to organize ourselves because this announcement has taken us all by surprise." He described how the College of Cardinals listened to the short statement "with great attention and with bated breath," but were not offered the opportunity to ask questions.

The church put on a united front, reassuring its flock that they would have a new pope before Easter, and cardinals began issuing statements praising the pope's courage and humility but admitting their surprise and sadness. Politicians soon followed with words of support and praise for Benedict's papal reign.

But not everyone shared their sympathies. Abuse victims' advocacy groups openly celebrated the resignation and blasted Benedict's papacy for failing to adequately tackle the crisis of sexual abuse by clergy. John Paul II's former secretary, Cardinal Stanislaw Dziwisz, of Kraków, made a thinly veiled critique when he remarked to Polish reporters that John Paul had remained in the position until death because he believed that "you cannot come down from the cross."

The most common reaction, however, was simple shock. The majority of people, Catholics and non-Catholics alike, was either not aware or did not believe that the Chair of Saint Peter could be abdicated. As Dziwisz implied, it was a burden popes should carry until death. Benedict himself had referred to the role as a death sentence.

HINTS AT A DECISION ALREADY MADE

In 2002 Benedict entered a series of intimate interviews with the German journalist Peter Seewald for the book *Light of the World*. When quizzed as to whether he had considered stepping down over the spate of child abuse allegations, Benedict answered, "When the danger is great one must not run away. For that reason, now is certainly not the time to resign. Precisely at a time like this one must stand fast and endure the difficult situation . . . One can resign at a peaceful moment or when one simply cannot go on. But one must not run away from danger and say that someone else should do it." Seewald then asked, "Is it possible then to imagine a situation in which you would consider a resignation by the Pope appropriate?" Benedict replied, "Yes. If a Pope clearly realizes that he is no longer physically, psychologically, and spiritually capable of handling the duties of his office, then he has a right and, under some circumstances, also an obligation to resign." At the time of the book's publication, the majority of readers focused on the "obligation to resign" as a thinly veiled critique of John Paul's reluctance to step down when he became so incapacitated. Now, with hindsight, it seems just as likely Benedict was referring to himself.

Describing his election in an interview with Seewald in 2010, Benedict remarked, "Actually I had expected finally to have some peace and quiet. . . . I had been so sure that this office was not my calling, but that God would now grant me some peace and quiet after strenuous years." So the same hesitancy expressed upon election in 2005 appears to have deepened into a resolute decision by as early as 2010—rather than post-Vatileaks, as many initially believed. This raises the question: Did something occur in 2010 that tipped the balance away from his carrying out the burden of his office?

To begin even to attempt at understanding his monumental decision, we must leave Pope Benedict and return once more to Joseph Ratzinger and his time as prefect of the Congregation for the Doctrine of the Faith, and then even further back, to his life in Germany.

A SCANDAL IN MUNICH

In January 2010, newspapers began reporting on a historic sexual abuse case spanning thirty years, from 1980 to 2010, in the archdiocese of Munich. As more and more details surfaced, connections emerged that brought the case to the door of Joseph Ratzinger, who—between 1977 and 1982—was archbishop of Munich.

The priest at the center of the scandal was Father Peter Hullermann, who in 1979 was accused of sexually abusing three boys in Essen, Germany. The victims' parents complained to Hullermann's superiors and wrote to the Munich archdiocese requesting that he be transferred there for therapy. Although Hullermann did not deny the accusations, letters from the archdiocese did not refer to

the priest as a pedophile and did not outline the offenses committed. But they did stress that "reports from the congregation in which
he was last active made us aware that Chaplain Hullermann presented a danger that caused us to immediately withdraw him from
pastoral duties," and suggested that he would be safe teaching "at a
girls' school."

The transfer was discussed during a regular meeting of senior
officials on January 15, 1980. The agenda simply stated that a young
priest needed "medical-psychotherapeutic treatment in Munich,"
along with accommodation and an "understanding colleague," but
Hullermann, referred to as "H," was otherwise described as a "very
talented man, who could be used in a variety of ways." Ratzinger
approved the request, and "H" was admitted to the care of psychiatrist Dr. Werner Huth. After just five days of treatment, Cardinal
Ratzinger's office received a copy from Vicar General Father Gerhard Gruber, which stated that "H" was being returned to full
duties in a parish outside Munich. When Dr. Huth learned of this,
he immediately informed Ratzinger's officials, "The risk of reoffend-
ing was undoubtedly so high that it would have been impossible to
continue doing any parish work. And I explained this to the local
bishop." His warnings were ignored. Huth was so concerned that
"he issued the explicit warnings—both written and oral—before the
future pope . . . left Germany for a position in the Vatican in 1982,"
but the decision to return Hullermann to parish duties, in direct
contact with children, went unchallenged.

Less than five years later, Father Hullermann was accused of
abusing more boys and was convicted of sexual abuse in Bavaria in
1986. He was given an eighteen-month suspended sentence with five
years' probation, along with another course of "therapy." Astonish-
ingly, he was still not defrocked and was allowed to continue working with altar boys until 2008, when the church issued an order that
he be moved to another parish and into a role that prohibited his
working with children. In reality, he had few restrictions and continued to celebrate mass with altar boys.

Only after the story was picked up globally was Hullermann suspended from his position, on March 15, 2010, thirty years after

he'd admitted to the first crimes alleged in Essen. By this point, the question everyone wanted answered was: What did the pope know?

The juggernaut of the Vatican Press Office suited up and went into battle to protect him at all costs, insisting that he bore no responsibility whatsoever. Former vicar general Gruber dutifully fell on his sword and took full responsibility, stating, "I deeply regret that this decision resulted in offenses against youths and apologize to all who were harmed by it." But the questions remained: If the memos confirming Hullermann's return to pastoral duties were sent to Archbishop Ratzinger, is it really conceivable that he would not have read them, having authorized the initial transfer of "H" to Munich to undergo therapy for crimes he had admitted? In an interview with *The New York Times*, abuse-scandal whistle-blower and former Vatican embassy lawyer in Washington, D.C., Father Thomas P. Doyle, refuted the denials as "nonsense," stating, "Pope Benedict is a micromanager. He's the old style. Anything like that would necessarily have been brought to his attention. Tell the vicar general to find a better line. What he's trying to do, obviously, is protect the pope."

The Vatican's next tactic was to allege that a smear campaign was being conducted against Benedict, and the press office issued a statement that it was "evident that in recent days there are those who have tried, with certain aggressive tenacity, in Regensburg and in Munich, to find elements to involve the Holy Father personally in issues of abuse. It is clear that those efforts have failed." Many considered this to be an insensitive and dismissive statement, one that made no mention of the victims. And the fact remained: if Ratzinger was unaware that Hullermann had returned to his pastoral duties in the community, after repeated warnings from a church-approved psychiatrist, it did not exactly reflect well on his management of a priest he already knew was a danger to the community. Indifference is hardly an excuse when it comes to the sexual abuse of children.

Despite the Vatican's staunch defense of the pope, new details continued to emerge daily, and by the end of March more than three hundred new victims had come forward with allegations of abuse in Germany. Furthermore, friends of the eighty-one-year-old Father

Gruber, Ratzinger's right-hand man in 1980, reported to *Der Spiegel* that he had been "asked" in no uncertain terms to take full responsibility for the entire scandal, therefore taking Pope Benedict "out of the firing line."

Only weeks earlier, Benedict had written an open letter to victims of abuse in Ireland, but now, on matters concerning his personal conduct, he remained silent.

A CONSPIRACY OF SILENCE

The year 2010 saw a staggering number of new cases of abuse reported. Sadly, although the particular revelations were new, the problem was not. The Hullermann case not only brought Pope Benedict himself to the forefront of scandal but also further exposed the conspiracy of silence within a Catholic Church that had failed to report pedophile priests to the police and instead repeatedly hushed up their crimes.

When Cardinal Ratzinger became Pope Benedict, he had condemned the "filth within the church." Now the perceived lack of decisive action was testing the public's patience. As prefect of the Congregation for the Doctrine of the Faith, he had been responsible for handling abuse cases on behalf of John Paul II's Vatican since 1982. Preferring to spend their energies quashing left-wing factions such as liberation theologists in Latin America, Ratzinger and John Paul could be accused of being, at best, completely blind to the crimes committed, and at worst, the architects of an insidious culture of cover-ups. Whistle-blowers from within the church now felt emboldened to share stories of how they had repeatedly warned the Vatican about both individual abusers and the vast extent of the problem, only to be met with more silence. Detailed reports had been delivered to the Holy See, and still nothing was done. Only when victims eventually found lawyers who would represent them in bringing their cases to courts of law was the church forced to address the issue.

The Vatican spent more than $2.5 billion settling historic abuse cases in the United States alone between 2004 and 2011. Individual bishops could not have authorized behind-closed-doors settlements of this magnitude. Ratzinger was "The Vatican's Enforcer." He was responsible for keeping the church in check, for handing down discipline, as cardinal and then as pope, and for excommunicating those who did not fall in line with John Paul's views. Yet abusers were protected.

And what of the victims? The pain expressed by Pope Benedict in interviews and speeches repeatedly focused first on his horror that the sanctity of the priesthood was being called into question, before expressing sympathy and concern for the victims. During the 2010 interview for *Light of the World*, Peter Seewald challenged the pope over comments made by former German constitutional judge Ernst-Wolfgang Böckenförde, who believed "the real reason for the decades-long failure . . . lies in deep-seated patterns of behavior according to a Church policy that places the welfare and reputation of the Church above all else. The welfare of the victims, on the other hand, automatically becomes a secondary matter, although actually they are first and foremost the ones in need of the Church's protection." Benedict's response? "Analyzing this is, of course, not easy. What does Church policy mean? Why didn't people react formerly in the same way they do now?" But the pope knew full well what the church's policy was. He knew it by heart and had personally ratified the perpetuation of the system of cover-ups that had lasted for decades.

THE WORST CRIME

While John Paul and Ratzinger were certainly responsible for years of ignoring and concealing abuse committed by clergy, the practice outlined in the "church policy"—the very one Pope Benedict found so hard to analyze—is part of canon law and dates back to at least 1867. A secret Vatican document circulated to all bishops, bearing the official seal of Pope John XXII—a document that Cardinal Ratzinger would, in a modified form in 2001, ratify and enforce as the church's instruction today—was obtained and published by *The Observer* newspaper in 2003. Entitled *Crimen Sollicitationis* (The Crime of Solicitation), the document showed that the methods employed throughout John Paul's papacy were, in fact, following time-honored official Vatican guidelines, instructing bishops, when dealing with pedophiles and those guilty of sex with other men, or sex with underage boys or girls or "brute animals," to "transfer [the offending priest] to another [assignment]" if warranted and deal with the matter "in a most secretive way," all parties to be "restrained by a perpetual silence," which is commonly regarded as "a secret of the Holy Office, in all matters and with all persons, under the penalty of excommunication. . . ." Regarding the secret oath just outlined, the keeping of the secret must be kept also "by the accusers or those denouncing [the priest]." Should the accusation be proved false, the bishops were instructed to destroy all documents, but with one copy of the report to be sent to the Holy Office.

Described by Daniel Shea, an American lawyer working for victims of abuse by Catholic priests, as a "blueprint for deception and concealment," the document makes for chilling reading. As Collins notes, "At first Rome tried to isolate sexual abuse as a problem in the English-speaking world resulting largely from secularism and 'pan-sexualism,' as one curial cardinal called it. . . . To non-Anglos it seemed as though the US situation was just another example of degenerate preoccupation with sex with a particularly vicious anti-Catholic prejudice built into it." But the document entitled "Instruction on the Manner of Proceeding in Cases of Solicitation" reveals that the practice of moving priests from parish to parish and protecting their sexual crimes has been common since at least 1962, with enforced papal secrecy surrounding allegations in place from as early as 1867.

Abuse of children, described by the Vatican in its "Instruction" as "the worst crime," was so common that the church hierarchy had well-oiled procedures in place for dealing with perpetrators. In a document produced in 1922, the Vatican stated that "the accusation itself was considered the most serious accusation one could bring against a Roman Catholic priest. Therefore, the procedure took care to ensure that a priest who could be a victim of a false or calumnious accusation would be protected from infamy until proven guilty. This was achieved through a strict code of confidentiality which was meant to protect all persons concerned from undue publicity until the definitive decisions of the ecclesiastic tribunal."

Jeffrey Ferro's book *Sexual Misconduct and the Clergy* refers to a text from the year A.D. 731 entitled *The Penitential of Bede*. The author, an Irish monk named Bede, "advises clerics who sodomize children to repent by subsisting on bread and water for three to twelve years." Moreover, in a series of essays, a former priest and vocal critic of the church's handling of abuse, Thomas Doyle, outlined that while the vow of celibacy did not become official until the Second Lateran Council, in the twelfth century, it had been a policy advocated in church legislation since the Council of Elvira, in the fourth century, with the earliest "explicit condemnation of sex between adult males and young boys" appearing in the *Didache* (A.D. 50), known as the *Teaching of the Twelve Apostles*.

Presented with a graphic history over nearly two thousand years, the question surely must be asked: How then could the church maintain such a policy of denial and secrecy around what it terms "the worst crime"?

Joseph Ratzinger would have known that, upon accepting the role of prefect of the CDF, a large part of his responsibilities would have been the handling of sexual abuse allegations. Here, surely, was an opportunity to heal the years of suffering of the victims by revising the procedures in place to promote greater transparency with the world outside the church.

Instead, in a letter explaining the "New Norms for Church Handling of Certain Grave Offenses," dated May 18, 2001, he, "having carefully considered opinions and having made the appropriate consultations," essentially reaffirmed the status quo. Ratzinger's letter issued new guidelines stating that cases of alleged abuse were now subject to a statute of limitations of ten years following the victim's eighteenth birthday, within which allegations may be considered by the church. It also stipulated that only priests were eligible to conduct "tribunals" when investigating allegations, and once local tribunals had been conducted, "all of the acts of the case are to be transmitted ex officio as soon as possible to the [CDF]." Finally, it reiterated that "cases of this kind are subject to the pontifical secret," meaning that clergy, victims, and witnesses would be excommunicated should they reveal any details.

Despite Ratzinger's updated ruling that *all* cases of abuse were to be sent to the CDF, those bishops and priests who were brave enough to report allegations to Rome frequently reported receiving no answer whatsoever, only silence—an icy silence that prompted many victims to go public with their allegations. And yet, even under the glare of global condemnation, there remained no Vatican encouragement to report pedophile priests to the police.

Also astonishing is that there is no mention of the victims in any of these legal guidelines, other than that they, too, are bound by papal secrecy. In a 2006 *Panorama* documentary entitled "Sex Crimes and the Vatican," Thomas Doyle scathingly concurs: "There's no policy to help the victims, there's absolutely no policy to help those who are trying to help the victims, and there's an unwritten policy to lie about the existence of the problem. Then as far as the perpetrators, the priests, when they're discovered the systemic response has been not to investigate and prosecute but to move them, to move them from one place to another in a secret way and not reveal why they're being moved."

Is Ratzinger's May 2001 letter further evidence of a man so deeply detached from humanity, so oddly removed from the world, so immersed in clerical detail and procedure and the application of rules that he lost sight of human hearts and souls and literally forgot to think of the victims of sexual abuse as people? Or was he a man so wholly conflicted, consciously torn between what he described in his 2005 speech as the "filth within the church" and his loyalty to and faith in the pope, that he found himself unable to deviate from his course?

UNEASY LIES THE HEAD THAT WEARS A CROWN

Benedict XVI encountered scandal after scandal during his papacy, but with the benefit of hindsight, it is clear that the accusation surrounding the case of Fr. Peter Hullermann brought the sexual abuse scandal much closer to home—as close as his own desk.

From his childhood in Nazi Germany right through to handling abuse cases at the CDF and then on through the myriad difficulties faced during his papacy, Benedict's survival mechanism was to detach, to focus on the doctrine, and to view everything in the abstract. Only when he was forced to remember his part, his hand, his responsibility in the "worst crimes," did the gravity of the issue seem finally to become real.

As we know, while it was Benedict's strong desire to preserve continuity after the death of John Paul II—giving a leader-style speech to this end—it was neither Benedict's intention nor his desire to become pope himself, and this, in part, perhaps contributed to his failures in office. The countless examples of his detachment from reality and from people left him completely out of his depth, all the more so when he seems to have been so badly supported. His resignation, revolutionary given his reputation for conservatism, was described by the Roman daily newspaper *La Repubblica* as "an eruption of modernity inside the Church." The irony is clear. As one professor of religion noted, "The theologian who held relativism as the worst foe of the church will be the pope who relativized the papacy." If the papacy was now just a job from which the incumbent could retire, how then would it maintain its status as a higher, even divine, calling? How much holier than his devoted followers is the Holy Father if he does not elevate himself by devoting his life—his *entire* life—to the church?

Benedict boarded a helicopter shortly after 5 P.M. on February 28, 2013, and was whisked away over the rooftops of Rome, to a chorus of church bells ringing out below, to the seventeenth-century Apostolic Palace of Castel Gandolfo to begin his new life as "simply a pilgrim beginning the last leg of his pilgrimage on this earth." At a little after 8 P.M., the Swiss Guards, protectors of popes for over five hundred years, took their leave of the papal summer residence. Benedict had ceased to be pope. He was the pope emeritus now and would, consequently, be protected by the Vatican security personnel at Castel Gandolfo until renovations were completed on the Mater Ecclesiae Monastery in the Holy City, where he would live out his retirement. His beloved piano was traveling with him (his favorite composer is Mozart) along with his papers and many books, all of which would remain with him until rooms had been enlarged, studies created, and spare bedrooms modernized to suit the needs of a former pontiff in the comfort he was accustomed to.

The Vatican's statements about the future of Benedict were

laconic, to say the least, and many were surprised at Benedict's decision to remain within its realm, having expected him to return to Germany. The thought of having an ex-pope and a sitting pope living side by side was more than a little strange, but the "experiment" had wider implications for ensuring Benedict's future protection: the Vatican, lest we forget, is a sovereign state, and within its walls Benedict retained immunity from prosecution, should any legal cases of sexual abuse be brought to trial.

With so little information divulged to the public about how the inner workings of this new era could play out, the outside world was left to speculate as the heavy wooden doors of Castel Gandolfo were pulled closed.

Those who remained on the inside could be sure of one thing: here, at last, was the opportunity for change.

6

CONCLAVE

The cardinals voting at the 2005 conclave that elected seventy-eight-year-old Pope Benedict XVI had been fully aware that his advanced age meant his papacy would not be particularly long. It was a relatively straightforward matter to put aside their differences for the good of the church and agree on the direction for its immediate, if not long-term, future. Now Benedict's dramatically early departure caught most in the curia off guard, and thoughts about a successor were far less defined than many would have wished.

Newspapers across the world published the same headline: the pope was leaving behind a church in crisis, besieged by scandal, and under threat from the spread of secularism. Old rifts about which direction the church should take were resurfacing. At their heart was a fundamental disagreement on the causes and solutions of the crisis. Traditionalists—Vatican II's followers of *ressourcement*—believed that the church should look inward and elevate itself above society, giving its followers a higher goal to strive for. Followers, they presumed, look to the church for unchanging and ageless truths, certain that an institution that is married to the spirit of the age will be a widow in the next. The reformists—in favor of *aggiornamento*—disagreed. They felt such insularity was the cause of the problem, not the solution to it, and that the church should meet the changing needs of its flock and open its doors in a spirit of nonjudgmental outreach, adapting to modern society to ensure its relevance in people's lives and therefore its own survival.

While the sides were poles apart, however, there were some areas of common ground. Both sides agreed, as eminent Vatican journalist and author John Allen explained to *The New York Times,* that they needed somebody who could "carry this idea of new evangelization, relighting the missionary fires of the church and actually make it work, not just lay it out in theory." They needed a pope who would be "the church's missionary in chief, a showman and salesman for the Catholic faith, who can take the reins of government more personally in his own hands."

Candidates aside, there was no time to lose. Preparations for the election of Benedict's successor began in earnest, and the Vatican announced that the conclave would begin on March 12, 2013. Even as the 115 cardinals from forty-eight countries began to pack their bags and gather their thoughts, the race for the 266th pope had begun.

THE ISSUES SEVEN YEARS ON

In the lead-up to the conclave to elect a successor to Benedict, John Allen who spoke with many cardinals in those turbulent days, wrote that the key requirements for the new pope were:

1. A man with global vision, especially someone who can embrace the two-thirds of the 1.2 billion Catholics in the world who live outside the West, a share that will be three-quarters by mid-century.
2. A pope for the "New Evangelization," meaning someone who has the capacity to arouse missionary fervor in Catholics and to reach out to the wider world, inviting people to take a new look at the Church.
3. A strong governor willing and able to bring 21st century best practices of business management to the Vatican, making the place more transparent and efficient, and holding people accountable for poor performance.

This time, with so many disputes over the causes and solutions to deep-seated problems, there was no front-runner. But there were many potential candidates.

Bookies began taking bets minutes after Benedict's announcement was made on February 12, but favorites continued to change right up until the day of the conclave, exactly one month later.

In his final year as pope, Benedict appointed twenty-four cardinals, just under one-fifth of the total electorate. This increased his total to a whopping ninety—roughly twelve per year, compared with John Paul's annual average of nine. Commentators felt that Benedict's flurry of appointments indicated that he was firming up the papacy for another European: eighteen of the new appointments came from Europe, and ten of those now held positions within the Vatican. But with so many new faces and little time for all members of the curia to get to know one another before the preconclave meeting began, there was an unusually high number of cardinals considered to be *papabile.*

THE *PAPABILE*

Percentage changes of 115 cardinal electors
at the 2013 conclave, compared with 2005

Western Europe	22 (19%) +4%	Eastern Europe	10 (9%) −1%
Italy	28 (24%) +7%	Africa	10 (9%) −1%
Latin America	19 (16.5%) −0.5%	Middle East & Asia	11 (10%) +1%
North America	14 (12%) 0%	Australia & New Zealand	1 (0.5%) −1.5%

With the church's "global vision" and "new evangelism" at the top of the agenda, it is perhaps prudent to consider 2013's candidates in terms not of their conservative or progressive views, but rather of their position within the Old or New World. Those from the Old World were perceived to have been cut from the same cloth as Pope Benedict. Candidates who heralded from the New World were the opposite. Most had a strong track record in drawing the faithful, boasting high attendance numbers to prove it. But the overwhelming majority had little to no experience of the inner workings of Vatican politics, casting doubt on their ability to successfully lead a church in crisis.

THE OLD WORLD

Comprising of cardinals from developed countries, the Old World candidates were facing such issues as the rise of secularism, declining church attendance, and scandals of sexual abuse by clergy. Their societies were wealthy and opinionated, which had consequently decreased the centrality of the church's status and made for more political questioning of archaic church doctrine in the modern world.

Cardinal Angelo Scola, Archbishop of Milan (age 71)

While there was no clear favorite coming into the conclave, Cardinal Angelo Scola was believed by many to be a strong contender. Theologically aligned with the outgoing Pope Benedict, Scola also possessed a strong intellect and an experienced understanding of Vatican politics. He surpassed Benedict, however, in his pastoral experience and popularity with followers and the media, and was viewed by many to be a skilled diplomat capable of fostering more positive relations with other religions.

But he was also one of many possible successors seen to be too similar to Benedict and thus incapable of implementing real change. Cardinal electors from outside the Roman Curia believed that, as archbishop of Milan, he was too entangled with the bureaucracy and petty infighting that was damaging the church as a whole. Also, the long line of Italian popes in times gone by had provoked a staunch resistance to returning so soon to a domestic successor to the Chair of Saint Peter.

Cardinal Gianfranco Ravasi of Italy (70)

Fiercely intelligent, popular with the people, and well respected by the church, Ravasi had held the position of president of the Pontifical Council for Culture, responsible for fostering relations between the church and other cultures, and other key roles within the curia since 2007. He had successfully navigated tricky political dealings

within the Vatican and escaped with his reputation intact. Ravasi
was both tech and media savvy—attributes that would benefit any
new pontiff in his attempts to evangelize the masses in the digital
age—and had been praised for his admission of church failings.

Opponents, however, were concerned that Ravasi's lack of pastoral experience and scholarly bent were reminiscent of the failings
of the outgoing pope and would leave him ill qualified to deal with
the practicalities of running the Catholic Church. Despite his popularity within the curia, his refusal to get drawn into curial politick-
ing meant there were few solid supporters likely to vote for him
ahead of other, more partisan candidates. As with Scola, his Italian
background worked to Ravasi's disadvantage.

Cardinal Marc Ouellet of Canada (68)

Head of the Congregation for Bishops, in charge of selecting new
bishops, Ouellet sat firmly on the conservative side of the divide. Intelligent, experienced, and widely traveled, he emerged quickly as a
front-runner owing to his theological prowess, masterful language
skills (he spoke six fluently), and firsthand experience of different
cultures.

It is agreed among Vatican reporters that the strength of a candidate's chances can be measured inversely by how much "whispering, rumor and character assassination that person generates."
Ouellet's position in the running was confirmed when negative
stories about his past began surfacing in the media, but his odds
were reduced as a consequence. The French Canadian cardinal
came under fire for his poor handling of sexual abuse cases in his
native Quebec, his failure to combat the sharp drop in church attendance, and his opposition to abortion even in cases of rape. Like
Ravasi, Ouellet was also seen by many to be far too similar to Pope
Benedict and lacking the necessary grit to tackle the crises facing
the church.

Cardinal Christophe Schönborn, Archbishop of Vienna (68)

A former student of Joseph Ratzinger in Regensburg during the
1970s, the archbishop of Vienna was a count before he was a cardinal,
descended from the princely House of Schönborn, an aristocratic

Austrian family that boasted "two cardinals and 19 archbishops, bishops, priests and religious sisters." Praised for his openness to dialogue on contentious issues, strong crisis management skills, and progressive views on homosexuality and the use of condoms by HIV/AIDS sufferers, Schönborn was seen as a courageous and intelligent candidate. He had publicly addressed the sexual abuse crisis in his native Austria as early as the 1990s, and as a result was one of three candidates endorsed as credible by the U.S.-based victim support network SNAP (Survivors Network of those Abused by Priests).

Many found his outspokenness refreshing in the context of the Vatican's traditional behind-closed-doors mentality, but Schönborn's opponents cited several publicized instances when he had openly intervened in curial matters outside his jurisdiction and aired disagreements with other cardinals via the media. This, they argued, made him a potentially dangerous candidate for the papacy.

Cardinal Péter Erdő of Hungary (60)

Cardinal Péter Erdő was one of the youngest cardinal electors attending the 2013 conclave. His swift rise to prominence had so impressed many within the curia that he was now considered a serious candidate. As archbishop of Budapest, he was a central figure in the bridge-building efforts with the Orthodox churches and had been praised for developing positive relations with Jewish leaders in Hungary. Erdő was another of the *papabile* who managed to walk the line skillfully between conservative and liberal factions. He spoke Italian and had held several high-ranking council positions during his career, all of which buoyed his potential in the eyes of Rome. Furthermore, his support was not limited to the Vatican. Through his role as president of the European Bishops—the body that represents bishops from all forty-five countries in Europe—Erdő had built strong relationships with colleagues in Africa and other developing countries when coordinating conferences and other events fostering ecumenical dialogue.

While Erdő's qualifications were extensive, there were some who feared that his young age—he was just two years older than John Paul II when he took office—would lead to another lengthy papacy. Also counting against him was his perceived lack of charisma, as the next pope had a lot of work to do in drawing followers back to the church.

Cardinal Timothy Dolan of the United States (63)

A highly regarded and enthusiastic evangelist, Dolan was described by John Allen as "easily the most charismatic, media savvy and engaging personality among the 115 cardinals" voting in the 2013 conclave. The archbishop of New York City was a consummate diplomat who appealed to both conservatives and moderates, and he had certainly displayed the necessary teeth required to handle the burdens of the papacy.

Although Dolan was considered to be the American cardinal with the greatest chance of success, his positive attributes were negated by a larger list of reservations. Despite his easy charm, he was a dominant force within the College of Cardinals. This, combined with the idea of a leading figure from the world's greatest superpower running the Catholic Church, filled many in the curia with horror. He had never worked inside the Vatican, and his domestic record in handling the sexual abuse crisis in his diocese was shaky—he was included in SNAP's "dirty dozen" list of inappropriate *papabile*. Many felt he did not have the management skills required to reform the papacy.

THE NEW WORLD

Cardinals from the New World brought concerns of their developing nations, including large-scale poverty and deprivation in often-corrupt and unstable societies. Evangelization was easy, but the Catholic Church was facing stiff competition from Pentecostal and Evangelical Christianity, which were rapidly increasing their numbers in several traditionally Catholic developing countries, such as the Philippines and Brazil, which, when combined with dwindling numbers of priests, was making for quite a challenging scenario.

Cardinal Oscar Rodríguez Maradiaga of Honduras (70)

A courageous and charming champion of the poor, Cardinal Rodríguez Maradiaga had long been touted as "such an obvious candidate to be the first pontiff from the developing world that he might as well start sizing curtains for the papal apartments." Supporters praised his diplomatic skills both in his personal crusade against the drug trade in Central America (he had to be protected by the military after threats were made against his life) and when representing the Vatican in meetings with the International Monetary Fund and the World Bank. Another of the *papabile* polyglots, Rodríguez Maradiaga was one of the great hopes for Catholics in developing nations and an ideal candidate to reignite the church's program of evangelism. Furthermore, his theological views managed to satisfy liberals, through his strong support of social justice, open dialogue on the use of condoms, and respect for the liberation theology so dreaded by Benedict and John Paul, and conservatives, through his staunch opposition to abortion.

Critics of Rodríguez Maradiaga felt that his lack of experience working within the curia would be detrimental to his papacy. Though seen as a possible successor to Pope John Paul at the 2005 conclave, he managed only three votes in the first ballot before falling away to zero in the second. In the lead-up to the 2013 conclave, SNAP issued a statement naming him as one of the twelve candidates identified as having a poor record in handling sexual abuse scandals. Doubts were reinforced when stories appeared in the media about comments Rodríguez Maradiaga had made in 2002 likening the criticism faced by the Catholic Church in the wake of the sexual abuse crisis to persecution faced under Hitler and Stalin. Rodríguez Maradiaga had suggested that, thanks to Jewish lobbying, American media were attempting to draw attention away from the Israeli-Palestinian conflict. Unsurprisingly, this caused angry protests by sexual abuse victims and the Jewish Anti-Defamation League.

Cardinal Peter Turkson of Ghana (64)

When news broke of Benedict's resignation, Cardinal Peter Turkson was immediately touted as the front-runner. His candidacy carried a significant level of symbolism, owing to what John Allen described as "the undeniable magic" surrounding "the notion of what's traditionally seen as the planet's ultimate First World institution being led by a black man from the southern hemisphere." Dubbed "Conservatism's Cape crusader" (a reference to his tenure on the cape coast of Ghana), Turkson was a charismatic and popular figure in Africa. He had risen through the curial ranks to hold several senior positions within the Vatican, and this, combined with his pastoral experience, suggested that he was well equipped both to take on evangelism in developing countries and to cope with the myriad difficulties associated with the papacy. A regular on television in his home country, Ghana's first cardinal spoke several local dialects, as well as English, French, Italian, German, and Hebrew, with an understanding of Latin and Greek thrown in for good measure.

After the initial flurry of enthusiasm, however, Turkson's chances faded. Whether stemming from excitement or arrogance, he made the rookie mistake of engaging in speculation surrounding his chances, and in an interview with the Associated Press following the resignation of Pope Benedict stated that he would happily assume the role "if it's the will of God" and that he believed "in a way the church is always and has forever been ready for a non-European pope." Indiscretions aside, many believed his outspoken views against homosexuality would lead to storms of controversy in more pluralist societies. In a preconclave interview with CNN's Christiane Amanpour, Turkson remarked that sexual abuse scandals would not spread to Africa because "African traditional systems kind of protect or have protected its population against this tendency." He sparked further outrage when, during a 2012 meeting with senior members of the curia, he screened a video predicting that soaring Muslim birth rates would quickly lead to a complete Muslim takeover of Europe.

Cardinal Jorge Bergoglio, Archbishop of Buenos Aires (76)

Cardinal Jorge Bergoglio had surprised many of his fellow electors when he received forty votes in the third ballot of the 2005 conclave, coming in as runner-up to Cardinal Ratzinger. Back once more on the *papabile* lists, albeit not among any commentators' top fives on account of his age and inability to pull in the necessary support last time around, Bergoglio was still favored by those who saw his pastoral abilities as an ideal quality for a future pontiff. Many lauded his rejection of the luxurious life afforded to an archbishop— chauffeur-driven limousines, palatial accommodation, and staff at his beck and call—in favor of a simple apartment and rides on the local buses. Bergoglio also drew support from both conservative and more moderate sides of the church. He was one of the few whose candidacy bridged both sides of the conservative-progressive divide.

In fact, the sheer strength of his candidacy in 2005 had given rise to a smear campaign by opponents within the church and back in his home country regarding his complicity with the Argentine military junta during the Dirty War, and many of the same cardinal electors would be called to vote in 2013. Although he had held several positions on curial councils, Bergoglio's lack of presence anywhere outside Argentina meant that voters knew little more about him than they had at the previous conclave. There had never been a Jesuit pope, and Bergoglio's age, at seventy-six, was a concern. Electing another elderly pontiff could lead to another sitting pope plagued by infirmity.

Cardinal Luis Antonio Tagle of the Philippines (55)

The youngest of all the candidates making the *papabile* lists, Cardinal Luis Antonio Tagle was very much a new generation of cardinal. He had a Facebook page and hosted programs on YouTube. Seen as the Great Asian Hope in the race for the Chair of Saint Peter, he preached a balanced view of Catholicism that might potentially satisfy opposing sides in the Roman Curia. Like other cardinals from developing countries, Tagle was a staunch campaigner for issues of social justice and a strong defender of the poor. A thoughtful and compassionate intellectual, he had studied in the United States and Rome before returning to pastoral life in his home nation. Like Argentina's Cardinal Bergoglio, he eschewed the ivory-tower isolation embraced by many senior clergy, preferring instead to ride the bus and invite homeless parishioners into the church to dine with him. Tagle's strong track record of handling sexual abuse cases in the Philippines also earned him a place on SNAP's list of three acceptable candidates for the papacy.

The Roman Curia was a deeply traditional place, however, and many of the attributes listed as qualifications were also interpreted as shortcomings. In particular, and similarly to Bergoglio, Tagle's complete lack of experience of the Vatican would make it nigh on impossible for him to spearhead the bureaucratic shake-up so desperately required in the wake of the Vatileaks scandal. His age was also a cause for concern, for any reforms Tagle might attempt to implement as pope would bring him face-to-face with senior figures within the church who had decades more experience than him and who were likely, in short, to eat him for breakfast. Likewise, as Benedict's resignation had called into question the entire tradition of lifelong papal service, the majority of cardinal electors did not welcome the idea of a younger pope taking office for ten to fifteen years and then resigning, or potentially sitting in the post for thirty years plus, if previous papal lifespans were anything to go by.

Cardinal Odilo Pedro Scherer of Brazil (63)

The archbishop of São Paulo was another respected candidate from the New World who benefited from ties to the Old. Cardinal Odilo Scherer came from a family of German immigrants and was educated in Rome. Having held pastoral roles in his home nation and senior roles within the Vatican, Scherer was seen as someone who could easily bridge the divide between Old and New. Confidently outspoken, but not in a divisive way, he was a keen supporter of reforms to bring the church into the twenty-first century, and Vatican pollsters recorded belief that he had the administrative skills to see them through.

Critics, however, were concerned whether this more formal cardinal had the necessary allure to capture the hearts of 1.27 billion followers. Many also felt that he had not adequately handled the rise of secularism and Pentecostalism in Brazil, home to the world's largest population of Catholics.

DAY ONE: THE FIRST BALLOT

The first day of the conclave followed the same regimented order as in 2005. At 9 A.M. the cardinal electors observed the *pro eligendo romano pontifice* mass (mass for the election of the Roman pontiff) inside St. Peter's Basilica. This was followed by lunch at Casa Santa Marta. Then the cardinals donned their brilliant scarlet cassocks and returned to the Apostolic Palace ready for the 3:30 P.M. procession.

As before, the cardinals stepped forward one by one and swore the oath under the gaze of Michelangelo's *Last Judgment*, declaring they would never reveal the secrets of the conclave. They were no doubt ordered to swear this with greater vehemence following the scandalous conclave diary that had been leaked to Italian media by that still unknown loose-lipped cardinal in 2005. When everyone had sworn, and the command *"Extra omnes!"* (Everybody out!) had been made, the doors of the Sistine Chapel were pulled closed, and at 5:35 P.M. on March 12, 2013, the conclave to elect the 266th pope began.

The crowds who had gathered in St. Peter's Square were not deterred by the freezing temperatures and torrential rain, and waited patiently, watching the chimney for signs of smoke. Inside the chapel, the cardinals, having observed a solemn period of deep meditation, proceeded to write the name of their chosen candidate on their ballot papers and brought them to the altar. After all ballots had been cast, the three elected scrutineers began their count.

A little over two hours later, at 7:41 P.M. local time, a trickle of unmistakably black smoke quickly turned into a thick plume, revealing to the world that no pope had been elected and that the Vatican had *finally* mastered the workings of its chimneys.

Sadly, the furor surrounding the secret conclave diary in 2005 meant there was no cardinal willing to leak the voting tallies to the press, so reports of exact numbers varied. Italian newspaper *La Repubblica* reported that Cardinal Scola was out in front, with thirty-five votes, followed by Cardinal Bergoglio, with twenty, and Cardinal Ouellet, with fifteen. Other news outlets reported that Scola and Ouellet were neck and neck, followed closely by Bergoglio in third position and the Brazilian Cardinal Scherer in fourth. In the last election, Ratzinger had stormed ahead in the first ballot, with forty-seven votes to Bergoglio's ten, but this conclave was very much anyone's game. Reports suggested that old grudges died hard between Italian cardinals and that there were no strategic alliances among nationalities.

Scola's performance was unsurprising and Ouellet's was impressive, but commentators were once again startled by the strong performance of the unassuming cardinal from Buenos Aires. Many had included Bergoglio on their *papabile* lists purely on the basis of his second-place finish during the 2005 conclave; they felt that he was not an obvious choice for the Italian cardinals and curia, who dominated the cardinal breakdown, and he had garnered only 40 votes out of 115 last time. In the lead-up to this conclave he ranked very low on everyone's lists. And yet here he was again.

Amid a swirl of intrigue and speculation, the cardinals departed the Sistine Chapel and returned to their residence for a dinner of bad food and discreet campaigning, during which Argentinian Leonardo Sandri advised his fellow countryman, "Prepare yourself, dear friend." The relief Bergoglio had felt when Ratzinger was named as successor to John Paul eight years earlier was a distant memory as he retired on what was to be his last night as a humble cardinal. He slept badly, his mind racing with the knowledge that, the next day, it was quite possible he would become pope.

DAY TWO: A DAY OF FIVE BALLOTS

With so much at play, the cardinals awoke on March 13, 2013, no surer than the world at large whether they would have a pope by the end of the day. The morning voting began at 9:30, and as early as 11:38 A.M. an ambiguously white-gray puff of smoke emerged, causing a frenzy of wild speculation. Was it white smoke? If white, it meant a two-thirds majority had already been reached. So soon? But yes, it was surely white smoke . . . but then, no. At last the smoke thickened, turned black: no decision had yet been made.

By lunchtime, however, the situation inside the chapel had most certainly changed. Canadian media reported that Scherer's campaign had faltered and that support for Cardinal Scola had dwindled "after many cardinals apparently decided they did not want a Vatican insider presiding over the Holy See." It was now a two-man race, with votes divided between Ouellet and Bergoglio, who was out in front with fifty.

Back at Casa Santa Marta, lunch was far from a relaxing affair. Cardinal Sean O'Malley of Boston sat next to his usually jovial friend but felt Bergoglio "seemed very weighed down by what was happening." In an interview after the conclave, the former archbishop of

Buenos Aires recalled that it was in this moment that he began to realize that he might be elected, and "he felt a deep and inexplicable peace, and interior consolation come over him, along with a great darkness, a deep obscurity about everything else. And those feelings accompanied him until his election later that day." After lunch, it transpired that Ouellet had been doing some reflection of his own. Having increased his votes after all three ballots, the Canadian decided to withdraw from the race, just as Bergoglio had done during the 2005 conclave when he asked his backers to vote for Ratzinger. The race was now effectively over.

When a fourth ballot was conducted that afternoon, Bergoglio's tally leapt to just below the seventy-seven votes required to secure the papacy. The rain began to fall heavily over the crowds gathered in St. Peter's Square, and a lone seagull perched on top of the chimney. As 6:15 P.M. came and went, commentators began to assume— correctly—that a fourth ballot had not produced a pope. What nobody knew was that a fifth ballot had been held immediately after the fourth, but there was a problem. The count was wrong: 116 ballots had been cast rather than 115. Someone had returned his ballot to the altar unaware that there was another, blank paper attached underneath. One could be forgiven for thinking a mistake this simple could be rectified by removing the blank ballot, but this was the Vatican, and it was decided that an entirely new vote must take place.

After the sixth ballot of the conclave had been counted, and counted again, the votes were read aloud: "Bergoglio, Bergoglio, Bergoglio." When the tally crossed the magic number of seventy-seven, tension broke and applause echoed around the chamber. The final votes were read out, and the new pope's supporters leapt to their feet to congratulate him; as Cardinal Dolan recalled, "I don't think there was a dry eye in the house." Sitting next to the bewildered Bergoglio was his great friend the Franciscan cardinal from Brazil, Claudio Hummes, who turned and hugged him before saying, "Don't forget the poor."

It was over. All 115 votes had been counted, and Bergoglio had taken ninety of them. The dean of the College of Cardinals, Cardinal Giovanni Battista Re, approached and asked in Latin, "Do you accept your canonical election as Supreme Pontiff?" to which Bergoglio replied, "I am a sinner, but I trust in the infinite mercy and patience of our Lord Jesus Christ." When asked what name he would take, and with the words spoken to him moments earlier by Cardinal Hummes still in his mind, Bergoglio replied, "I choose the name Francis, in honor of Saint Francis of Assisi."

And with that, a sinner became pope.

But the question remains: Just what were the sins that cast such long shadows across his soul?

7

A DIRTY SECRET

To fully understand Jorge Bergoglio's transgressions, we must first provide a context. The 1970s and early 1980s represented a climax of many years of violent political struggle and coups d'état that had cost thousands of Argentine citizens' lives since the country won its freedom from the Spanish Empire at the end of the Argentine War of Independence in 1818. Violence as a means of restoring order had become an endemic part of society, and the military coup of March 1976 proved to be no different.

The United States was informed about the approaching coup by the junta leaders, who reassured the American ambassador, Robert Hill, that they had studied General Augusto Pinochet's successful U.S.-backed coup in Chile in 1973, and theirs would "not follow the lines of the [Pinochet] takeover," during the first two months of which 1,850 suspected leftists were murdered and a further thirteen hundred of the forty thousand arrested "disappeared."

To an Argentine people weary of the escalation of political violence and the disastrous government of Isabel Perón, the coup staged on March 24 brought a sense of relief and optimism. The Americans were impressed with the outcome, which Hill described as "probably the best executed and most civilized coup in Argentine history." Two days after the takeover, U.S. Secretary of State Henry Kissinger stated in his staff meeting, "Whatever chance they [the junta] have, they will need a little encouragement . . . because I do want to encourage them. I don't want to give the sense that they're harassed by the United States."

The new Argentine military government was led by General Jorge Rafael Videla, who had been selected as president from among the three coup leaders. Its grip on power was brutal. Those Argentinians who had the courage to resist it were subject to a brutal campaign of violence, kidnapping, torture, and, in the case of the thirty thousand "disappeared," murder.

Subversives at the top of the list included communists, trade union members, and anyone who had voiced antipathy to the regime, but in the way of such things, the targeting of subversives became a broadly indiscriminate policy of the policing of thought. For example, more than sixty students from one Buenos Aires high school were "disappeared" between June and September 1976, simply because they had been members of the student council.

In November 1976, Amnesty International dispatched a delegation of independent observers to Argentina to assess the worsening situation. In its extensive 1977 report—following which Amnesty was awarded the Nobel Peace Prize that year—it was revealed that the junta admitted to "the existence of between 2,000 and 10,000 political prisoners" (Amnesty believed the figure to be around 5,000 to 6,000) and that "the total capacity of the prisons was between 4,000 and 5,000." With the drastic increase in the prison population, the regime was forced to think of creative ways to mask its activities and hide detainees.

The solution it settled on was to establish approximately 520 clandestine detention centers across the country, the most notorious of which was the Navy School of Mechanics (ESMA), where Jorge Bergoglio's old friend Esther Ballestrino de Careaga was held and tortured before her final death flight. Argentina having sheltered many exiled Nazis following the end of the Second World War, the Argentine junta not only borrowed the idea for a network of secret concentration camps but also adorned the walls with swastikas and forced prisoners to shout, "Heil Hitler." According to Esther's daughter, Ana María, who survived her abduction, "They put on cassettes of Hitler speeches to drown out the screams while they tortured us."

THE WORLD WATCHED ON

As the junta continued to conceal the scale, and destroy any physical evidence, of the crimes being committed, the Argentine public was left to interpret whispered rumors. Those who were certain of the crimes, having experienced the loss of a friend or loved one, were often batted away when they requested information from the military. The authorities would either deny all knowledge or, sometimes, say that the individuals had fled the country.

These underlying conflicts within the national consciousness were exacerbated when Argentina played host to the FIFA World Cup in June 1978. In scenes eerily reminiscent of the 1936 Olympic Games in Nazi Germany, the rest of the world became complicit in upholding a murderous regime by attending a sporting event that had clearly been politicized to legitimize the position of the government. The military dictatorship understood the potential domestic and global leverage that the tournament could bring to the regime, and so proceeded to appropriate what was called a "World Cup of Peace" as a shining example of the government's success at restoring order.

The regime's confidence was misplaced when it came to foreign journalists, many of whom, having been invited to cover the soccer, spent a great deal more time shining a spotlight on the atrocities. Amnesty International printed posters in Spanish, English, and German, declaring, FOOTBALL YES—TORTURE NO, and particular coverage was given to the protests of the Mothers of the Plaza de Mayo, who timed their weekly protest, during which hundreds marched in the square wearing white head scarves, each carrying a picture of her missing children, to coincide with the opening ceremony of the World Cup on June 1, 1978. It was a symbolic gesture that was not lost on the press.

In the United States, Jimmy Carter's presidential administration was at such a loss as to how to deal with the Argentine situation that it even considered approaching Pope John Paul II to put pressure on the junta. In a confidential memo entitled "The Tactic of Disappearance" from the American embassy in Buenos Aires to the secretary of state in Washington and the Vatican office of the U.S.

embassy in Rome, it was suggested that the State Department "encourage the Vatican and the Argentine Church to intervene with the Argentine authorities. The Papal Nuncio here understands the issues and is already involved in trying to get the [Government of Argentina] to examine the morality and wisdom of the tactic of disappearance. . . . The Church and the pope have far more influence here than the [United States government] and can be the most effective advocates of a full return to the rule of law."

The church did little to pressure the government, publicly at least—later, it was claimed that efforts were made behind closed doors. The papal nuncio at this time, Archbishop Pio Laghi, became well aware of the disappearances after the military provided him in December 1978 with lists of the names of fifteen thousand people it had "taken care of." But neither he nor the Vatican attempted to make this information public. Laghi's record, therefore, divides opinion, with some praising him for his endeavors to obtain from the junta information about disappeared persons and even, in some cases, to secure their release. Others have been highly critical, accusing him of being wholly complicit with the regime and even reporting that he regularly played tennis with one of the main leaders of the coup.

But Pio Laghi was, of course, not the only priest accused of being unsettlingly close to the Argentine military rulers.

"I DID WHAT I COULD"

Two principal events occurred during the early years of the junta's reign that have called into question the actions of the man who would, almost forty years later, be elected 266th leader of the Catholic Church: the abduction and torture of Jesuit priests Orlando Yorio and Franz Jalics, and the abduction and murder of Esther Ballestrino de Careaga.

During a criminal investigation of the junta's concentration camps in 2010, Archbishop Bergoglio was called as a witness to the events and was questioned for four and a half hours by human rights lawyers and three judges. During his testimony—Bergoglio had previously refused two court summonses—he was accused by lawyers of being evasive and repeatedly refused to name names when questioned about the sources of his information. Among other things, Bergoglio described the events surrounding the kidnapping of Esther Ballestrino de Careaga and detailed the attempts he made to gather as much information as possible about her disappearance. When challenged by lawyers, who asked if, "given their friendship, [he] should have done more for Ballestrino de Careaga," he replied, "I did what I could." For many people, what he did was nowhere near enough.

The most damning accusations centered on the case of two Jesuit priests, Orlando Yorio and Franz Jalics, former theological teachers of the young Bergoglio, who were arrested on May 23, 1976, in the Buenos Aires *villa miseria* known as Rivadavia del Bajo Flores, where they worked. Like many Jesuits during this time, they had embraced the reforms of Vatican II that encouraged them to promote a church of the poor, and they were known as "slum priests." There was a good deal of crossover between this outreach work and the formation of organizations such as the left-wing, and occasionally Marxist, Movement of Priests for the Third World. And it was exactly this gray area that endangered the lives of many clergy.

After they were arrested, Yorio and Jalics were hooded and chained before being taken to the infamous ESMA detention center. Here they were stripped naked and tortured by military police over a period of five days, in an attempt to elicit a confession that they were colluding with left-wing guerillas, before being moved to a house in Don Torcuato, twenty-two miles outside of Buenos Aires. While many prisoners gave false confessions to spare themselves further brutality, Jalics and Yorio maintained that they had committed no crimes, even after they'd been administered so-called truth serums. Yorio later recalled that after he had spent many days insisting he was innocent, his torturer made a chilling and revealing comment about the true vision of Videla's society: "We know you're not violent. You're not guerrillas. But you've gone to live with the poor. Living with the poor unites them. Uniting the poor is subversion."

On October 23—five months after their abduction, having been held in chains and blindfolded—the pair was drugged, stripped naked except for their hoods, and transported by helicopter to an airfield, where they were dumped. Regaining consciousness and removing their hoods hours later, they discovered they were the only people there—but they were free. Jalics and Yorio walked until they found a farm and soon after, according to Bergoglio's testimony at the 2010 ESMA trial, Yorio telephoned him. Bergoglio stated that "at that point one had to take all possible precautions," and so he told the priests, "Do not tell me where you are, and do not move from where you are. Send me a person to tell me where we can meet."

Who can say why the priests were not loaded onto the death flight and thrown from the air with other detainees? Perhaps their captors could not stomach killing priests as part of a holy war to purge their Christian civilization of communists.

When the pair returned home, they began speculating over what had led to their abduction and torture. Their suspicions fell heavily at the door of their provincial superior, the head of the Jesuits in Argentina, Jorge Mario Bergoglio. A week before their abduction, their priestly licenses had been withdrawn and they had been ordered to close down the religious community they had founded in Bajo Flores three years earlier. The philosophical underpinning of the venture was deemed too politically close to liberation theology, with its Marxist undertones.

The two first fell afoul of Bergoglio during an earlier purge of left-wing associations within the Jesuits toward the end of 1974. Yorio and Jalics did not take kindly to the upstart provincial superior, a former student of theirs, dictating what work they were allowed to do within the community, and the pair refused to disband their project, even after Bergoglio's decision was endorsed by the superior general of the Jesuits, Pedro Arrupe, at the beginning of 1976. By February 1976, Bergoglio told the two priests he was under "tremendous pressure from Rome and sectors of the Argentinian Church." Arrupe had decided that they must choose whether they wished to continue as priests within the Society of Jesus, and therefore close down the community, or leave the Jesuits entirely. According to Yorio, "he [Bergoglio] had told the general that this order was tantamount to expelling us from the Society, but that the general's mind was firm in the matter." The ultimatum left them completely torn, and Bergoglio suggested that they request a leave of absence to give themselves some time to consider their options.

The death squads had already gunned down another slum priest, Father Carlos Mugica, outside his church, and accounts of violence against clergy were increasing. Supporters of Bergoglio insist that not only did he help hundreds of people escape persecution by the junta, but also that it was not ideological objections that caused him to close down the community but, rather, a fear for the priests' safety. These reports do chime with the fact that Bergoglio himself played a vital role in securing the exhumation of Mugica's remains in April 1999 from the middle-class cemetery where he had originally been buried and their transfer to Villa 31, where he was laid to rest in the slum he had given his life for.

However, others discount these efforts, made over twenty years after the events, and believe that Bergoglio's motivations were not so pure. The priests claimed that in the subsequent meeting between them and Bergoglio on March 19, 1976, five days before the coup, Bergoglio informed them it had been decided they were to be expelled from the society. The future Pope Francis remembered the occasion quite differently, maintaining that he suggested they resign and the pair agreed.

Upon learning that Yorio and Jalics were no longer members of the Society of Jesus, the archbishop of Buenos Aires, Juan Carlos Aramburu, withdrew their licenses, to prevent them from celebrating mass and carrying out priestly activities in the diocese.

A few days later, they were abducted.

Bergoglio first heard that the men had been kidnapped when one of their neighbors telephoned him that same day. He testified at the November 2010 federal court hearing that he sprang immediately into action, informing the relevant Argentine and Roman clergy and contacting the families of the victims. He then had what he described as a "very formal" meeting with President Videla, during which "he [Videla] took notes and he said that he would make enquiries." After this somewhat unsatisfactory conversation, Bergoglio decided to appeal to Videla via a different route: "The second time, I managed to find out which military chaplain was going to celebrate

Mass in the residence of the Commander in Chief. I persuaded him to say he was sick and to send me in his place. That Saturday afternoon, after the Mass, which I said before the whole Videla family, I spoke with him there. There I had the impression that he was going to take action, and take things more seriously."

By this time, rumors around Flores were suggesting that a naval task force had snatched Yorio and Jalics. Bergoglio approached Admiral Emilio Massera, head of the navy, to plead the priests' case. The tone of this meeting was similar to that of his first conversation with Videla. Massera listened to Bergoglio's assurances that the men had not been involved in anything subversive, and he agreed to look into the matter and get back to him. After several months of silence, Bergoglio was "almost certain" that the navy was responsible and so met with Massera again in an interview he described as "very ugly." The admiral kept Bergoglio waiting for ten minutes, then the two men had a heated exchange during which Massera attempted to dismiss him, stating, "I've already told Tortolo [archbishop of Buenos Aires] what I know." Infuriated by Massera's evasive response, Bergoglio declared that he knew where the priests were. He said, "Look, Massera, I want them to appear," and then "got up and left."

During Bergoglio's retelling of events thirty-four years later, lawyers found him evasive, and in their closing statement to the court described his as "one of the most difficult testimonies" they had faced on account of "dozens of references made" that indicated "a great knowledge on facts that are investigated here but also a great reluctance to provide all the information." When explaining his understanding that a naval task force had snatched the priests, Bergoglio would give no greater detail other than he had heard it through the grapevine, or "vox populi," as he termed it. Luis Zamora, one of the attorneys questioning Bergoglio, was frustrated by this lack of detail and pushed him for greater clarity:

Zamora: Maybe you can tell us what was going around as vox populi, because publicly people couldn't know this.
Bergoglio: The people that one asked said it was the navy, it was navy infantry.

Zamora: Whom did you ask?

Bergoglio: The people that had influence, the people that you could consult, that had connections with judges, with some military guy, with a policeman, with the interior ministry. Everything pointed to the navy.

Zamora: Do you remember any name from these people who so easily accessed power?

Bergoglio: No.

Zamora: Were they ecclesiastical superiors? The cardinal?

Bergoglio: It was everyone that one could go to in a moment of desperation, you know? They were friends, acquaintances, "I have an acquaintance, I'm going to find out." These type of things.

Zamora: That they were kidnapped by the navy is a very important piece of information. Let's see if you can try hard, Mr. Bergoglio. This is a very important piece of information that you are giving us that can help us understand the origin, to identify those that you talked about, that you believe were trustworthy, as you indicated to Massera, that it was a serious source, not just anyone, yeah?

Bergoglio: It was said as "vox populi." The whole world agreed. It was not that one person said it. Everyone said, "It was the navy infantry." I don't remember well if they identified the agents that participated in the operation as naval infantry, I think they also identified themselves as a task force from the navy.

Bergoglio continued with his testimony, recounting how, when he met with Yorio and Jalics after they were released, the priests expressed near certainty that they had initially been held and tortured at ESMA, having heard planes taking off and landing nearby— Buenos Aires's domestic airport is located near the naval center. When asked by Zamora if he made "any denouncements for the lives of those people," Bergoglio answered, "We did everything via the ecclesiastical hierarchy." Zamora probed further: "Why not the legal hierarchy, since it was a crime?" Bergoglio simply replied, "Due to our discipline, we preferred to do it via the ecclesiastical hierarchy."

In Bergoglio's defense, one could argue that denouncing these crimes to the "legal hierarchy" was not a realistic option under the junta's rule. After all, the military had made substantial amendments to the constitution that "legalized" many of the gross abuses of human rights committed during the process of reorganization and had effectively assumed control of the justice system as well. This was a fact that Alicia Oliveira, a judge and close friend of Bergoglio's, was all too familiar with after the junta sacked her immediately after taking power on March 24, 1976. Despite being castigated by the military, she continued to work as a human rights lawyer and held the impressive statistic of having written the most habeas corpus writs issued to the courts on behalf of detainees and disappeared persons during the Dirty War.

Nonetheless, even without a fair and unbiased justice system to rely on, Bergoglio's decision to handle issues via the "ecclesiastical hierarchy" was, it will be seen, a hollow option.

THE TRUTH WILL OUT

In 2006, the church published a collection of internal documents and correspondence sent during the Dirty War, entitled *The Church and Democracy in Argentina*. Such collections are sporadically produced by various sectors of the Catholic Church, so on the surface this one appeared to be no great exception. The duties of editing, writing an introduction, and overseeing the selection of material fell to the president of the Argentine Episcopal Conference, who was at this time none other than Cardinal Jorge Mario Bergoglio, archbishop of Buenos Aires. But what set off this particular publication from the rest was that it included a memorandum dated November 15, 1976, detailing the minutes from a meeting between the military junta and Cardinal Juan Aramburu, archbishop of Buenos Aires; Cardinal Raúl Primatesta, president of the Argentine Episcopal Conference; and Monsignor Vicente Zazpe, archbishop of Santa Fe, in which the church outlined its concerns regarding the current state of the country. The meeting was described in the 2006 book this way: "On November 15, 1976, representatives of the Argentine Episcopal Conference, speaking with representatives of the military junta, expressed that although the church is careful not to be manipulated by anyone in political campaigns on the occasion of the defense of human rights, it cannot cede anything in this field."

What was not immediately apparent to readers would become clear only when the Argentine investigative journalist and former *montoneros* guerilla Horacio Verbitsky published the entire original memorandum in a 2010 piece for the Argentine newspaper *Página/12*. The truth was particularly damning for Cardinal Bergoglio, because it revealed the document had been heavily redacted for its 2006 publication. Verbitsky published the two copies side by side in response to a comment made by Bergoglio in the 2010 book *El Jesuita,* in which he stated, "Contrary to the suggestions of certain ill-intentioned journalists, they're complete, with no omissions. The church spoke out."

This was, speaking plainly, a lie. In the unredacted documents is proof of what the church had always denied: that it had indeed colluded with the regime and turned a blind eye to the brutalities being committed to save itself from a confrontation with the junta.

The extracts below are taken from the original:

OBJECT OF THE MEETING:
First of all, clarify the position of the church.
We do not intend to take a position of criticism of government actions, an attitude that does not correspond to us, but only to warn of the dangers that we have come to see.

What is the aim of the church?
First, not to mix politically—Faced with this, the bishops are aware that a failure [of the junta] would, very likely, lead to Marxism, and therefore, we accompany the current process of reorganization of the country, undertaken and led by the armed forces, with understanding, and in time with adhesion and acceptance . . .

What we fear:
Seeing us forced into a dilemma
   —Or a conscientious silence of our consciences, which, however, would not serve the process [or reorganization]

–Or a confrontation that we sincerely do not want
–In both of the two cases the country loses

Proposition:
  –A communication channel, which can serve as an authorized consultation, unofficially.

Although the memo does express concerns over the kidnappings, torture, and general repression of freedoms, it rationalizes that these crimes were probably committed by a few bad apples at the "inter-mediate level" and even praises the junta for its "notable efforts" so far at acceptable "reorganization." The memo as a whole firmly contradicts Bergoglio's assertion of 2010: "At the beginning, little or nothing was known; we became aware gradually. I myself, as a priest, knew that something serious was happening and that there were a lot of prisoners, but I realized it was more than that only later on."

If the meeting did take place on September 15, 1976, as the orig-inal internal church memo states, then Yorio and Jalics were still missing but Bergoglio had definitely already informed his superi-ors of suspected naval involvement and of his meetings with Valida and Massera. If it, in fact, occurred on November 15, 1976, then nearly ten priests and seminarians had already been murdered, in-cluding one bishop, and the church would have been well aware of the release of the two priests three weeks prior and of the priests' belief that they had been held and tortured at the ESMA naval camp. Either way, the information the church had in its possession was highly incriminating, yet none of it was discussed with the junta.

An addendum in the 2006 publication declares that the church could not "cede anything" when it came to the defense of human rights. If this was truly the case, why, then, did it remove large sections of the original document? What to make of the church's proposal of an unofficial direct channel of communication—one that, later, did not prevent the murders of 150 Catholic priests as well as "hun-dreds of nuns and lay catechists" by the end of the Dirty War? That church leaders kept their "communication channel" open throughout the junta's rule was proven by another leaked document dated April 10, 1978, detailing a meeting between the same three senior clerics, but this time with President Videla himself. Over lunch, the president frankly admitted that the disappeared persons had indeed been murdered, but he dismissed the church's suggestion that his government should publish a list of the victims' names because "it gives rise to a series of questions about where they are buried: in a common grave? In that case, who put them in that pit?" It goes without saying that a record of this conversation did not appear in the 2006 church publication.

The Catholic Church had denied the existence of any documentation that would aid criminal prosecutions against the perpetrators of the Dirty War. Again, this document was discovered by Verbitsky's tireless campaigning for justice and relentless pressure on the church to acknowledge its true crimes during this time. This evidence had not been lost; it had been carefully filed in the episcopal archives under the record number 10,949. One can only begin to imagine what is contained in the other 10,948 documents, which still remain locked in the archives despite the Vatican's announcement in October 2016 that it had digitized records from the church of Argentina and would release them to the victims and relatives of those involved, at the request of Pope Francis. The documents have yet to be published, almost two years later.

When the drama of their release subsided, Yorio and Jalics finally began to consider their abduction in the cold light of day. As more time passed, their thoughts turned to the disturbing possibility that someone within the church had handed them over to the authorities, and their suspicions fell heavily on Jorge Bergoglio. According to Vallely, Yorio confided in friends that "his interrogators had asked questions based on theological information and spiritual confession he thought only his Provincial could have known." Their speculations only increased when, in 1977, Admiral Massera was awarded an honorary professorship from the University of El Salvador—the same institute that Bergoglio had purged of leftist Jesuits in 1973, replacing them with the Iron Guard. Coincidentally, it was around the same time that Yorio submitted a detailed twenty-seven-page report to the Vatican outlining his and Jalics's ordeal. No official action was taken in response to the allegations. In a 1999 interview with Verbitsky, Yorio said, "I don't have any evidence to think that Bergoglio wanted to free us, quite the contrary." He died a year later, still convinced of Bergoglio's guilt.

The Hungarian-born Jalics remained a Jesuit but left Argentina almost immediately after his and Yorio's release. Following a short spell in the United States, he relocated to Germany and began running retreats based on the Jesus Prayer—*Lord Jesus Christ, Son of God, have mercy on me, a sinner*—"since [he] survived psychologically in captivity by reciting it over and over." Jalics had Argentinian citizenship, but when his Argentinian passport expired in 1979, he was terrified at the prospect of returning to renew it and so asked Bergoglio to act on his behalf, despite his suspicions. The provincial superior duly sent the requested official letter to the Argentine Foreign Ministry, but the passport application was refused on account of Jalics's previous record.

The reason would not be known were it not for the efforts of Verbitsky, who discovered an official memo dated December 4, 1979, and signed by the director of Catholic worship at the Foreign Ministry. In it, he explained that he had refused the renewal based on information personally relayed to him by Father Bergoglio, who had made a special request for the application to be declined. The evidence presented included Jalics's conflicts of obedience.

On April 15, 2005, shortly after Verbitsky published this new evidence, a criminal lawsuit was filed against Bergoglio over his alleged involvement in the kidnap and torture of Fathers Olando Yorio and Franz Jalics. This was just three days before the conclave that saw Joseph Ratzinger beat out strong competition from Cardinal Bergoglio to become pope. A strong and vocal contingent of Catholics, at both the conclave and back home in Argentina, was deeply opposed to the man they saw as a collaborator. Alicia Oliveira believed the leaked dossier that found its way into the inboxes of cardinal electors at the 2005 conclave came from Bergoglio's enemies within Opus Dei, while others believed it was the work of high-ranking Argentine Jesuits with whom Bergoglio had fallen out during his time as provincial superior.

The motives and names of those priests remain a mystery to this day, and the lawsuit was eventually dismissed, but the allegations of

Bergoglio's complicity would continue to haunt him, even before another case that suggested his complicity surfaced.

VOWS OF SILENCE

"Bergoglio's silence is thunderous and shameful.
Where is Bergoglio? Does he have nothing to say
about this trial?"

These questions were asked by the witness Estela de la Cuadra de Fraire during her testimony at the trial of a police chaplain, the Reverend Christian von Wernich. He was found guilty on October 10, 2007, of involvement in forty-two kidnappings, thirty-one cases of torture, and seven murders during the Dirty War. Von Wernich received a life sentence for his crimes.

The trial lasted several months, during which the testimonies of hundreds of victims and witnesses described in detail how von Wernich worked alongside the police in torture sessions held at several of the secret concentration camps. After gaining detainees' trust, he would extract confessions and then pressure them into revealing information about other potential "subversives." The priest also developed relationships with the families of four kidnapped young left-wing guerilla fighters, collecting considerable sums of money—fifteen hundred dollars per family in 1977—on the promise that he would buy their way out of prison and smuggle them out of the country. When the desperate parents handed over their savings, it never even occurred to them to consider that a priest would conspire with the military; told by the chaplain that their sons were now in hiding, they believed it. The families later discovered that the men had been executed and that Father von Wernich was among those to witness the executions.

Another of his victims was Estela de la Cuadra de Fraire's sister Elena, who was abducted, along with her husband, Héctor Baratti, in February 1977. She was twenty-three years old and five months pregnant. As militant members of the Marxist-Leninist Communist Party and vocal campaigners for human rights, they and other family members had been identified by the junta as enemies of the state.

Elena's brother Roberto José had already been "disappeared" in September 1976, and her parents were distraught at the prospect of losing another child and their grandchild.

The de la Cuadras searched tirelessly for information and finally caught a break in May 1977, when a series of anonymous phone calls and notes slipped under the door of the family home began to offer hope. Several of the messages reported the same thing over a period of two months: the couple was alive and Elena was still pregnant. In July, the family received word that Elena had given birth to a baby girl on June 16, but the child had been taken away after just four days. It was a bittersweet blow, but the knowledge that the baby was alive spurred the family to continue searching and prompted Elena's mother, Alicia, to begin protesting alongside the Mothers of the Plaza de Mayo, where she cofounded the sister group Grandmothers of the Plaza de Mayo with other women whose grandchildren had been taken when their daughters gave birth in prison.

When the news dried up, the de la Cuadras, like many families of the disappeared, turned to the church for help. Their local priest suggested they speak with Monsignor Emilio Grasselli, private secretary to the head of the military chaplaincy, Archbishop Adolfo Servando Tortolo, who informed them that he had no information on their son, Roberto José, because he had disappeared "a long time ago," but that Elena was being detained outside La Plata.

That was all they could get from Grasselli—it would later transpire that he kept a list of the disappeared for the chaplaincy, with crosses marked next to the names of those confirmed dead by the military.

The family then sent Soledad, another of the de la Cuadra sisters, who lived in exile in Italy, the information and asked her to visit the Rome office of the superior general of the Jesuits, Pedro Arrupe, with whom the family had a long-standing relationship. Arrupe obliged and passed their case to the provincial superior for Argentina, Jorge Bergoglio.

Elena's father, Roberto, met with Bergoglio to explain the situation, and Bergoglio suggested that Mario Picchi, auxiliary bishop of La Plata, could possibly help, as he was well connected with the military in that area. Bergoglio gave de la Cuadra a brief handwritten note of introduction to take to Picchi. It read, "He [de la Cuadra] will explain to you what this is about, and I will appreciate anything that you can do."

Batted from one office to another, ad nauseam, Roberto Senior traveled to La Plata and, again, explained the details of his missing children. Picchi assured him, "It's okay, I'm going to see Tabernero." This was Colonel Reynaldo Tabernero, deputy chief of the Buenos Aires police. His chief was Colonel Ramón Camps, after whom the network of torture centers known as Camps Circuits was named— and for whom Christian von Wernich worked as chief confessor.

When Picchi reported back to the family, he did not have good news. Tabernero had informed him that Elena's child had been given to a "good family" who would raise her well. When asked about Roberto Junior, they were told not to inquire again. Picchi also checked with Enrique Rospide, an intelligence liaison, who confirmed what Tabernero had said, adding that the situation with the adults, including Elena and Héctor, was "irreversible."

In 2010, the National Commission for the Right to Identity and the Grandmothers of the Plaza de Mayo received information about a young woman who could potentially be the daughter of a disappeared person. After an investigation, the case was referred to the specialist unit of the attorney general's office, which was dealing with the appropriation of children during the Dirty War. The young woman, now living abroad, voluntarily submitted herself for DNA testing, and on August 21, 2014, it was confirmed that she was the daughter of Héctor Baratti and Elena de la Cuadra.

It was later revealed that Elena had given birth on the floor of the kitchen at a police station on June 16, 1977. Witnesses who survived the torture camps recalled Elena and Héctor pleading with von Wernich to spare their child, to which he replied, "The sins of the parents shall be visited upon the children." The reality was clear. There was no way the couple would ever be released, and they would soon be executed. In the final moments with their baby, they placed all their hopes that she might still be saved into the last free choice they had left: their daughter's name. They christened her Ana Libertad: Anna Freedom.

Her father's remains were discovered in an unmarked mass grave and identified by forensic anthropologists in 2009. He had been thrown from a death flight into the sea.

Her mother's body was never found.

Reverend Rubén Capitano, a priest who had studied with von Wernich as a young seminarian, gave perhaps one of the most honest testimonies ever given by a cleric when he said, "The attitude of the church was scandalously close to the dictatorship to such an extent that I would say it was of a sinful degree. [The church] was like a mother that did not look for her children. It did not kill anybody, but it did not save anybody, either." Such thoughts would always be shared by the de la Cuadra family after they went to Jorge Bergoglio for help looking for their own child.

On the surface, the case is just another example of Bergoglio using the "ecclesiastical hierarchy" to deal with inquiries into disappeared persons. This would have remained the opinion were it not for a second testimony he was ordered to give in 2010 at the federal court investigation into the death of Elena de la Cuadra and many others held prisoner at ESMA. Just as he had tangled himself up in a web of lies when he fervently declared that the internal Catholic documents had been published complete and uncensored, Bergoglio was once more revealed to be lying about the true chronology— how much he knew and when he discovered it. When questioned by lawyers as to when he first heard that the junta was removing babies born to detained mothers and selling them off to wealthy families, he replied, "Recently, about ten years ago [2000]," before correcting himself and saying, "No, it must have been around the time of the military junta trial [which began in 1985]."

Admittedly, the handwritten note Bergoglio sent to Picchi does not give any details of Elena's pregnancy, only that her father would fill the priest in on the situation when they met. The de la Cuadra family is adamant, however, that Roberto Senior would have informed Bergoglio of Elena's condition, just as they informed Picchi before he returned with devastating news.

THE ROAD TO CÓRDOBA

The charges laid against Jorge Mario Bergoglio are inextricably linked to the people he is accused of harming, and so long as pain is still felt by those alive to speak out, there will be no clean slate for him. Suspicions have and will always linger over what he did or did not do during the Dirty War. In situations such as this, "innocent until proven guilty" will never apply, perhaps in part because the secrecy with which the junta carried out its campaign of genocide on the Argentine people has created a culture of suspicion within the society as a whole. A lack of answers will always lead to speculation. But what is especially remarkable is that out of the ashes, Bergoglio was able to emerge reborn and go on. While grief still lingered in the hearts of many parents and children, Bergoglio was off in Rome being elected pope. So one has to ask, how on earth does someone with such a checkered past manage to succeed to the ultimate office within the Catholic Church?

There is one period in Bergoglio's life that stands out from all the others as a true Damascene moment worthy of Saint Paul himself. This occurred in 1990, when he was removed from his teaching post in Buenos Aires and exiled to the Jesuit residence in the city of Córdoba.

Several other priests were exiled at the same time, to other provinces and even as far as Europe, as the new provincial superior, Víctor Zorzín, carried out his own "purge" of the Jesuits. But this time, instead of removing leftists, as Bergoglio had done, Zorzín was expunging Bergoglians. As for Bergoglio himself, the theory went that by removing the man considered by many to be the cause of the internal backbiting and friction that had built up since the conference at Medellín, they could return the Jesuits to a unified and peaceful society. Therefore, those loyal to the newly labeled persona non grata were instructed not to have any contact with him—according to his biographer and friend Elisabetta Piqué, "Bergoglio's telephone calls were censored and his correspondence controlled"—and malicious rumors were spread about the reason for his banishment. Father Angel Rossi, a young Jesuit who had been accepted into the society by Bergoglio in 1976, recalled hearing that Bergoglio had fallen so spectacularly from grace that "the man who had been provincial of the Society so young, so brilliant, had ended up in Córdoba because he was sick, crazy."

Bergoglio was not, as gossip would have people believe, suffering some kind of breakdown, but a darkness came over him in the two years he spent in Córdoba. When reflecting on this period five months after becoming pope, he explained, "I lived a time of great interior crisis when I was in Córdoba." In an attempt to explain what he went through, he said in a 2010 interview, "What hurts me the most are the many occasions when I have not been more understanding and impartial. . . . But I must emphasize, I was always loved by God. He lifted me up when I fell along the way, He helped me travel through it all, especially during the toughest periods, and so I learned."

Listening to the sorrows and sins of regular parishioners was the ideal cure for any form of self-pity with respect to his own circumstances. He engaged on a meaningful and personal level with the local population—a somewhat ironic twist of fate considering the years he spent restricting the *villa miseria* priests back in Buenos Aires. Primarily, however, it was, as Bergoglio recalled, "a time of purification that God sometimes permits. It is a dark time, when one does not see much. I prayed a lot, I read, I wrote quite a bit and lived my life. It was something of the inner life. Beyond being a confessor or a spiritual director, what I did in Córdoba had more to do with my inner life."

THE POSTER BOY FOR ATONEMENT

Day by day he pieced himself back together, but as he did so, he began to understand that the pieces no longer fitted the man he had been before; sides that had once been straight were now curved, and vice versa. His published theological reflections from this time are profoundly connected to feelings of exile and pain, loneliness and marginalization. Although he maintained the rather Victorian etiquette, so favored by the Catholic Church, that it is not polite to talk about oneself, his later insistence that these works were produced with a general view of faith, rather than a personal reflection on his own suffering, is belied by the tone of passages such as "Between feelings and thoughtlessness, between grace and sin, between obedience and rebellion, our flesh feels the exile to which it is subject, the walk it is obliged to make, and it struggles for itself, to defend this hope."

Torn between such conflicting emotions, Bergoglio returned to his Jesuit roots and behaved almost as if he were once more a young man studying for his formation. He swept floors and tended to the sick, washing them and changing their bedsheets; he walked among the people in the streets and presided over many spiritual retreats; and through doing so, he established a humility that, he said, he had never known existed. Years later, in an interview with Father Antonio Spadaro, Bergoglio, now Pope Francis, reflected on the reasoning of those who had wished to punish him, and admitted, "My authoritarian and quick manner of making decisions led me to have serious problems and to be accused of being ultraconservative. . . . To be sure, I have never been like Blessed Imelda [a proverbial goody-goody], but I have never been a right-winger. It was my authoritarian way of making decisions that created problems."

The silence afforded to him during the two years in Córdoba changed Bergoglio fundamentally, and this was reflected in the memories of those who knew him during this time. There is one image that is repeated again and again: of Father Jorge always asking people if they needed anything. He was now nearly fifty-five years old and had finally been freed from the pressures of ecclesiastical politics that had so dominated his life. With a new perspective, he was able to see just how far removed from society the small and insular world of the church had been, and he wrote that "the lack of poverty encourages division [among men and communities]." The humble man, who lives in simplicity and poverty, is far richer in his experiences of the world.

The sound of Jorge Mario Bergoglio's footsteps in Córdoba echo loudly through his years as bishop and then archbishop; cardinal and then pope. His period of atonement saw him confess his sins to God and, in the process, completely revitalize his view of the world and his commitment to the new role he now intended to play. But moments of atonement and the confession of sins within the Catholic

Church are and have always been a silent peace made with God: "the grace of silence." They are private and will remain so for the rest of a sinner's life. Therefore, what frustrated and angered those waiting for some acknowledgment or apology who listened to his terse testimony during the 2010 trials—"I did what I could" and "due to our discipline, we preferred to do it via the ecclesiastical hierarchy"—is precisely the concept that the church has followed since its inception: you confess your sins to God and you are forgiven. And although sinners carry that knowledge deep in their hearts—the knowledge of pain caused to others or actions not taken—that is where it remains. There are no public declarations, only the offer of a chance to continue life with the blessing of absolution.

And that is exactly what Jorge Bergoglio did.

8

HABEMUS PAPAM . . . ITERUM

The ballot papers were loaded into the stove, along with the Vatican's new *fumo bianco* cartridge, to avoid any color confusion, and at 7:06 P.M. unmistakably white smoke billowed from the chimney and into the rainy night sky. The pealing of bells from St. Peter's mingled with the jubilant cheers of the sodden crowds in the square.

While emotions were erupting outside, Francis was seated quietly in the Room of Tears. Considering the magnitude of the election, precious little time for reflection is afforded a new pope, as impatient tailors wait nervously outside the door, needles at the ready to adjust the white papal cassock. While members of the Gammarelli family busied themselves around Francis, the master of Pontifical Liturgical Ceremonies entered to assist him in donning the red velvet and white ermine *mozzetta* so favored by Benedict, along with the gold, jewel-encrusted pectoral cross, papal cuff links, and red leather shoes. But Francis was not Benedict. He was a man who had rejected luxury his whole life: to embrace it now would be sheer hypocrisy. Instead, the Italian media reported him—although the quotes were believed to be false—thanking the assistant who was helping to dress him, before saying, "It's not carnival time."

He returned to the chapel dressed simply in the white cassock, his plain black orthopedic shoes, and his cardinal's silver pectoral cross. His modest appearance was a surprise, to say the least, and there were more to come. When Francis reentered the Sistine Chapel, he was instructed to officially receive his fellow cardinals from the same ornate throne as Benedict had done eight years ear-lier. Again, he politely declined the formality: he preferred to stand, and rather than allowing his brothers to kiss his ring and declare their loyalty, he disarmed them once more by kissing their hands. It was a moving gesture. Cardinal Dolan recalled, "He met with us on our own level. It's very difficult to explain. You obviously get to know your brother cardinal. But all of a sudden the identity is different."

With congratulations over, it was time for Francis to reveal him-self to the world. But he had one more important gesture to make. On his way to the balcony, he paused at a telephone and requested to be connected to Castel Gandolfo. He wished to speak to Benedict. There was no reply, but Francis insisted they try again. It turned out that the pope emeritus and his staff were all gathered around the television, eager for their first view of the successor. Benedict was finally pried away, and the two men spoke kindly, "exchanging good wishes and assurances of mutual prayer."

Over an hour had passed since white smoke had billowed out. St. Peter's Square was overflowing, and crowds of people hoping to catch a glimpse of their new pope now spilled out down the side roads. There were screams of delight when the red velvet curtains twitched. Out stepped Cardinal Jean-Louis Tauran to utter the words everyone had been waiting for: *"Habemus papam!"* As quickly as they had erupted, the cheers fell away when Tauran announced that Cardinal Jorge Mario Bergoglio had been elected pope.

"Who is he?" many asked. After some furious googling, which revealed the scant facts that an Argentinian Jesuit had been elected, the crowds happily chanted, "FRANCISCUM! FRANCISCUM! FRANCISCUM!" for ten long minutes.

Finally, at 8:22 P.M. the curtains were drawn back and the smil-ing but nervous face of Pope Francis beamed down from the bal-cony. His wave was tentative and brief. Francis lowered his arms as his smile faded. For well over a minute he stood there, motionless. As if in a trance, he gazed through his small round spectacles at the crowds enveloped in a darkness now punctuated by thousands of twinkling camera flashes. When a microphone was placed in front of him, the new pope awoke from his reverie and said in Italian,

"Brothers and sisters, good evening!" Cheers echoed around the square. Breaking the tension with a kind of joke, Francis continued: "You know that it was the duty of the conclave to give Rome a bishop. It seems that my brother cardinals have gone to the ends of the earth to get one . . . but here we are. . . . I thank you for your welcome."

Conscious that Benedict was watching, the new pope began his speech with a prayer for the old pope: "First of all, I would like to offer a prayer for our bishop emeritus, Benedict XVI. Let us pray together for him, that the Lord may bless him and that Our Lady may keep him." This was followed by some general words about the journey they were all about to take together. According to Vatican tradition, a newly elected pontiff blesses his people, but Francis, as his brother cardinals had already discovered, was anything but traditional and instead said, "Now I would like to give the blessing, but first—first I ask a favor of you: before the bishop blesses his people, I ask you to pray to the Lord that he will bless me: the prayer of the people asking the blessing for their bishop. Let us make, in silence, this prayer: your prayer over me."

The clamor had, overwhelmingly, been for change. Here change was. A self-confessed "sinner" pope, lowering his head with humility and asking his people to pray for him. The silence in the square was spellbinding. Gone were the princely pontifical ways; and as Cardinal Oscar Rodríguez Maradiaga recalled from his position next to Francis on the balcony that night, "You can't imagine the response from that huge crowd that was in St. Peter's Square, because they expected a theological message and they found somebody that is warm, that is there, that is one of us." It was a powerful statement to the world but also to the Vatican, and it illustrated that Francis intended to be true not only to his humble origins and principles but also to those of his namesake.

WHAT'S IN A NAME?

Jorge Mario Bergoglio was a pope of many firsts: the first Jesuit pope; the first pope from Latin America; the first non-European pope in over twelve hundred years; the first pope to have never studied or worked in Rome; and, significantly, the first pope to choose the name

Francis. And the first pope for a long time to have a former pope still around. The choice of name was a daring move laden with symbolism, and depending on which side of the Vatican's political divide one sat, it could be interpreted as hopeful or ominous for the future of the Catholic Church.

Saint Francis of Assisi was born into a wealthy family in the Umbrian town of Assisi in 1181 and enjoyed a carefree and lavish youth, never wanting for anything. But by twenty-five he had tired of parties and what he later described as living in sin, and when Assisi declared war on the neighboring town of Perugia, he seized the opportunity to prove himself as a noble young knight. He rode out of Assisi resplendent in a suit of armor decorated with gold. After a day on the road, however, God came to him in a dream and commanded him to return home. He did so and was mocked for his cowardice. Humiliated, Francis began to withdraw from his former life and to immerse himself in prayer. During a pilgrimage to Rome, he was so moved by the poverty he witnessed that he exchanged clothes with a beggar outside St. Peter's Basilica and spent a day among the poor, begging for alms.

As he wandered the hills, searching for guidance from God, a vision came to him and told him three times, "Francis, go and repair My house, which, as you can see, is falling into ruins." Returning to Assisi in rags, Francis was disowned by his father and so renounced his former life to live as a beggar. Devoting himself to poverty and penitence, he spent two years helping to rebuild local churches before founding the Franciscan Order in 1208. It had only one rule: "to follow the teachings of our Lord Jesus Christ and to walk in his footsteps."

Followers continued to increase in number after his death in 1226, and he was canonized in 1228. Francis, "one of the most cherished saints in modern times," remains revered for his "generosity, his simple and unaffected faith, his passionate devotion to God and man, his love of nature and his deep humility."

When the new pope declared that he wished to be named Francis, those who knew him thought it a perfectly pitched choice for the cardinal who had already shunned the luxurious lifestyle of an archbishop. But for members of the curia who lived like kings within the Vatican walls, it was a concerning move that prompted more than a few quizzical sideways glances.

Fundamentally, the trappings of the papal office could not be more different from the life of poverty led by Saint Francis. It is pomp and ceremony; it is red leather shoes and fur-trimmed velvet; it is assassination attempts and armored cars; it is governance and power; it is management and administration; and, cripplingly, it is a gilded cage from which the dove of peace looks out over the world, unable to fly among the people. It is one thing for a pope to reject limousines in favor of the bus, but quite another for him to overturn the tradition and institution he had just been appointed to lead.

As a cardinal, Jorge Bergoglio had not been shy in expressing his opinions about such worldly excess:

> The cardinalate is a service, it is not an award to be bragged about. Vanity, showing off, is an attitude that reduces spirituality to a worldly thing, which is the worst sin that could be committed in the Church. . . . An example I often use to illustrate the reality of vanity, is this: look at the peacock; it's beautiful if you look at it from the front. But if you look at it from behind, you discover the truth . . . Whoever gives in to such self-absorbed vanity has huge misery hiding inside them.

These words, taken from an interview in February 2012, now seem prescient. They can easily be interpreted as characterizing the pope or the Vatican as the peacock behind which the murky scandals of sexual abuse and Vatileaks corruption lurked. When coupled with Saint Francis of Assisi's determination to "go and repair [God's] house, which, as you can see, is all in ruins," they indicated that the church at last had an opportunity to effect great change. The only question now was how those within its walls would embrace it.

AND THE DUST FINALLY SETTLED

Tears and celebrations continued to flow throughout the night in Vatican City. When a somewhat bewildered Francis stepped down from the podium and was ushered to the official papal limousine that would take him to dinner, again he refused, saying he preferred to ride the bus with his brother cardinals: "We have come together, we go together." Back at Casa Santa Marta, he could finally relax. Over the celebratory dinner, including ice cream and sparkling wine, he joked during his toast, "May God forgive you for what you've done." Cardinal Dolan recalled that this "brought the house down."

After the guests had retired to bed, Francis, unable to sleep, changed out of his papal robes and back into his plain black trousers and coat, and made his way downstairs. According to Paul Vallely's biography, "Startled officials found themselves being asked if there was a car available. The new Pope wanted to go for a drive, he said. A driver was summoned and, in a small unmarked car, the man who hours earlier had pointedly styled himself only as Bishop of Rome, toured the streets of that city watching the celebrating crowds."

Perhaps Francis felt this was his last opportunity to move unnoticed through life, absorbing the perspective afforded to him as a simple cardinal on the streets of Buenos Aires. Or perhaps he was curious to experience the natural outpouring of joy now that the cameras had stopped rolling. Whatever the reason, he drank in these last few hours of freedom like a man about to endure what his predecessor had described as a death sentence.

The following morning, Francis woke early. After prayers, he made a visit to the Basilica of Santa Maria Maggiore to pay homage to the Virgin Mary. Crowds of people surged around him, but the new pope requested his security team not to prevent them from entering the chapel with him. On his way back to the Vatican, he requested another unscheduled stop, this time at the hostel he had stayed at during the two weeks prior to the conclave. Declining the offer of an assistant to pack his bags, Francis explained that he wished to gather his belongings himself and to thank the staff for all their help. More shocking still, he insisted on paying his bill, explaining that he, more than anyone, "had to set a good example."

At 5 P.M. Francis returned to the Sistine Chapel to celebrate mass with the cardinal electors. He did not read from the prepared Latin homily offered to him, but spoke from the heart in Italian. Nor did he speak from the papal throne. Instead, he stood at the lectern just as a parish priest would when delivering a sermon to his congregation. In his speech he outlined three building blocks that would be at the heart of his pontificate:

1. Journeying
Our life is a journey, and when we stop moving, things go wrong.

2. Building
We speak of stones: stones are solid; but living stones, stones anointed by the Holy Spirit. Building the Church . . . on the cornerstone that is the Lord himself. There is another kind of movement in our lives: building.

3. Professing
We can walk as much as we want, we can build as many things, but if we do not profess Jesus Christ, things go wrong. We may become a charitable NGO, but not the Church . . . When we are not walking, we stop moving. When we are not building on the stones, what happens? The same thing that happens to the children on the beach when they build sand castles: everything is swept away, there is no solidity.

Francis then summarized his message:

Journeying, building, professing. But things are not so straightforward, because in journeying, building, professing, there can sometimes be jolts, movements that are not properly part of the journey: movements that pull us back. . . . My wish is that all of us, after these days of grace, will have the courage, yes, the courage, to walk in the presence of the Lord, with the Lord's Cross; to build the Church on the Lord's blood which was poured out on the Cross; and to profess the one glory: Christ crucified. And in this way, the Church will go forward.

The election of Pope Francis was itself an unmistakable signal that a large majority of cardinals wished for real reform within the church. Francis was acutely aware of this and, through the words of his first homily, was signaling to those who had voted for him that he had heard them loud and clear. No member of the curia or even from the old-guard Western nations could have dreamt of instigating any form of quantifiable shake-up. It had to come from the New World. Now, to many in that room, it *had* come. Francis was the man to bring change and hope.

THE FRANCIS EFFECT

The potential impact of a Latin American's election as pope should not be underestimated. The symbolism of Francis's choice of papal name and his dedication to fighting social injustice and human rights abuses set him worlds apart from the many popes before him. As a Jesuit, his freethinking and acute understanding of evangelism in developing societies opened up a world of new opportunities in the church's fight against the global rise of secularism.

The United States, in particular, was continuing to reel from the impact of secularism. In a survey conducted by the Pew Research Center in 2014, nearly one-third of all American adults (31.7 percent) stated that they were raised Catholic, but of that figure, 41 percent—equating to 12.9 percent of the total population—no longer identified with the religion. This makes lapsed Catholics the fourth-largest "religious" group in America behind Protestants (46.5 percent), practicing Catholics (20.8 percent), and those who identified as "nothing in particular" (15.8 percent). In real terms, for every one person who joins the Catholic Church in America, a staggering six people leave it. In the years between 2007 and 2014, the number of people not affiliated with any religion rose by 6.7 percent of the total population—some fifty-six million people. They now outnumber both Catholics and Protestants, with only Evangelical Christians maintaining a higher share of the population.

In Britain, most people under the age of forty now say they have no religion. In fact, "No religion" is a more common response to polls than "Christian." This loss of faith is a concern not only for

Christians: secularism is also on the rise within Muslim-majority countries. As Ahmed Benchemsi reported in the *New Statesman,* a poll in 2012 found that 5 percent of Saudi citizens—more than a million people—self-identify as "convinced atheists," the same percentage as in the United States. Nineteen percent of Saudis—almost six million people—think of themselves as "not a religious person." (In Italy, the figure is 15 percent.) These numbers are even more striking considering that many Arab countries, including Saudi Arabia, the United Arab Emirates, Sudan, and Yemen, uphold the sharia rule punishing apostasy with death.

This rise in disbelief in the developed world rocked the church to its foundations, yet a solution remained elusive. By electing a man so clearly cut from a different papal cloth, the sense of hope was palpable. Francis had seemingly done the impossible and managed largely to satisfy both traditional and progressive wings of the church. In his biography, *Pope Francis: Untying the Knots,* Paul Vallely describes him as a man of many contradictions:

> Jorge Mario Bergoglio is a doctrinal traditionalist but an ecclesiastical reformer. He is a radical but not a liberal. He seeks to empower others and yet retains a streak of authoritarianism. He is a conservative yet was on the far left of his nation's reactionary Bishops' Conference. He combines religious simplicity with political guile. He is progressive and open, yet austere and severe. . . . He has opposed same-sex marriage and gay adoption but he has kissed the feet of homosexuals with AIDS. He is of the South, yet has deep roots in the North: a Latin American whose parentage is Italian and who has studied in Spain, Ireland and Germany. He is a diocesan priest and yet also a member of a religious order. He is a teacher of theology but a pastor with the common touch. In him humility and power come together.

It is quite possibly *because* of these contradictions that Francis seems to have benefited from a surge of confirmation bias among the cardinal electors during the 2013 conclave. Based on their own desires for the future of the church, they saw the side of Francis they wanted to see—something that was impossible when electing Pope Benedict, unquestionably an archconservative. Francis's enigmatic and humble demeanor, combined with his virtual invisibility during the run-up to the election, allowed individual voters to assume what kind of pope he would be.

Once the furor of his election had died down, however, the reality of electing a man so paradoxical meant the church was at a loss to decipher exactly which Francis he would turn out to be. Cardinals and media alike were now forced to become detectives, and every movement he made or word he uttered was studied in microscopic detail for possible clues. There was one word in particular that stuck in the mind of many who sat within the Sistine Chapel, watching the master of ceremonies ask Francis if he would take up the papacy: *sinner.*

9

THE SUPERSTAR POPE

It was perhaps a combination of the mystique of Francis's arrival as virtually unknown cardinal from Latin America, his radical steps of humility, and his admissions of sin in his first year that set such a high benchmark of expectation from the public and ruffled the feathers of conservatives within the Catholic Church. How could he possibly sustain such a glittering start?

We have already seen that his decision to dispense with the luxuries of the papal apartments, limousines, and extravagant clothing as favored by his predecessors struck an immediate chord with many of his followers, but what really set him apart in his first year was his highly visible ease with people. In the first month alone, he preserved his "slum bishop" tradition of washing the feet of twelve marginalized people during Holy Week. This time, he went to a prison and included not just two women among the twelve but also two Muslims. The stiffness of Benedict's relationship with the people was suddenly a distant memory, and the new pope was all smiles and natural warmth. Francis took advantage of the glaring spotlight he now found himself in and showed unrivaled determination to draw the world's attention to issues he believed pressing. There was one in particular that weighed on him, and so on his first official visit outside the Holy City, in July 2013, Francis traveled to the tiny Sicilian island of Lampedusa. Located seventy miles off the coast of Tunisia, this small spit of rock, just four miles long, with its white-sand beaches and turquoise waters, had become a focal point of the ever-growing crisis in which hundreds of thousands of refugees were risking their lives on perilous sea voyages to reach the shores of Europe—a crossing many thousands would never survive.

In a poignant illustration of this unrelenting catastrophe, a ship carrying more than 160 Eritreans had docked into port shortly before the pope's arrival, and the Italian coast guard had the previous day rescued a boat carrying 120 people, including four pregnant women, after its engines had failed just off the coast.

Francis traveled out on a rescue boat to lay a wreath of white and yellow flowers for those who had lost their lives at sea. Then he addressed the fifteen-thousand-strong crowd of locals and migrants with a moving and powerful homily:

> I felt I had to come here today, to pray and to offer a sign of my closeness, but to also challenge our consciences lest this tragedy be repeated. . . .
>
> Has any one of us grieved for the death of these brothers and sisters? Has any one of us wept for these persons who were on the boat? . . .
>
> We are a society which has forgotten how to weep, how to experience compassion—"suffering with" others: the globalization of indifference has taken from us the ability to weep!

Francis repeated the charge of "globalized indifference" four times during his address, which he delivered wearing purple mourning dress and standing on a makeshift altar made from the driftwood of shipwrecked refugee boats. By any standards, it was a strikingly political display for a pope who, while expressing his affection for the Muslims present, who were about to begin fasting for Ramadan, also begged forgiveness "for those who by their decisions on the global level have created situations that lead to these tragedies." But this was no publicity stunt, and the refugee crisis has remained one of the pope's causes célèbres throughout his time in office. Every year, he has made multiple calls to action and traveled to numerous locations at the center of the crisis to continue drawing world attention to the issue. He has also publicly criticized the exploitation of Africa and its natural resources by the global elite; and labeled President Donald

Trump's policy of separating migrant children from their parents as "immoral" and "contrary to our Catholic values." He expressed "deep concern" following the violent clashes that erupted after the United States relocated its Israeli embassy from Tel Aviv to Jerusalem. And he described the U.S. president as "not Christian" in his desire to build a wall at the Mexican border.

The mercy he has shown to refugees and the poor has also led to fervent criticism of global capitalism. In a year when the World Bank estimated that 767 million people were living on less than $1.90 a day, Francis issued his first apostolic exhortation, entitled *Evangelii Gaudium* (The Joy of the Gospel), in November 2013, and did not shy away from identifying the failings of capitalist societies to fight poverty and injustices. In a style not dissimilar to John Paul II's targeting of communism, Francis launched a blistering attack on economies of "exclusion and inequality" in which "everything comes under the laws of competition and the survival of the fittest, where the powerful feed upon the powerless." But he did not just speak in Orwellian tones of "big powers bad, small people good." No, he had done his homework and identified specific examples of economic models he believed to be crippling the global population:

> Some people continue to defend trickle-down theories which assume that economic growth, encouraged by a free market, will inevitably succeed in bringing about greater justice and inclusiveness in the world. This opinion, which has never been confirmed by the facts, expresses a crude and naïve trust in the goodness of those wielding economic power and in the sacralized workings of the prevailing economic system. Meanwhile, the excluded are still waiting. . . . This imbalance is the result of ideologies which defend the absolute autonomy of the marketplace and financial speculation. . . . Debt and the accumulation of interest also make it difficult for countries to realize the potential of their own economies and keep citizens from enjoying their real purchasing power.

The pope went on to blast corruption, tax evasion, and "the new idolatry of money" as the cause of the increasingly vast gulf between rich and poor. He declared that the people should say "no to a financial system which rules rather than serves" and called on political leaders to implement a "vigorous change of approach" to bring about financial reforms.

As with his campaigning for refugees, this was not flash-in-the-pan populist rhetoric. These issues have remained at the top of his agenda and have acted as a foundation for the implementation of reforms of the Vatican Bank, exposed for its own deep-rooted corruption in the Vatileaks scandal. Despite some inevitable backlash, his stance on capitalism and deep concerns over the impacts of climate change have won him considerable support with ideologically liberal people outside the church, as well as those reformers inside. The media widely report him as the most universally popular pope ever—John Paul II was indeed a much-loved figure, but his popularity was more closely confined to the Catholic faithful—and some believe him to be more popular *outside* the church than with his own clergy.

A POPE IN NAME ONLY?

Ever since his first speech from the balcony to the joyous crowds in St. Peter's Square, Pope Francis has gone to great lengths to reform the papacy, not just through outward reform but through a redefinition of the pope's own status and role. For instance, on the five occasions Francis referred to himself during his Urbi et Orbi apostolic blessing on March 2013, he referred to himself simply as "Bishop of Rome." Pope Benedict XVI, on the other hand, tried out a wide range of grander monikers in his early speeches: Successor to the Apostle Peter, Pontiff, Bishop of Rome, Pastor of the Universal Church, among others. He eventually confirmed his preference to utilize a maximum of eight, while dropping some in March 2006, when he published his *Annuario Pontificio* (Pontifical Yearbook), the annual statistical guide to the Catholic Church and a who's who of its hierarchy, released each March.

The supremacy of the pope has been a highly contentious part of Christian and Catholic history right through to the present day, when it is viewed as an essentially unaccountable position of authority. In the modern era, the concept of papal infallibility was cemented with the decrees of Popes Pius IX in 1870 and Paul VI in 1964, along with the apostolic letter *Laetamur Magnopere* on the Catechism of the Catholic Church, issued by John Paul II in 1997. Francis is keenly aware of the matter of infallibility, but the paradox remains that were he to attempt to implement any kind of doctrinal reform, he would, in effect, be declaring that all popes who had ruled before him were wrong. Also, he is presented with another challenge: the ambiguous status of the former pope, now Pope Emeritus Benedict XVI.

If a pope resigns, does he remain infallible? As the eminent Vatican journalist Sandro Magister notes, "The pope is invested with his power of primacy . . . directly from Christ through acceptance of the legitimate election made by the organ of the college of cardinals." But what happens after he steps down? Are the divine powers removed? The answer to this theological conundrum caused a lively debate among academics, with some, such as Enrico Maria Radaelli, even declaring it a "murderous blow to dogma" in his thirteen-page article on Benedict's resignation:

> . . . Resigning means losing the universal name of Peter and going back to the private being of Simon, and this cannot be, because the name of Peter, of Cephas, of Rock, is given on a divine plane to a man who, in receiving it, no longer makes only himself, but "makes Church." Without counting the fact that since the self-removed pope cannot in reality resign, the incoming pope, despite himself, will be nothing but an antipope. And reigning will be he, the antipope, not the true pope.

When Francis published his own *Annuario Pontifico* two months later than expected, in May 2013, there was much speculation as to the cause of this delay. Many concluded that there had been some serious debate about how exactly to handle the situation of having two living popes. Many were surprised to discover that the new pope had completely reformed his own status and stripped himself of the eight titles that Benedict XVI had published in his own final edition less than a year earlier. On the same page of the new *Annuario Pontifico,* the new pope is referred to simply, in two lines of text on the entire page, as "Francis/bishop of Rome." Biographical information on the following page does include the other titles, but this was a highly symbolic move and many believe a strong statement that he intended to assert his difference from his predecessor, who was referred to as "supreme pontiff emeritus." What is also intriguing, as Magister pointed out, is that in public Francis has always referred to Benedict as "bishop emeritus," so "it can therefore be presumed that the title of 'supreme pontiff emeritus' . . . was personally desired by Joseph Ratzinger and the current pope simply decided not to oppose it."

Francis might have decided not to oppose the outgoing pope's request, but he has still chosen not to use that title. This suggests that despite the Vatican's wish to project an image to the public of a warm and respectful relationship between the two popes, the coexistence has not been as harmonious as the church would have us believe. Such a conclusion is hardly surprising, however, considering the decision by the self-proclaimed supreme pontiff emeritus to remain living in the Vatican and to continue wearing his white papal cassock, albeit without the white *mozzetta*.

And it is not just titles, vestments, and lodgings that have sparked rumors of a rift. On two occasions, Benedict has written letters of support for cardinals with whom Francis has had very public confrontations.

The first saw the pope emeritus write a loving tribute for the funeral of Cardinal Joachim Meisner in July 2017, despite Meisner's coauthoring of a letter criticizing the sitting pope for his April 2016 apostolic exhortation on the family, *Amoris Laetitia* (The Joy of Love), which allowed for divorced and remarried persons to receive communion. Francis did not respond to the letter, nor to the subsequent request for an audience, but two of the cardinal authors have since died, and the response remains outstanding.

Always known for his gaffe-prone approach to politics, Benedict again managed to blithely stir up controversy by writing a glowing foreword for the German edition of Cardinal Gerhard L. Müller's book *Catholic Dogmatics for the Study and Practice of Theology*, six months after the cardinal was not renewed in his role as prefect for the Congregation for the Doctrine of the Faith by Pope Francis in July 2017, a role to which he had been appointed by Benedict, and was replaced by his Spanish Jesuit deputy, Archbishop Luis Ladaria. The conservative Müller had been strongly opposed to Francis's proposals to allow divorced and remarried Catholics to receive communion and has been a vocal critic of the pope since his removal from office.

But the embarrassing incidents did not end there. Having been asked by Monsignor Dario Viganò, the pope's director of Vatican communications, to write another foreword, this time for an eleven-volume collection of books called *The Theology of Pope Francis,* Benedict responded on February 7, 2018, with a letter marked "private and confidential," in which he declined. Upon receiving this reply, Viganò decided to slip an edited version of the pope emeritus's statement to the press on March 12 but made no mention of the original request to write the foreword, perhaps to head off further speculation that might arise from the publication of the book *without* an introduction from Benedict. Or perhaps it was an attempt to level the playing field, theologically speaking, and to bolster Francis's talents, in comparison to those of his predecessor, by including a glowing compliment from such an eminent theologian as Benedict:

> Thank you for your kind letter of 12 January and the attached gift of eleven small volumes edited by Roberto Repole.
>
> I applaud this initiative that wants to oppose and react to the foolish prejudice in which Pope Francis is just a practical man without particular theological or philosophical formation, while I have been only a theorist of theology with little understanding of the concrete life of a Christian today.
>
> The small volumes show, rightly, that Pope Francis is a man of profound philosophical and theological formation, and they therefore help to see the inner continuity between the two pontificates, despite all the differences of style and temperament.

When the media responded with requests for a copy of the full letter so they could publish it in its entirety, the Vatican said it was unable to send a scan of the original letter but did have a photograph, which it could send out as *proof* that the words had definitely come from Benedict.

Unfortunately, the press immediately cried foul when the artfully staged picture of the letter arrived, for it showed not only a second paragraph that had been intentionally blurred to make it unreadable, but also a glimpse of Benedict's signature halfway down a second page, the text of which had been entirely obscured by the eleven-volume pile of books, conveniently placed on top to prevent the press from reading it. It was a bizarre decision and one that incensed the media. The Associated Press stated, "The manipulation changed the meaning of the image in a way that violated photojournalist industry standards. . . . Those quotes suggested that Benedict had read the volume, agreed with it and given it his full endorsement and assessment."

Backed into a corner, the Vatican was compelled, two days later, to admit to the redaction and reveal the text of the blurred paragraph, which was described as "the letter in its entirety." What had seemed a positive message of support had become something else entirely. In fact, Benedict had politely declined to write anything whatsoever for the book, explaining:

> I don't feel like writing a short and dense theological passage on them because throughout my life it has always been clear that I would write and express myself only on books I had read really well. Unfortunately, if only for physical reasons, I am unable to read the eleven volumes in the near future, especially as other commitments await me that I have already made.

But wait, there's more. Not only was Benedict too busy to read and endorse the books on Francis's theology, but it also transpired that Sandro Magister had discovered a further redacted page of the letter, and this contained highly critical comments about one of the writers who had been chosen to author a volume, whom Benedict considered to be a critic of papal authority. It was all humiliating for the Vatican. First it had cherry-picked passages and

misled the press, and then it had lied by claiming the previous release was the "letter in its entirety." All this made it doubly embarrassing when the Vatican finally released the complete letter . . . again:

> Only as an aside, I would like to note my surprise at the fact
> that among the authors is also Professor Hünermann, who
> during my pontificate had distinguished himself by leading
> anti-papal initiatives. He played a major part in the release of
> the *Kölner Erklärung* [Cologne Declaration,] which, in rela-
> tion to the encyclical *Veritatis Splendor* [Truth Shines,] viru-
> lently attacked the magisterial authority of the Pope, especially
> on questions of moral theology. Also the *Europaische The-
> ologengesellschaft* [European Theological Society], which he
> founded, was initially conceived by him as an organization
> in opposition to the papal magisterium. Later the ecclesial
> sentiment of many theologians prevented this orientation,
> allowing that organization to become a normal instrument of
> encounter among theologians.

Time and again, we find a church seemingly incapable of learning that small lies lead to bigger ones, which then oblige cover-ups
and, in most cases, result in exposure and disgrace. Whether through
arrogance or stupidity, the publication of a clearly doctored photograph was an insult to the intelligence of both the media and 1.28
billion Catholics, a gross violation of Benedict's trust, and a blatant
example of willful deceit. And lest we forget, this was not the first
time Bergoglio had been caught redacting documents to fit a particular narrative—a fact that made his homily on Palm Sunday, just
eight days later, all the more puzzling. Rather than taking this opportunity to publicly make amends or offer an apology, Francis instead issued a thinly veiled attack on those he deemed responsible
for propagating a torrent of negative gossip regarding his pontificate
and his relationship with Benedict. Magister described it as a "thunderous" denouncement of "fake news." What the pope said was this:

> It is a cry that emerges in moving from the facts to an account
> of the facts; it comes from this "story." It is the voice of those

who twist reality and invent stories for their own benefit, without concern for the good name of others. This is a false account. The cry of those who have no problem in seeking ways to gain power and to silence dissonant voices. The cry that comes from "spinning" facts and painting them such that they disfigure the face of Jesus and turn him into a "criminal." It is the voice of those who want to defend their own position, especially by discrediting the defenseless.

The speech was a continuation of the message issued by Pope Francis on January 24, 2018, regarding "fake news and journalism for peace" in advance of World Communications Day in May 2018. In the letter, Francis likened what he described as the "snake-tactics" of those spreading disinformation and fake news to those used by Satan in the Garden of Eden, who he declared had, "at the dawn of humanity, created the first fake news (cf. *Gen* 3:1–15), which began the tragic history of human sin." In the era of Donald Trump's war with the media, the topic was timely and a bold one for a pope to speak out on; the issue was also one that Francis was clearly concerned about. However, the fact that the "lettergate" scandal was bookended by these two searing indictments of malicious journalism and fake news left many confused by what appeared to be blatant hypocrisy.

It had been just over five years since Francis was elected pope, and some began to wonder whether this was evidence of cracks beginning to appear. He had thus far weathered the multitude of storms that had blown his way, but it would be little surprise if his strength was starting to yield under the immense pressures, both positive and negative, that had surrounded him since the very beginning of his papacy.

"WHO AM I TO JUDGE?"

Those five words have become synonymous with the papacy of Pope Francis. In one of his famously relaxed and informal papal plane press conferences, where he is said be completely open to all questions and where he displays a wry, razor-sharp wit, when asked where he gets the energy to handle his exhausting schedule, he quipped, "He meant to ask, 'What drug is he on?'" Francis was responding to allegations of a so-called "gay lobby" within the church and to accusations that Monsignor Battista Ricca—whom the pope had personally appointed to be his man inside the Vatican Bank—had, among other things, been in an openly homosexual relationship with a Swiss Army captain while living at the Holy See's nunciature in Uruguay.

> So much is written about the gay lobby. I still haven't found anyone with an identity card in the Vatican with "gay" on it. They say there are some there. I believe that when you are dealing with such a person, you must distinguish between the fact of a person being gay and the fact of someone forming a lobby, because not all lobbies are good. This one is not good. If someone is gay and searching for the Lord and has good will, then who am I to judge?

The compassion expressed by Francis was considered by many to be a true watershed moment in the church's teaching on the subject of homosexuality. There was further praise when, in April 2018, Pope Francis met with Juan Carlos Cruz, a victim of sexual abuse by a Chilean priest, and said of his homosexuality, "You know, Juan Carlos, that does not matter. God made you like this. God loves you like this. The Pope loves you like this and you should love yourself and not worry about what people say."

When compared to the teachings of his predecessor, this was most certainly groundbreaking. Pope Benedict had stated in 2010 that homosexuality was "contrary to the essence of what God originally wanted." This was, in fact, a somewhat softened stance from his time at the CDF, when he labeled it "an intrinsic moral evil." Benedict himself further contradicted Francis in a 2016 interview with Peter Seewald for the book *Last Testament: In his Own Words*, when he confirmed the existence of a "gay lobby" and boasted about how he and others had successfully dismantled the group. But to those familiar with Catholic teachings, Francis's words were not revelatory reforms of doctrine; they simply adhered to the 1992 Cat-

echism of the Catholic Church approved and promulgated by Pope
John Paul II. This colossal document refers to homosexuality as "acts
of great depravity . . . contrary to natural law . . . [and] under no
circumstances can they be approved"—but it also states that homosexual people should still be "accepted with respect, compassion,
and sensitivity. Every sign of unjust discrimination in their regard
should be avoided."

The difference between the bishop of Rome and the supreme
pontiff emeritus, therefore, may be one of degree and not of kind.

In a 2013 article, *New Yorker* journalist James Carroll raised the
point that while "many observers insist that in a Church understood
as *semper idem*—always the same—the most that even an apparently innovative figure like Francis can effect is 'pastoral' adjust-
ments in discipline or practice: a merciful easing up on rules
without repealing them. Even if he wanted to, Pope Francis could
not alter the basic beliefs of the Church." There is also the possibility
that, if he really wished to shake things up, Francis could go down
the Vatican II route and organize another global council on the
future of the church. What had been decided at the Second Ecumenical Council was certainly revolutionary on paper, but the interpretation of the official conclusions differed widely, and Vatican
II still has the ability to polarize clergy to this day. Besides, there
was nearly a century between the first and second Vatican councils,
and it is unlikely that many would agree to another one just over
fifty years since the last concluded, in 1965.

Since Carroll's article was written, Francis has nevertheless
used his position to effect change in doctrine and has proved strong
enough to stand firm against the ecclesiastical backlash—as in the
case of his apostolic exhortation *Amoris Lætitia*, on family life, in
which he explicitly reversed the teachings of his predecessors and
pushed for an end to the use of condemnations that described "all
those in any 'irregular' situation [as] living in a state of mortal sin
and . . . deprived the sanctifying grace."

The task of uniting both conservative and liberal views under his
banner is, of course, impossible. Conservatives find his reforms too
radical, and liberals find them not radical enough. But it appears that
Francis is well aware he will never be able to satisfy everyone and

must therefore make decisions irrespective of their popularity and based on what he believes to be right. This has, conversely, left some people feeling let down by the pope's essentially traditional opinions on issues such as same-sex marriage, the ordination of women priests, abortion, and homosexuality, as they now know that if he believes in something strongly enough, he will advocate for the necessary changes. The ambiguity of those early days of the Francis papacy is now gone, and with it, too, the hopes of many who support reforms on these issues.

His predecessor, Pope Benedict, fought against reforms of the church that would see it adapt to the realities of modern society: that people are gay, women have abortions, people get divorced, and so on. But the church faithful essentially knew what they were getting with him and were not surprised when he stuck rigidly to traditionalist principles. Like the cardinal electors at the 2013 conclave, however, the media and the public have developed a form of confirmation bias toward the superstar Pope Francis, and this has given rise to further disappointment when he stands with the church on its conservative policies.

On the other hand, Francis seems to understand more than most the detrimental impact the scandal of sexual abuse by clergy has had on the church—an impact that cannot be overstated. People not only want the church to be better, but they also *need* it to be. No greater test of faith has occurred in modern history or, one could argue, in the church's entire history. The freedom and liberty of modern society mean that a great many followers of Catholicism are in an unprecedented position: they feel confident enough to be critical of the church. And so, the moral quandary of an institution that dictates how its followers should live their lives and yet, at the same time, is confronted with, as Cardinal Ratzinger even admitted, the "filth" within its own walls, puts the church in an extremely vulnerable position. Francis's response of openness and compassion has found synergy with followers' newly emboldened critique, while at the same time being met with accusations of heresy from conservative members of the clergy. In short: damned if you do, damned if you don't.

As the biographer and journalist Andrea Tornielli notes, "One of his most interesting traits is . . . that the more the media portray the figure of the Pope as a superstar, a pop Pope, the more he tries to prove himself the opposite." Francis's desire to disassociate himself from the concept of papal infallibility and supremacy has left him exposed to insurrection and condemnation that few would have dared utter publicly, let alone in a twenty-five-page open letter such as the one delivered to him on August 11, 2017, in which sixty-two conservative members of the clergy declared the pope's teachings and behavior to be heretical and even Lutheran in their outlook.

But as Tornielli points out, "It is the conservative critics who shout the loudest." Perhaps this accounts for the much more moderate tone used in Francis's March 2018 apostolic exhortation, *Gaudete et exsultate* (Rejoice and be glad). It contains no changes to doctrine or expressions of consternation outside of his existing favorite causes. The overall message is of love, holiness, compassion, and kindness. But while no one could call these weak pronouncements, there's a certain thinness to his message, and it is hard not to feel disappointment that the pressure of his antiliberal opponents could potentially put an end to Francis's Promethean struggle.

How much pressure a pope can take will continue to be the subject of great speculation, not least because Francis, like Benedict before him, did not want to be elected as pope in the first place. He wanted to retire and had made all the necessary preparations to do so. Desires such as this run deep and cannot easily be displaced, no matter how important an honor is bestowed upon a person.

Two months after the release of *Gaudete et exsultate*, on May 15, 2018, Pope Francis, now eighty-one years old, spoke during a Tuesday morning mass at his Santa Marta residence. Although the Vatican has not published the full transcript of his mass, it would seem it has learned its lesson in seeking to hide remarks. After his homily, audience members were left wondering if the pope had begun to consider his own "great refusal." When reading from Acts of the Apostles, Francis referred to the story of Paul's decision to leave Ephesus and go to Jerusalem, saying:

> It's a decisive move, a move that reaches the heart, it's also a move that shows us the pathway for every bishop when it's time to take his leave and step down. . . . When I read this, I

think about myself, because I am a bishop and I must take
my leave and step down. . . . I am thinking of all bishops. May
the Lord grant all of us the grace to be able to take our leave
and step down in this way [like Paul], with that spirit, with
that strength, with that love for Jesus Christ and this faith in
the Holy Spirit.

The gasp of "Oh no" could be heard around the world: "Here we
go again!" Will he also throw in his skullcap and retire, thus turning papal retirement from a crisis to a convention? It is not out of
the question.

But before it's assumed that Francis is preparing the world for
the day when he will use the path cleared by Benedict, a closer
reading of his words also suggests that a resignation ought to proceed only if instruction to do so is received from the Holy Spirit. We
must assume, at this point, that no such instruction has been sought
or received.

Still, a new age for faith is with us, when everything seems to be
up for grabs. In such times, the Catholic Church finds itself with two
living papal touchstones. One, retired but with many secret followers still, is devoted to his scholarship and contemplation; the other,
at large, is almost rampantly social, able to inspire and hold fast more
than 1.28 billion followers, steering them, with demonstrations of
humility and empathy and fallibility and headline-grabbing reasoning, back toward the faith that has been burning for two thousand
years—the faith of Saint Francis, who cast off his rich apparel and
embraced the nakedness of poverty.

Being pope is the job nobody wants. It's especially a nightmare
for an elderly man faced by seemingly intractable problems and
pockets of intractable opposition. Francis, in speaking of retirement,
suggests that a very relieving precedent has now been established
and is available to him. Still, were he to retire tomorrow, his legacy
would be profound. He has already rocked the boat of Christ's teaching, calling for an end to the days of harsh judgment and inquisition, demanding more tolerance, humility, and transparency, and
reminding the faithful that we are all sinners, up to and including
the two popes in Rome.

THE ODD COUPLE

Before we take leave of these two elderly men, living now as unlikely neighbors, a few words on how—at the time of this writing—they spend their days, revealing a little of what is known about their one-on-one meetings over the ensuing years since the first days of the Francis papacy in 2013.

The two popes first embraced as such when the papal helicopter bearing the ten-day-old pope, Francis, landed on the grounds of Castel Gandolfo, where Benedict had been sequestered since his retirement.

Benedict was at the helipad to greet and congratulate his fellow pope. Both wore the white robes and caps of papal office. They kissed, embraced warmly, and looked deeply into each other's smiling eyes as the world's cameras whirred, recording the moment. What a burdensome destiny the two now shared, what an odd brotherhood with linked destinies; and where would destiny—or, if you will, God's plan—take them both? Into what unknown waters?

Francis had brought a gift that day, an icon of the Madonna, and told Benedict that it was known as the Madonna of Humility. "I thought of you," Francis said. "You gave us so many signs of humility and gentleness in your pontificate." Benedict's reply? *"Grazie. Grazie."* And then they retreated from the cameras and went indoors.

When they went to pray in the chapel, Benedict offered the place of honor, a kneeler before the altar, to Francis. But Francis, seeing Benedict retreat to the back, followed him and knelt beside the elder pontiff, saying, "We are brothers, we pray together." The two prayed from the same pew.

Benedict then offered his pledge of obedience to the new pope, while Francis thanked Benedict for his ministry.

After this, they went into the palace to eat lunch.

As they talked, *papa a papa,* Francis may have dropped the bombshell that he didn't intend to use the magnificent palace as his summer retreat, having already a plan to open it—for the first time in its 420-year history—to the public, thus ending an ancient tradition himself. Perhaps he also mentioned that he wouldn't be using the chandelier-lit Papal Apartments in the Vatican, either, preferring to stick to the busy premises of the fluorescent-tube-lit Hotel Santa Marta he'd been using since the conclave. (Both of these promises are ones he has made good on.) And perhaps he used the same words he gave to a journalist sometime later: "I cannot live alone, surrounded by a small group of people. I need to live with people, meeting people."

At first the Vatican said that what passed between them would never be known, but this was until, in an interview in 2016, Archbishop Georg Gänswein, who now serves both popes as personal secretary, revealed that Benedict passed Francis a top-secret dossier that day. Wrongly suspected of being about the reform of the curia, it was in fact the report on the Vatileaks scandal that Benedict had commissioned.

If Benedict's cloistered retirement behind the walls of the Mater Ecclesiae has the air of a prison sentence, it may also seem that way to the pope emeritus. Quickly dashed were his early hopes of returning to Bavaria to live out his days with his brother, when it was realized that he could not be protected there: surely he would find himself speaking with an ungovernable array of people, drawn into saying things that might clash with Francis. No. No pope could roam free. And so the doors of the walled garden were closed around him, hiding him from prying eyes.

Holy Days—Easter and Christmas—as well as personal milestones like birthdays, are occasions when visits between the two men are most likely now to take place. The world's press is often invited to record the fond greeting before the two retire indoors. The Holy See Press Office often afterward supplies a few morsels of information: when Francis turned eighty, on December 17, 2016, among the seventy thousand email messages wishing him a happy birthday, as well as telephone calls and telegrams from world leaders and religious figures, he received a "very affectionate" written message, three small gifts, and a personal phone call from his predecessor that were "particularly appreciated" by the current pontiff.

And when Benedict turned ninety, on April 16, 2017, he spent the day in the monastery with his then-ninety-three-year-old brother,

Georg. He drank a little beer, nibbled pretzels, and watched the news on TV in German. Four days earlier, Francis had visited to wish the nonagenarian a happy birthday.

Benedict still enjoys summer breaks to visit Castel Gandolfo. The nuns set out a small box of bread on the edge of a goldfish pond so he can feed the fish. He loves this.

In February 2018, Benedict, in a rare public statement, said he is frail but at peace with the prospect of death. Gänswein confirms this. In a recent interview with the Italian newspaper *Il Messaggero*, Gänswein said that Benedict occasionally talks about it, describing his journey as "on a pilgrimage toward home," but it's not an obsession for him. "I can say," Gänswein adds, "that he's a serene person. He has a soul at peace, and a happy heart."

These days, Benedict, blind in one eye, and also with difficulties walking, is otherwise in good health. "Certainly, he's a man who by now is old," Gänswein says. "It's tough on him to walk, and he uses a walker. He can't work on scholarly texts like he used to do, but he still writes, and a lot. He has an enormous amount of correspondence from all over the world. He gets books, essays and letters, and he replies."

He "replies"? As what? In what capacity? As pope? Sharing infallible views? Was this the promised *silenzio incarnato*? Part of what may help keep the aged Ratzinger on track, according to Gänswein, is the regularity with which he divides each day—beginning, as it always has, he said, with the celebration of morning mass. And each Sunday, Pope Benedict still delivers a homily at mass for his small household, sometimes as few as four people: Gänswein and several female members of Memores Domini, a community of consecrated laywomen associated with the Communion and Liberation movement. The onetime leader of the biggest religion on earth, Benedict now directs his words to four friendly faces. But he does not regret this meteoric reduction in audience size. Rather, he welcomes it.

Pope Francis, at the same time, also delivers each day a small homily at morning mass at the Santa Marta residence on Vatican grounds, where he resides. These transcripts of his sermon are published, for they are considered divinely inspired. His audience remains gargantuan, but he keeps his homily short. No sermon should be more than ten minutes long, he has ordered. Make your point, clearly, quickly, then get off the stage: let the people—with their own sea of troubles—return to their lives, some hunger in them hopefully satisfied.

EPILOGUE

The Dawn of the Age of Disbelief

When the geneticist Francis Crick cracked the genetic code of life—DNA—he was so sure that science had finally defeated religion that he offered a prize for the best future use for Cambridge's college chapels. The winning entry? Swimming pools. But Crick's 1953 presumption of a watery fate was premature, for it remains impossible to take a dip at St. Catherine's Chapel Tepid Baths: but was he *wrong*?

In New York City, near Forty-fourth Street and Sixth Avenue, there is a digital sign, billboard-size, which has become known as the National Debt Clock. It shows the U.S. national debt inevitably rising, rising, the glowing numbers cycling so fast that the right-hand columns are indecipherable, merely a blur. Its effect is to alarm, to bring to life an issue so serious (more serious by the millisecond) that only a visual representation can even begin to bring home the enormity of the problem.

Imagine a similar clock—an International Faith Clock—calibrated to track the current state of *belief*: of belief that there is a God, a presiding deity, provisioned with human emotions; God as switchboard operator for all universal communications, as the source of all love, the begetter of all things bright and beautiful, whose idea and handiwork the universe is. Imagine such a clock hanging high over Times Square, or St. Peter's Square, or Red or Trafalgar or Tiananmen Square: What news would it impart?

In the developed world at least, the rise in the number of people turning away from—or simply not engaging with—the Christian faith would make at least the extreme right-hand columns a blur, the numbers of believers falling, falling, falling . . .

It is now clear: more and more people demand to be free to make up their own mind on matters of faith and morality. Increasingly they do not require their temples to tell them what to do or to supply them with ultimate answers. They navigate by stars other than the *axis mundi* so beloved of Pope Benedict. Angels will no longer suffice; Hell is no deterrent.

In such times, unmatched in human history, what is the role for the Catholic Church, or any church, and what is the best approach for its supreme leaders to take if they are to stay relevant, vital, necessary?

As I conclude this book, what strikes me now—which was not apparent to me at the outset—is not how very different these men are, but how much they share. *Both* grew up under the authoritarian regimes of murderous dictators, *both* have been accused of being bystanders to brutality. Their responses, in common, have fallen short of the mea culpa one might have expected with the benefit of hindsight and self-reflection, and offer mostly a familiar wall of silence, a wall mirrored by the Catholic Church itself in its handling of sexual abuse cases. Were these men shaped in this regard by the veiled culture of the church they both adore? Or did real life get to them first, teaching them, in terrifying times, that a little secrecy goes a long way in the management of human affairs?

Silenzio incarnato though they may remain on these matters, one sees them straining to break free of their vows. Benedict's resignation—to my mind—is a loud (and arguably noble) admission of guilt and complicity and incapacity; and in the case of Francis, the Argentinian came closest to a full reckoning when the then-Cardinal Bergoglio presided over the reburial ceremony of Father Carlos Mugica. Not yet pope, more at liberty to speak freely, he gave a searing and heartfelt address from the pulpit at the late priest's slum church. His words are the closest he has come to explicitly acknowledging his guilt over the part he played during the Dirty War: "For the death of Fr. Carlos; for his physical assassins; for those who planned his death; for the silence kept by most of the society, acting as accomplices and for all the opportunities we, as members of the Church, had to denounce his assassination but we did not, for lack of courage, Lord have mercy."

In Benedict's case we have his act of resignation, which would normally speak louder than words, if he had not provided the recondite words himself, located deep in his 2009 book, *Caritas in Veritate*:

"Truth may be vital, but without love it is also unbearable."

Lord have mercy.

The writers of all the sacred texts were poets. Whether these texts—the Bible, the Qu'ran, the Vedas, the Torah, the Upanishads, the Sutras—contain only divinely inspired and therefore purely literal truth ought never to have warranted a debate, let alone a single war. (Holy wars, seen this way, are nothing but violent disagreements over who has the superior poem.) But what inspired poems they do remain: odes to the unknowable; the most durable and beloved texts in human history. Were we able to look far into the future of the Catholic Church and learn that its fate was to become nothing more than a sacred book club, where fans gathered once a week to discuss their favorite characters and chapters, debate passionately the themes, and draw real life-lessons from shared readings, it could do a lot worse. The lesson taught by all these texts will never dim or lose its relevance; for that lesson is simply: be good, be kind, be sensitive, be just, be respectful, and take care of each other . . . for God's sake.

The British poet Philip Larkin, himself an atheist, once interrupted a perfectly lovely bicycle ride through a small English village to pop into an empty church, an "accoutred frowsty barn," and rendered his impressions in his poem "Church Going." Finding the church musty and "unignorably" silent, he inspects briefly the altar, the lectern, the baptismal font, and later the graveyard, where so many dead lie round, and concludes the old place was not worth stopping for, only to then admit that he often does so. Why keep coming back? Looking for what? What persists here that is still pleasing? A nostalgia for what once was? A vacancy in himself that old instinct says might still be filled here? Larkin has little use for religion as such: ". . . superstition, like belief, must die / And what remains when disbelief has gone?" And yet he concedes that these places can never be obsolete, "Since someone will forever be surprising / A hunger in himself to be more serious / And gravitating with it to this ground / Which, he once heard, was proper to grow wise in / If only that so many dead lie round."

What indeed remains in this skeptical age when disbelief itself fails? For disbelief, in the face of wonder, also requires effort to maintain. Wonder and magic can surprise us still, catch at us, tug at the threads of our cynicism. More often than we might care to admit, we still find ourselves struck in the contemplation of an enchanted, inexplicable moment, when the only word in the language still best suited to describe it is *God*.

Only the current pope emeritus knows whether the benefits to the church from his departure outweigh, in his mind and in his soul, the damage he must surely feel he has done to the immemorial status of the papacy. Whatever the reasons behind it, it seems only natural to conclude that Pope Benedict was aware of its likely consequences, at least in the matter of his successor. After all, Cardinal Bergoglio had been the runner-up to Benedict at his own papal election, and there was every chance the Argentinian would prevail in the new contest. What's more, Bergoglio's resignation letters, twice submitted to Benedict and held on file, unsigned, unanswered, suggest that Benedict could easily have eliminated the Argentinian from papal consideration if he'd wanted to, and thus significantly reduced the possibility of radical change within the church—change to which, Ratzinger's record tells us, he was strongly resistant. Why were these resignation letters sent to Ratzinger left unsigned by him? It seems quite possible that Benedict, after deciding he would step down, chose to make Bergoglio's candidacy at least *possible,* leaving the actual choice of the next pope to the cardinals and, of course, to God.

So what thoughts occupy Benedict, now that he is (for the most part) *silenzio incarnato*? With what does he reproach himself as he moves about his monastery garden, takes grandfatherly naps, and writes at his desk late into the night? Does he watch and marvel at the cult of Francis, who waves so confidently to the millions? Is he in awe of the man's charisma, the transformative campaigns and stunning pronouncements? Or does he, instead, blame himself for creating the opportunity for unnecessary and damaging change, for uninsured freethinking, when, with a stroke of his pen a few years earlier, he might have seen Cardinal Bergoglio now tucked up harmlessly in Room 13 at the retirement home for priests on calle Condarco 581 in Flores, Buenos Aires?

It is my conjecture that Joseph Aloisius Ratzinger debated long and hard the implications of the kind of change his resignation might invite and stepped down only when he had made his peace with the idea of Bergoglio, the reality of Bergoglio, the need for Bergoglio, the dangers of Bergoglio. This debate may still occupy the frail pope emeritus; he may be playing, in secret, both parts in the theological debates he has always enjoyed, making the case for and against an *unchanging* church that preaches simple, timeless truths; for and against a *dynamic* church that adapts its rules to meet the complex, changing needs of its people. The insignia for the papacy is two crossed keys: one to bind, one to set free; to define what is sin and what is permitted. While Ratzinger has long held and used the first key, it must seem to him that Pope Francis has run off with the second and is now in a frenzy of unlocking. (Only today, as I write, Francis has just changed Catholic teaching on the death penalty, calling it "inadmissible.") Who is right? Will the church that is married to the spirit of the age indeed be a widow into the next? Will Francis's flexibility be its downfall; or will it be its saving, and will it become, in its outreach and modernizing appeal, the mother of new millions, inspiring the disaffected back into her arms? The conservative line of argument may be reduced to a simplification: that, finally, people crave a monolithic master and will bend at the knee for nothing less. People revere that which is bigger than themselves. Liberal thought takes the opposing view: people tire of masters who appear unmoved by all entreaties.

In my mind's eye I see Benedict giving both sides of the argument full weight, before setting down his pen empty of its last ink. I imagine, on his desk, Bergoglio's resignation letters still lying there, so very shrewdly never signed by Benedict, and it is only then that I realize this clever old man actually reached his decision long ago, when no one in the world was watching.

Francesco, rebuild my church.

ACKNOWLEDGMENTS

My continued thanks to Rebecca Cronshey, whose skills at research verge on the miraculous, and Jane Parkin for her early editorial input. A debt also to Alexander Lucie-Smith for casting a knowledgeable eye over these pages.

NOTES

PROLOGUE

x "I saw and . . . great refusal": Dante Alighieri, translated by Allen
Mandelbaum, *The Divine Comedy: Inferno* (University of California
Press, 1980), Canto III, pp. 22–23.

xiv "My pope is Benedict": Edward Pentin, "Ex-Nuncio Accuses Pope
Francis of Failing to Act on McCarrick's Abuse," *National Catholic
Register*, August 25, 2018.

xiv "foolish prejudice": "Benedict affirms continuity with Pope Francis,"
The Tablet, March 13, 2018, https://www.thetablet.co.uk/news/8716
/benedict-affirms-continuity-with-pope-francis.

xiv "having a wise . . . home": Edward Pentin, "Pope Francis on Pope
Emeritus: 'The Wise Grandfather at Home,'" *National Catholic Register*, June 27, 2016, http://www.ncregister.com/blog/edward-pentin/pope
-francis-on-pope-emeritus-the-wise-grandfather-at-home/.

1. CONCLAVE

1 "acute inflammation . . . laryngo-spasm": Official statement by Vatican
spokesman Joaquín Navarro-Valls, quoted in "Pope John Paul rushed to
hospital," BBC, February 2, 2005, http://news.bbc.co.uk/1/hi/world/europe
/4228059.stm.

2 "[looking] to be . . . head": John Hooper, "Pope Blesses Easter Faithful
but Is Unable to Speak," *Guardian*, March 28, 2005.

2 On the morning of . . . Last Rites: Official statement by Vatican spokesman Joaquín Navarro-Valls, Holy See Press Office, Libreria Editrice
Vaticana, April 1, 2005.

2 "the most telling . . . reporters": John Allen Jr., *The Rise of Benedict
XVI: The Inside Story of How the Pope Was Elected and What It Means
for the World* (London: Penguin Books, 2005), p. 38.

2 "serene and lucid": Stanislaw Dziwisz, Czeslaw Drazek, Renato Buzzonetti,

Angelo Comastri, *Let Me Go to the Father's House: John Paul II's Strength in Weakness* (Pauline Books and Media, 2006), p. 86.

2 "a small . . . expiring": Ibid.

2 "I have looked . . . you": Official Account of John Paul II's Last Days, Libreria Editrice Vaticana, 2005.

3 the *novemdiales* . . . period of festivity: Francesca Prescendi (Geneva), "Novendiale sacrum," in *Brill's New Pauly,* antiquity volumes edited by Hubert Cancik and Helmuth Schneider, English edition by Christine F. Salazar; classical tradition volumes edited by Manfred Landfester, English edition by Francis G. Gentry, http://dx.doi.org/10.1163/1574-9347 _bnp_e825640 (published online 2006).

4 "As a gift . . . and gives peace": John Paul II, Eucharist Celebration for the Repose of the Soul of Pope John Paul II: Regina Caeli, Libreria Editrice Vaticana, April 3, 2005.

4 "is considered . . . among equals": The Cardinals of the Holy Roman Church [From the Latin Code of Canon Law 1983]—Can. 352 §1., in the College of Cardinals General Documentation, Libreria Editrice Vaticana, February 17, 2014.

5 "three bags . . . Pope John Paul II's reign": Allen, *The Rise of Benedict XVI,* p. 59.

5 "human, not . . . terms": Sister Mary Ann Walsh, RSM, ed., with reporting by Catholic News Service, *From Pope John Paul II to Benedict XVI: An Inside Look at the End of an Era* (Oxford: Sheed and Ward, 2005), p. 23.

6 the pope . . . his wishes: John Paul, Universi Cominici gregis Apostolic Constitution, Libreria Editrice Vaticana, 1996.

6 "a man's chances . . . in the press": George Weigel, "The Pignedoli Principle," *The Catholic Difference,* May 3, 2001, https://web.archive .org/web/20151031122412/http://eppc.org/publications/the-pignedoli -principle/.

7 "an underlying . . . local ordinaries": Michael J. Lacey and Francis Oakley, *The Crisis of Authority in Catholic Modernity* (Oxford: Oxford University Press, 2011), pp. 15–16.

7 The Vatican . . . "unbelievable" to him: Joaquín Navarro-Valls, Vatican Press Conference, Libreria Editrice Vaticana, April 25, 2014.

7 "the anger . . . John Paul II": David Gibson, *The Rule of Benedict: Pope Benedict XVI and His Battle with the Modern World* (Harper San Francisco, 2006), p. 32.

8 "secularism . . . center and the periphery": Allen, *The Rise of Benedict XVI,* p. 80.

9 "a weakened . . . the pope": Paul Collins, *God's New Man: The Election of Benedict XVI and the Legacy of John Paul II* (London: Continuum, 2005), p. 13.

9 "forced to mark time . . . of the Pope": Ibid.

10 "there [was] a real danger . . . relativism": Ibid., p. 36.

10 "As soon as he . . . course in the faith": Pope Benedict XVI, *Light of the*

World: The Pope, the Church, and the Signs of the Times: A Conversation with Peter Seewald (San Francisco: Ignatius Press, 2010), pp. 4–5.

11 "to promote . . . in all of the Catholic world": http://www.vatican .va/roman_curia/congregations/cfaith/documents/rc_con_cfaith _pro_14071997_en.html.

11 "[drag] the Catholic Church . . . dialogue with it": Collins, *God's New Man*, p. ix.

11 "developed a culture . . . irrelevant": Joseph Ratzinger, Speech at Subiaco, Italy, April 1, 2005, in ibid., p. 122.

12 "How much filth . . . every side": Joseph Ratzinger, Meditations of the Cross, Good Friday, March 25, 2005, in John Thavis, *The Vatican Diaries*, p. 292 (New York: Penguin Books, 2013).

12 "high marks . . . charisma": Walsh, ed., *From Pope John Paul II to Benedict XVI*, p. 82.

12–13 "the most powerful . . . divided: John L. Allen Jr., *Conclave: The Politics, Personalities, and Process of the Next Papal Election* (New York: Doubleday, 2002), p. 201.

13 "had real . . . stances": Collins, *God's New Man*, p. 48.

13 "the great . . . decades": Allen, *Conclave*, p. 169.

14 "assumed . . . Brazilian dictatorship": U.S. Embassy to the Vatican, "Toward the Conclave Part III: The Candidates," WikiLeaks, April 15, 2005, 05VATICAN466_a, https://wikileaks.org/plusd/cables /05VATICAN466_a.html.

14 "roly-poly, affable" . . . John Paul: Allen, *Conclave*, p. 176; Walsh, ed., *From Pope John Paul II to Benedict XVI*, p. 81.

14–15 "now that these . . . anymore": Sandro Magister, "Progressives, Moderates, Neocons: Notes Before the Conclave," *L'Espresso*, April 14, 2005, http://chiesa.espresso.repubblica.it/articolo/28458%26eng%3dy .html.

15 "A single African child . . . universe": Allen, *Conclave*, p. 176.

16 "If we elect a pope . . . support": Allen, *The Rise of Benedict XVI*, pp. 82–83.

16 "unwavering commitment . . . doctrinal views": Ibid., p. 104.

17 "a climate of . . . John Paul II": Gibson, *The Rule of Benedict*, p. 99.

17–18 "intervened . . . not always manage": Allen, *The Rise of Benedict XVI*, pp. 94–95.

18 "complicity in the . . . subversive": Paul Vallely, *Pope Francis: Untying the Knots* (London: Bloomsbury, 2014), p. 1.

19 "Ever since the . . . dinner table": Ibid., p. 3.

20 In his book . . . Holy Spirit guide them": Gibson, *The Rule of Benedict*, p. 103.

21 *Results of the first ballot of the papal conclave, 2005:* Anonymous to Lucio Brunelli, *Limes,* http://www.limesonline.com/cosi-eleggemmo -papa-ratzinger/5959 (originally published September 2005).

22 "a true . . . 'left'": Ibid.

22 "He had . . . do this to me'": Ibid.

23 *Results of the second ballot of the papal conclave, 2005:* Ibid.

24 *Results of the third ballot of the papal conclave, 2005:* Ibid.

24 "the picture of calm": Gibson, *The Rule of Benedict,* p. 105.

24 According to the diarist . . . start afresh: Anonymous to Lucio Brunelli.

25 "there was sort . . . everyone clapped": Cardinal Cormac Murphy-O'Connor, interview with BBC, March 1, 2013, http://www.bbc.co.uk/news/world-europe-21624894.

25 "want to be . . . else": Magena Valentié, "El hogar que ya no espera al padre Jorge," *La Gaceta* (Argentina), March 16, 2013, https://www.lagaceta.com.ar/nota/536881/mundo/hogar-ya-no-espera-al-padre-jorge.html.

2. FRANCIS

26 "My strongest . . . grandmother": Austen Ivereigh, *The Great Reformer: Francis and the Making of a Radical Pope* (Sydney: Allen and Unwin, 2014), p. 13.

26–27 "the single greatest . . . five years": Ibid.

27 "family legend . . . back in Piedmont": Paul Vallely, *Pope Francis: Untying the Knots,* pp. 21–22.

28 "priest-eater": Ivereigh, *The Great Reformer,* p. 14.

28 "loved all . . . memories": Vallely, *Pope Francis: Untying the Knots,* p. 22.

28 "always a joyful . . . presents": Omero Ciai, "Pope Francis as a Child," *La Repubblica* (Italy), March 17, 2013.

29 "when we got . . . to cook": Andrea Tornielli, *Francis: A Pope of a New World* (San Francisco: Ignatius Press, 2013), p. 74.

29 "always with . . . text": Ivereigh, *The Great Reformer,* p. 17.

30 "be a friend . . . to Christ": The Salesians of Don Bosco in Great Britain, http://www.salesians.org.uk/.

30 "I learned to study . . . everything easier": "Father Bergoglio's 1990 Recollection of His Salesian Education," *Zenit,* February 4, 2014, https://zenit.org/articles/father-bergoglio-s-1990-recollection-of-his-salesian-education/.

31 "mostly played . . . afternoons together": Tornielli, *Francis: A Pope of the New World,* p. 77.

31 "always liked to . . . gentleman": Ibid.

31 "if you don't . . . a priest": Ibid., p. 78.

31 "had dared . . . a boy": Philip Sherwell and Aislinn Laing, "Pope Francis: Amalia, the Childhood Sweetheart Whose Snub Created a Pope," *Telegraph* (UK), March 14, 2013.

31 "were still . . . love": Ibid.

31 "never saw him . . . separate us": Ibid.

32 "I'm so grateful . . . endeavor": Sergio Rubin and Francesca Ambrogetti, *Pope Francis: Conversations with Jorge Bergoglio,* translated by Laura Dail Literary Agency Inc. (London: Hodder and Stoughton,

2013), p. 14. Originally published as *El Jesuita: Conversaciones con Jorge Bergoglio* (Ediciones B: Argentina, 2010).

32   "an extraordinary boss": Ibid.

32   "the seriousness . . . work": Ibid.

32   "I realized . . . of the Church": Javier Cámara and Sebastián Pfaffen, *Understanding Pope Francis: Key Moments in the Formation of Jorge Bergoglio as Jesuit,* Luis Fernando Escalante, CreateSpace, an Amazon .com Company, 2015, p. 31.

33   "I would wait . . . *La Vanguardia*": Ibid., p. 32.

34   "it was the . . . free people": John L. Allen Jr., *The Francis Miracle: Inside the Transformation of the Pope and the Church* (New York: Time, 2015), pp. 121–22.

34   In an interview . . . dying relative: Uki Goni, "Pope Francis and the Missing Marxist," *Guardian* (UK), December 11, 2013, https://www .theguardian.com/world/2013/dec/11/pope-francis-argentina-esther -careaga.

34   "truly enviable . . . ahead of us": Ivereigh, *The Great Reformer,* p. 32.

34   "He supported us . . . to assist": Ibid.

35   "militantly religious": Ibid., p. 33.

35   "I went in . . . was headed": Ibid., pp. 35–36.

35–36 "It was the surprise . . . you first": Rubin and Ambrogetti, *Pope Francis: Conversations with Jorge Bergoglio,* p. 34.

36   "passive solitude": Ibid.

36   "I'm going to . . . with people": Ivereigh, *The Great Reformer,* p. 36.

36   "were not . . . political restlessness": Vallely, *Pope Francis: Untying the Knots,* pp. 30–31.

36–37 "defensive and . . . or left": Ivereigh, *The Great Reformer,* p. 28.

37   "aimed at restricting . . . religious institutions": Ibid., p. 29.

38   "You said you . . . of the soul": Vallely, *Pope Francis: Untying the Knots,* p. 30.

38   'Since I saw . . . Perpetual Help.': Cámara and Pfaffen, *Understanding Pope Francis,* p. 34.

38   "I definitely knew . . . being uprooted": Rubin and Ambrogetti, *Pope Francis: Conversations with Jorge Bergoglio,* p. 37

38   "Why don't we . . . December 12, 1995": Letter from Fr. Jorge Bergoglio to Fr. Cayetano Bruno, October 20, 1990, published in Fr. Alejandro León, ed., *Francis and Don Bosco* (Quito, Ecuador: CSPP José Ruaro/CSRFP, 2014), p. 16.

38–39 "Fr. Pozzoli said . . . typical of him": Ibid.

39   "extremely upset . . . a plundering": Rubin and Ambrogetti, *Pope Francis: Conversations with Jorge Bergoglio,* p. 37.

39   "Well, if God . . . blessed be": Ivereigh, *The Great Reformer,* p. 39.

39   "I loved . . . much": Rubin and Ambrogetti, *Pope Francis: Conversations with Jorge Bergoglio,* p. 14.

40   "a normal . . . life": Ivereigh, *The Great Reformer,* p. 48.

40 "We are so . . . that path": Jorge Bergoglio and Rabino Abraham Skorka, *On Heaven and Earth,* translation by Image, a division of Random House, Inc. (London: Bloomsbury, 2013), p. 47.

40 "When I was . . . rediscover his place": Ibid., pp. 47–48.

41 "when one . . . in that direction": Ibid., p. 47.

41 "To tell the truth . . . focus on missionary works": Rubin and Ambrogetti, *Pope Francis: Conversations with Jorge Bergoglio,* pp. 35–36.

41 "When he first got ill . . . to die": Jimmy Burns, *Francis: Pope of Good Promise* (London: Constable, 2015), p. 94.

41 "every day . . . scar tissue": Rubin and Ambrogetti, *Pope Francis: Conversations with Jorge Bergoglio,* p. 23.

41 "said something . . . imitating Christ'": Ibid., p. 24.

41–42 "pain is not a virtue . . . life fulfilled is a gift": Ibid., pp. 24–25.

42 "Two years' novitiate . . . tertianship": Ivereigh, *The Great Reformer,* p. 57.

42 A self-described . . . come back": Rubin and Ambrogetti, *Pope Francis: Conversations with Jorge Bergoglio,* p. 158.

43 "go out to . . . with people": Ivereigh, *The Great Reformer,* p. 36.

43 "The boys . . . themselves with": Ibid., p. 70.

44 "Fr. Pozzoli . . . he said nothing": León, ed., *Francis and Don Bosco,* p. 17.

44–45 "I did not want . . . different way": Ibid.

45 "the most important . . . twentieth century": John W. O'Malley, S.J., *What Happened at Vatican II* (Cambridge, MA: Harvard University Press, 2010), p. 1.

45 "on the side . . . the world": Ibid., p. 74.

46 "[Bergoglio] was serious . . . to doubt it": Elisabetta Piqué, *Pope Francis: Life and Revolution* (London: Darton, Longman and Todd, 2014), p. 55.

47 "against men . . . or religion": Declaration on the Relation of the Church to Non-Christian Religions, *Nostra Aetate,* proclaimed by His Holiness Pope Paul VI on October 28, 1965 (Libreria Editrice Vaticana).

47 "Church of the poor": Pope John XXIII, "Radio Message to All the Christian Faithful One Month Before the Opening of the Second Vatican Ecumenical Council," Libreria Editrice Vaticana, September 11, 1962.

48 "engender new injustices . . . results": "Encyclical of Pope Paul VI on the Development of Peoples," Libreria Editrice Vaticana, March 26, 1967.

48 "1,500 priests from . . . understandable response": Vallely, *Pope Francis: Untying the Knots,* p. 43.

48 "the activity of . . . the people": Ivereigh, *The Great Reformer,* pp. 95–96.

49 "The option . . . Medellín": Jorge Bergoglio, transcript of 2010 judicial inquiry, Bergoglio Declara ante el TOF, https://www.yumpu.com/es/document/view/14836117/declaracion-bergoglio-esma

-abuelas-de-plaza-de-mayo. English translation in Ivereigh, *The Great Reformer*, p. 95.

50 a promotion that . . . his age: Father Antonio Spadaro, "Interview with Pope Francis," Libreria Editrice Vaticana, August 19, 2013.

52 "sterile inter-ecclesiastical . . . strategy": Allen, *The Francis Miracle*, p. 20.

52 "a sweeping purge . . . Buenos Aires": Burns, *Francis: Pope of Good Promise*, p. 135.

52–53 'bloodless, serene and . . . government': Ibid., p. 151.

53 "the killing . . . unaccounted for": Marchak, *God's Assassins*, p. 155.

53 In declassified . . . campaign": F. Allen Harris to Mr. Bumpus, Mr. Floor–Disappearance Numbers—memorandum AT056, December 27, 1978, ed. Carlos Osorio, 2006 U.S. Department of State Argentina Declassification Project, 2002), Digital National Security Archive accession number NSAEBB185, https://nsarchive2.gwu.edu//NSAEBB/NSAEBB185/19781227%20Disappearance%20Numbers%200000A8B1.pdf.

53–54 "priests of the church . . . them": Marchak, *God's Assassins*, p. 236.

54 leading figures . . . public functions: Burns, *Francis: Pope of Good Promise*, p. 171.

54 during the Dirty . . . exiled: Ivereigh, *The Great Reformer*, p. 136.

54 "The two objectives . . . been suspect": Ibid., p. 137.

54 "it was a high-wire . . . people": Ibid.

55 "He went from . . . detail with us": Ibid., p. 187.

55 "against the rector . . . in Latin America": Ibid., p. 173.

56 "I remember . . . for Argentina'": Rubin and Ambrogetti, *Pope Francis: Conversations with Jorge Bergoglio*, p. 158.

56 Unexpectedly . . . in Bavaria: Vallely, *Pope Francis: Untying the Knots*, pp. ix–xii.

57 "spirituality and . . . Paul II himself: Ibid., p. 54.

57 "My mind . . . always wrong": Ibid., p. 164.

58 "At mid-morning . . . Aires'": Ibid.

60 "When he arrived . . . is that": Fr. Tello, quoted in "El Papa Villero," *Qué Pasa* (Chile), February 20, 2014, http://www.quepasa.cl/articulo/actualidad/2014/02/1-13835-9-el-papa-villero.shtml/.

60 "regularly ignored . . . payments": Ivereigh, *The Great Reformer*, p. 244.

61 "the auditor's . . . affair": Ibid.

61 "[This is] scarlet . . . Church": The College of Cardinals General Documentation, Holy See Press Office, Libreria Editrice Vaticana, updated February 17, 2014.

62 "extraordinary consistory . . . millennium": John Paul II, Sixth Extraordinary Consistory, Remarks of the Holy Father, Libreria Editrice Vaticana, 21 May 2001.

63 "Nowadays the war . . . First Fathers": Jorge Bergoglio, "Report After the Discussion, X Ordinary General Assembly of the Synod of

Bishops," Holy See Press Office, 12 October 12, 2001 (Libreria Editrice Vaticana), http://www.vatican.va/news_services/press/sinodo/documents/bollettino_20_x-ordinaria-2001/02_inglese/b21_02.html.

63 "Midway through November . . . Ratzinger": Sandro Magister, "Bergoglio in Pole Position," *Chiesa, L'Espresso* (Italy), November 28–December 5, 2002, wwwespresso.repubblica.it.

64 "assumed a key . . . of them": Eduardo Duhalde, "Aquel Hombre Que Estuvo en las Horas Más Difíciles," *La Nación* (Argentina), March 18, 2013, https://www.lanacion.com.ar/1564280-aquel-hombre-que-estuvo-en-las-horas-mas-dificiles.

66 "authoritative source" . . . Ratzinger: Marco Tosatti, "Ecco Come Andó Davvero il Conclave del 2005," *La Stampa* (Italy), October 3, 2013, http://www.lastampa.it/2013/03/07/esteri/ecco-come-ando-davvero-il-conclave-del-3TekbdbFe00nzWPyxlJSSP/pagina.html.

66 "[Bergoglio was] safe . . . curia": Luca Brunelli, "Così Eleggemmo Papa Ratzinger," *Limes* (Italy), September 23, 2005, http://www.limesonline.com/cosi-eleggemmo-papa-ratzinger/5959.

67 "what upset Bergoglio . . . life's work": Ivereigh, *The Great Reformer,* p. 285.

67 "I am convinced . . . been evident": Guzmán M. Carriquiry Lecour, "La Revolution de la Gracia," *Tierras de América*, February 18, 2014, http://www.tierrasdeamerica.com/2014/02/18/la-revolucion-de-la-gracia-asi-preparo-la-providencia-el-nuevo-pontificado/.

68 "The difference . . . the issue: Burns, *Francis: Pope of Good Promise,* p. 234.

68 "the Devil's envy . . . God's plan": Cardinal Bergoglio to the Carmelite Nuns of Buenos Aires, in "La Carta Completa de Bergoglio," July 8, 2010, Todo Noticias (Argentina), https://tn.com.ar/politica/la-carta-completa-de-bergoglio_038363.

69 "It's worrisome to . . . devil' ": Anthony Failoa, "Jorge Mario Bergoglio, Now Pope Francis, Known for Simplicity and Conservatism," *Washington Post,* March 13, 2013.

69 "spent many years . . . university": Ivereigh, *The Great Reformer,* pp. 302–3. This is obviously a confidential source who has requested not to be named, as Ivereigh just refers to him as "a senior priest."

69 "had compassion . . . wounds": Luke 10:33.

69–70 "made the decision . . . margins": Ivereigh, *The Great Reformer,* p. 305.

70 "are offered . . . in early 2013": Ibid., p. 340.

71 "I want . . . this world": Vallely, *Pope Francis: Untying the Knots,* p. 125.

3. CONCLAVE

72 "a little forlorn": Allen, *The Rise of Benedict XVI,* p. 116.

72 "the silence . . . but calm": Cardinal Cormac Murphy-O'Connor, in-

terview with BBC, March 1, 2013, http://www.bbc.co.uk/news
/world-europe-21624894.

72 "a courageous . . . civilization": Pope Benedict XVI, General Audi-
    ence, April 27, 2005 (Libreria Editrice Vaticana), http://w2.vatican.va
    /content/benedict-xvi/en/audiences/2005/documents/hf_ben-xvi
    _aud_20050427.html.

73 "Actually, at that . . . other": Pope Benedict XVI, *Light of the
    World,* op. cit., p. 4.

73 "just finished . . . been elected": Thavis, *The Vatican Diaries,* op.
    cit., p. 23.

74 Finally, when the . . . new pope: Allen, *The Rise of Benedict,* op. cit.,
    p. 117.

75 God's Rottweiler . . . Papa-Ratzi: Cardinal Joseph Ratzinger with
    Vittorio Messori, *The Ratzinger Report: An Exclusive Interview on
    the State of the Church* (San Francisco: Ignatius Press, 1985), p. 9.

75 "deep snow . . . that reigned": Joseph Cardinal Ratzinger, *Milestones:
    Memoirs 1927–1977* (San Francisco: Ignatius Press, 1997), p. 8.

76 "the triangle . . . rivers": Ibid., p. 7.

76 "many beautiful . . . church life": Ibid., p. 9.

76 "unemployment was rife . . . another": Ibid., p. 8.

76–77 "shrill campaign posters" . . . am Inn: Ibid., p. 12.

77 "obliged to . . . activities": Ibid., p. 14.

77 "warn and aid . . . danger": Ibid.

78 Hitler's "rhetorical . . . top: Ibid., p. 16.

78 "true home": Ibid., p. 22.

78 "could not compete . . . diligence": Ibid., p. 17.

78 "no one could . . . meaning": Ibid., pp. 17–18.

79 "there was no . . . maturation": Joseph Ratzinger, *Salt of the Earth:
    An Interview with Peter Seewald* (San Francisco: Ignatius Press,
    1997), p. 53.

79 "started down the . . . discovery": Ibid., p. 20.

79 "perfectly ordinary . . . himself included: Ibid., p. 54.

79–80 On March 12 . . . from visiting: Ibid., pp. 24–25.

80 "No foreign . . . country yesterday": "A Black Day for Germany,"
    Times (London), November 11, 1938.

80 "Do not buy . . . and home": John L. Allen Jr., *Cardinal Ratzinger: The
    Vatican's Enforcer of the Faith* (New York: Continuum, 2000), p. 15.

80–81 "good Germans . . . fight back": Ibid., p. 32.

81 "urged . . . into the spiritual life": Ibid., p. 25.

81 "it was not . . . the daughters, nuns": Georg Ratzinger and Michael
    Hesemann, *My Brother the Pope* (San Francisco: Ignatius Press,
    2011), p. 102.

81 Ratzinger recalls following . . . surrounding mountains: Ratzinger,
    Milestones, pp. 25–27.

81 "the war . . . Phony War: Ibid., p. 27.

82 "brought to their . . . time": Ibid.

82 "with unfailing . . . for them": Ibid.

82 "just go once . . . of it": Ratzinger, *Salt of the Earth,* p. 52.

82 "huge transports . . . soldiers": Ratzinger, *Milestones,* p. 28.

83 "brought many . . . as myself": Ibid., p. 31.

83 "fanatical ideologues . . . respite": Ibid., p. 33.

83 "in two years' . . . time": Laurence Rees, *War of the Century: When Hitler Fought Stalin* (London: BBC Books, 1999), p. 14.

84 "hear the . . . distance": Ratzinger, *Milestones,* p. 33.

84 "who had orders . . . murderers": Ibid., p. 36.

84 "put back on . . . our meadow": Ibid., p. 37.

85 "the moral failings . . . specifically": David Gibson, *The Rule of Benedict: Pope Benedict XVI and His Battle with the Modern World* (Harper San Francisco, 2006), p. 138.

85 "was reading great . . . conjugations": Allen, *Cardinal Ratzinger,* p. 15.

85 "those who cannot . . . repeat it": George Santayana, *The Life of Reason: Reason in Common Sense* (New York: Scribner, 1905), p. 284.

85 "What the Nazi . . . history": Gibson, *The Rule of Benedict,* p. 137.

86 "better Germany . . . world": Ratzinger, *Milestones,* p. 42.

86 "despite many . . . eternity": Ibid.

86 "more fully familiar . . . as a profession": Ibid., p. 47.

86 "I looked . . . renowned teachers": Ibid., p. 48.

86 "radical change . . . and obsolete": Ibid., p. 57.

86 "lay in ruins . . . at Fürstenried": Ibid.

87 "radiant summer day": Ibid., p. 99.

87 "We should not . . . way'": Ibid.

87 "learned firsthand . . . the sacrament": Ibid., pp. 99–100.

87 "I had to give . . . and so on": Ibid., p. 101.

87 "practical training . . . of our families": Ibid.

88 "I suffered a . . . parish work": Ibid., p. 102.

88 "a minor act of rebellion": Allen, *Cardinal Ratzinger,* p. 35.

88 "rightly and deservedly . . . Catholic faith": *Aeterni Patris: Encyclical of Pope Leo XIII on the Restoration of Christian Philosophy,* Libreria Editrice Vaticana, August 4, 1879.

88 "anyone who departed . . . with heresy": Allen, *Cardinal Ratzinger,* p. 35.

88 "decided Augustinian": Ratzinger, *Salt of the Earth,* p. 33.

88 "the intellectual ferment": Allen, *Cardinal Ratzinger,* p. 35.

89 "accepted it enthusiastically . . . February 1957: Ratzinger, *Milestones,* pp. 107–9.

89 "theologians were like . . . *Time*": Gibson, *The Rule of Benedict,* pp. 161–62.

89 "some sniper shots . . . quarters": Ratzinger, *Milestones,* p. 112.

89 "Ambitious young clerics . . . habits": Allen, *Cardinal Ratzinger,* p. 50.

90 "legend in . . . circles": Ibid., p. 52.

90 "positioned to be . . . began": Ibid.

90 "people who wanted . . . lost": Ibid., p. 57.

90 "I see no . . . [over the years]": Richard N. Ostling, "Keeper of the Straight and Narrow: Joseph Cardinal Ratzinger," *Time*, December 6, 1993.

90 "deeply troubled by . . . he detected": Ratzinger, *Milestones*, p. 134.

91 "At almost a moment's . . . by the Marxist": Ibid., p. 136.

91–92 "The destruction . . . at stake": Ibid., p. 137.

92 "This was deeply . . . resist another": Allen, *The Rise of Benedict XVI*, p. 151.

92 "knew what was . . . his integrity": Ratzinger, *Salt of the Earth*, p. 78.

92 "if the principles . . . invalidate them": Gibson, *The Rule of Benedict*, p. 172.

92 "remains true . . . a mob?": Ibid.

92 "Time and again people . . . Grand Inquisitor": Hans Küng, *My Struggle for Freedom: Memoirs*, John Bowden, trans. (London: Continuum, 2003), p. 457.

92 "in support of . . . theologian": Allen, *Cardinal Ratzinger*, p. 50.

93 "controversies experienced during . . . awaited him: Ibid., pp. 137–40.

93 "Father Ratzinger . . . the council was over": Ralph M. Wiltgen, *The Rhine Flows into the Tiber: The Unknown Council* (New York: Hawthorn, 1967), p. 285.

93 "a time of . . . work": Ratzinger, *Milestones*, p. 149.

93 "conservative standard-bearer" . . . affirmed: Gibson, *The Rule of Benedict*, p. 173.

94 "I did not . . . a bishop": Ratzinger, *Milestones*, p. 151.

95 "under some pretext . . . was staying": Ibid., p. 152.

95 "said to have . . . archdiocese": Allen, *Cardinal Ratzinger*, p. 120.

95 "the weeks before . . . of consecration": Ratzinger, *Milestones*, p. 152.

96 "young and intelligent conservative": Allen, *Cardinal Ratzinger*, p. 121.

96 "deep orthodoxy . . . shared: Ibid.

96 "too much baggage . . . in Poland": Ibid.

96 "simple, pastoral . . . Second Vatican Council": Collins, *God's New Man*, p. 167.

96 "cautioned against . . . the left": Allen, *Cardinal Ratzinger*, p. 122.

96–97 "the smiling pope . . . *Accepto*": Jason Evert, *Saint John Paul the Great: His Five Loves* (Lakewood, CO: Totus Tuus Press and Lighthouse Catholic Media, 2014), p. 54.

97 "Lord, save me": *Urbi et Orbi*, radio message of His Holiness John Paul I, August 27, 1978 (Libreria Editrice Vaticana).

97 "My name is . . . coming" Evert, *Saint John Paul the Great*, p. 54.

99 "would be no . . . rolled in": Allen, *Cardinal Ratzinger*, p. 130.

99 "attempts to emphasize . . . the job: Ibid.

99 "When someone moves . . . earlier convictions?": Ibid., p. 51.

99–100 "sought . . . social change": Allen, *The Rise of Benedict XVI*, p. 155.

100 "perversion of the Christian message": Joseph Ratzinger, Prefect, *Instruction on Certain Aspects of the "Theology of Liberation,"* Sacred Congregation for the Doctrine of the Faith, XI.1, August 6, 1984 (Libreria Editrice Vaticana), http://www.vatican.ca/roman_curia .congregations/cfaith/documents/rc_con_cfaith_doc_19840806 _theology-liberation_en.html.

100 "noninfallible": Gibson, *The Rule of Benedict*, p. 197.

100 "choosing a leading . . . leader": Collins, *God's New Man*, p. 177.

100 "willingness to polarize . . . himself": Allen, *Cardinal Ratzinger*, p. 260.

101 "intellectual assaults": Ratzinger, *Salt of the Earth*, p. 92.

101 "The paradox . . . lectern": Gibson, *The Rule of Benedict*, p. 207.

101 "too easily . . . timidity": Ibid., p. 210.

102 "There is an . . . generations": Collins, *God's New Man*, p. 68.

102 "because of our esteem . . . Church": Pope Paul VI, Apostolic Letter, *Apostolica Sollicitudo*, September 15, 1965 (Libreria Editrice Vaticana).

102 "The theory of . . . pope's": Allen, *Cardinal Ratzinger*, p. 57.

103 "asserted . . . teach authoritatively": Ibid., p. 63.

103 "the biggest problem . . . dioceses": Ibid., pp. 43, 45.

105 "It is truly ironic . . . children": Nicholas P. Cafardi, *Before Dallas: The U.S. Bishops' Response to Clergy Sexual Abuse of Children* (Mahwah, NJ: Paulist Press, 2008), p. 63.

106 "a strong tendency . . . evil": Cardinal Joseph Ratzinger, Letter to the Bishops of the Catholic Church on the Pastoral Care of Homosexual Persons, October 1, 1986 (Rome: Congregation for the Doctrine of the Faith, Vatican Press Office), http://www.vatican.va/roman_curia /congregations/cfaith/documents/rc_con_cfaith_doc_19861001 _homosexual-persons_en.html. Heng Sure, "Pope Benedict XVI's Buddhist Encounter," *Dharma Forest* (blog), http://paramita.typepad .com/dharma_forest/2005/04/pope_benedict_x.html.

4. THE RELUCTANT POPE

108 "up until now . . . than he: Walsh, ed., *From John Paul II to Benedict XVI*, p. 102.

108 "Five days after . . . into the background": Gibson, *The Rule of Benedict*, p. 217.

109 "there the architecture . . . pope": Quote in Sandro Magister, "The 'Reform of the Reform' Has Already Begun," *Chiesa, L'Espresso* (Italy), April 28, 2005, http://chiesa.espresso.repubblica.it /articolo/29626%26eng%3Dy.html). Pope Benedict XVI quoted as saying to the master of ceremonies.

109 "pray for me . . . capacity": Pope Benedict XVI, Homily of His Holiness Benedict XVI, Libreria Editrice Vaticana, April 24, 2005.

109 "advertisement . . . millennium ago": Collins, *God's New Man*, p. 198; Gibson, *The Rule of Benedict*, p. 218.

109 "SANTA POPE...LOOK: "'Santa Pope' Woos Vatican Crowds," BBC News, December 22, 2005, http://news.bbc.co.uk/1/hi/world/europe/4551348.stm; Jonathan Petre, "Pope Delights Crowds with Santa Look," *Telegraph* (UK), December 22, 2005, https://www.telegraph.co.uk/news/worldnews/europe/italy/1506119/Pope-delights-crowds-with-Santa-look.html.

110 "real program . . . the Lord": Pope Benedict XVI, Homily of His Holiness Benedict XVI, April 24, 2005 (Libreria Editrice Vaticana), http://w2.vatican.va/content/benedict-xvi/en/homilies/2005/documents/hf_ben-xvi_hom_20050424_inizio-pontificato.html.

110 "dictatorship of relativism": Cardinal Joseph Ratzinger, Mass, Pro Eligendo Romano Pontifice, Libreria Editrice Vaticana, April 18, 2005.

110 "the truth . . . of persons": Chris Gowans, "Moral Relativism," in Edward N. Zalta, ed., *The Stanford Encyclopedia of Philosophy*, Summer 2018 ed., https://plato.stanford.edu/entries/moral-relativism/.

110 "the dissolution . . . human rights: Cardinal Joseph Ratzinger, Speech to the LUMSA Faculty of Jurisprudence, Rome, November 10, 1999, http://www.ewtn.com/library/Theology/LAWMETA.HTM.

111 "The majority . . . factors": Ibid.

111 "every aspect . . . crisis": Gibson, *The Rule of Benedict*, p. 257.

111 "subtle seductions . . . properly": Letters from Cardinal Ratzinger to Gabriele Kuby, March 7, 2003, https://www.lifesitenews.com/news/pope-opposes-harry-potter-novels-signed-letters-from-cardinal-ratzinger-now; Gibson, *The Rule of Benedict*, p. 257.

111 "as gaffe-prone . . . to another": Nick Squires, "Pope Benedict XVI Resigns: A Papacy Marred by Crises and Controversies," *Telegraph* (UK), February 11, 2013.

111–12 "grave sins . . . culture'": "Instruction Concerning the Criteria for the Discernment of Vocations with Regard to Persons with Homosexual Tendencies in View of their Admission to the Seminary and to Holy Orders," November 4, 2005 (Congregation for Catholic Education, Rome), http://www.vatican.va/roman_curia/congregations/ccatheduc/documents/rc_con_ccatheduc_doc_20051104_istruzione_en.html.

112 "I would like . . . peoples": Pope Benedict XVI, General Audience.

112 "structures of faith contained in the Bible": Lecture of the Holy Father, *Faith, Reason and the University: Memories and Reflections*, Alua Magna of the University of Regensburg, September 12, 2006 (Libreria Editrice Vaticana), http://w2.vatican.va/content/benedict-xvi/en/speeches/2006/september/documents/hf_ben-xvi_spe_20060912_university-regensburg.html.

112 "the essential relationship between faith": Pope Benedict XVI, Meeting with the Representatives of Science, University of Regensburg, September 12, 2006 (Libreria Editrice Vaticana).

112 "It would have . . . pontificate": Paul Badde, *Benedict Up Close: The Inside Story of Eight Dramatic Years*, trans. Michael J. Miller (Inondale, Alabama: EWTN Publishing, 2017), p. 62.

113 "sincerely regrets . . . his intentions": Official Statement by Holy See Press Office, September 16, 2006.

113 "unhappiness . . . twenty years": Vallely, *Pope Francis: Untying the Knots,* pp. 9–10.

113 "mission of dialogue . . . Church: Apostolic Journey of His Holiness Benedict XVI to Turkey, Libreria Editrice Vaticana, November 28–December 1, 2006.

114 "remarkable flowering . . . mutual trust": Ibid.

114 "the genocide . . . Nazi ideology": Address of His Holiness Benedict XVI at the viewing of a film on the life of Pope John Paul II, Libreria Editrice Vaticana, May 19, 2005.

114–15 "What earlier . . . harmful": Letter of His Holiness Benedict XVI to the Bishops on the Occasion of the Publication of the Apostolic Letter *Motu Proprio Data Summorum Pontificum* on the Use of the Roman Liturgy Prior to the Reform of 1970, Libreria Editrice Vaticana, July 7, 2007, http://w2.vatican.va/content/benedict-xvi/en/letters/2007/documents/hf_ben-xvi_let_20070707_lettera-vescovi.html.

115 "We are extremely . . . wrong time": Jason Burke, "Pope's Move on Latin Mass 'a Blow to Jews,'" *Guardian* (UK), July 8, 2017.

116 "hugely against six . . . chambers": Richard Williamson interviewed in 2008 on *Uppdrag Granskning,* SVT (Sweden), January 21, 2009.

116 "The Vatican . . . an individual": Statement by Father Federico Lombardi, head of the Vatican Press Office, January 24, 2009, published by Philip Willan; "Pope Readmits Holocaust-Denying Priest to the Church," *Independent* (UK), January 25, 2009, https://www.independent.co.uk/news/world/europe/pope-readmits-holocaust-denying-priest-to-the-church-1515339.html.

116 "the biggest . . . modern times": Olivia Balch, John Hooper, and Riazat Butt, "Vatican Crisis over Bishop Who Denies the Holocaust," *Guardian* (UK), February 7, 2009, https://www.theguardian.com/world/2009/feb/07/vatican-pope-holocaust-bishop.

116 "welcoming an open . . . anti-Semitism": Shira Medding, "Pope Outrages Jews over Holocaust Denier," CNN, January 26, 2009, http://edition.cnn.com/2009/WORLD/europe/01/26/pope.holocaust.denial/index.html.

116–17 "If a decision . . . been sufficient": Statement by Angela Merkel, February 3, 2009, http://www.dw.com/en/merkel-urges-pope-to-reject-holocaust-denial/a-3998869.

117 "I have been told . . . unity?": Letter of His Holiness Pope Benedict XVI to the Bishops of the Catholic Church Concerning the Remission of the Excommunication of the Four Bishops Consecrated by Archbishop Lefebvre, Libreria Editrice Vaticana, March 10, 2009.

118 "Summary . . . its objectives": U.S. Embassy to the Vatican, *The Holy*

See: A Failure to Communicate, WikiLeaks cable: 09VATICAN28_a, dated February 20, 2009, 16:00, https://wikileaks.org/plusd/cables /09VATICAN28_a.html.

118–19   The report went on . . . bad news": Ibid.

119   "deeply disturbed . . . a domestic level: Pastoral Letter of the Holy Father Pope Benedict XVI to the Catholics of Ireland, Libreria Editrice Vaticana, March 19, 2010

120   "personal and political axes": John Allen Jr., "Puccini Meets Watergate in 'Vatileaks' Scandal," *National Catholic Reporter,* February 27, 2012, https://www.ncronline.org/news/vatican/puccini-meets -watergate-vatileaks-scandal.

121   "One of the . . . harm": Ibid.

5. THE RESIGNATION OF A POPE

122–23   "Dear Brothers . . . it is": Pope Benedict XVI, Declarito, Libreria Editrice Vaticana, February 10, 2013, http://w2.vatican.va/content /benedict-xvi/en/speeches/2013/february/documents/hf_ben-xvi _spe_20130211_declaratio.html.

123   "The cardinals . . . and sadness": John Hooper, "Pope Benedict XVI Announces Resignation—As It Happened," *Guardian* (UK), February 11, 2013, https://www.theguardian.com/world/2013/feb/11 /pope-resigns-live-reaction.

123   "The pope took us by surprise": John Hooper, Pope's Resignation— Eyewitness Account, *Guardian* (UK), February 11, 2013, https:// www.theguardian.com/world/2013/feb/11/pope-resigns-live -reaction.

124   "you cannot come down from the cross": Philip Pullella, "Pope's Sudden Resignation Sends Shockwaves Through Church," Reuters, February 11, 2013, https://www.reuters.com/article/us-pope-resigns /popes-sudden-resignation-sends-shockwaves-through-church -idUSBRE91A0BH20130211.

124   "When the danger is . . . do it": Benedict XVI, *Light of the World,* p. 29.

125   "Actually I had expected . . . years": Ibid., p. 3.

126   "at a girls' school": Leaked memo published by *New York Times,* March 25, 2010, https://www.nytimes.com/2010/03/26/world/europe /26church.html.

126   "medical-psychotherapeutic . . . ways": Ibid.

126   "The risk of . . . local bishop": Interview with Dr. Werner Huth, "What the Pope Knew," *Panorama,* BBC, September 13, 2010.

126   "he issued . . . unchallenged: *New York Times,* March 25, 2010, https://www.nytimes.com/2010/03/26/world/europe/26church.html.

127   "I deeply regret . . . by it": Nicholas Kulish and Rachel Donadio, "Abuse Scandal in Germany Edges Closer to Pope," *New York Times,* March 12, 2010, https://www.nytimes.com/2010/03/13/world/europe /13pope.html.

127 "nonsense . . . protect the pope": Ibid.

127 "evident that in . . . have failed": "Vatican Sees Campaign Against the Pope," *New York Times*, March 13, 2010, https://www.nytimes.com /2010/03/14/world/europe/14pope.html.

128 "asked" in no . . . line": Conny Newman, "Was Munich's Vicar General Forced to Serve as Ratzinger's Scapegoat?," *Der Spiegel* (Germany), April 19, 2010, http://www.spiegel.de/international/germany/catholic-abuse -scandal-was-munich-s-vicar-general-forced-to-serve-as-ratzinger-s -scapegoat-a-689761.html.

129 "the real reason . . . decades: Benedict XVI, *Light of the World*, pp. 27–28.

130 "brute animals," to . . . Holy Office: "Instruction on the Manner of Proceeding in Cases of Solicitation," From the Supreme and Holy Congregation of the Holy Office (Vatican Press Office, 1962), http://image .guardian.co.uk/sys-files/Observer/documents/2003/08/16/Criminales .pdf.

130 "blueprint for deception and concealment": Anthony Barnett, "Vatican Told Bishops to Cover Up Sex Abuse," *Observer* (UK), August 16, 2003; "Instruction on the Manner of Proceeding in Cases of Solicitation," obtained by the *Observer*, https://www.theguardian.com/world /2003/aug/17/religion.childprotection.

130 "At first Rome tried to . . . into it": Paul Collins, *God's New Man*, pp. 93–94.

130 "the worst . . . tribunal": *The Norms of the Motu Proprio*, official publication by the Congregation for the Doctrine of the Faith (Vatican Press Office, 2010).

131 "advises clerics . . . years": Jeffrey Ferro, *Sexual Misconduct and the Clergy* (New York: Facts on File, 2005), p. 107.

131 It also . . . any details: Cardinal Joseph Ratzinger, "Letter Explains New Norms for Church Handling of Certain Grave Offenses," Congregation for the Doctrine of the Church, Vatican Press Office, May 18, 2001.

132 "There's no policy . . . moved": Father Tom Doyle, in "Sex Crimes and the Vatican," *Panorama*, BBC, October 1, 2006.

132 UNEASY LIES THE HEAD THAT WEARS A CROWN: William Shakespeare, *Henry IV, Part 2*, act III, scene 1.

133 "an eruption . . . Church": Jerome Taylor, "Italy Hails 'an Outbreak of Modernity in the Church' as Pope Benedict XVI Announces He Will Resign Because of Ill Health," *Independent* (UK), February 11, 2013, https://www.independent.co.uk/news/world/europe/italy-hails-an -outbreak-of-modernity-in-the-church-as-pope-benedict-xvi -announces-he-will-resign-8489837.html.

133 "The theologian . . . papacy": Marco Ventura, professor of law and religion at Siena University, Italy, quoted in "See You Later," *Economist*, February 16, 2013, https://www.economist.com/news/international/21571864 -papal-resignation-ecclesiastical-earthquake-how-church-interprets -it-will.

133 "simply a pilgrim . . . earth": Greeting of His Holiness Benedict XVI to the faithful of the diocese of Albano, Libreria Editrice Vaticana, February 28, 2013.

6. CONCLAVE

136 "carry this idea . . . hands": Rachel Donadio and Elisabetta Povoledo, "Successor to Benedict Will Lead a Church at a Crossroads," *New York Times*, February 11, 2013, https://www.nytimes.com/2013/02/12/world /europe/with-popes-resignation-focus-shifts-to-a-successor.html.

136 A man with . . . performance: John L. Allen Jr., "Papabile of the Day: The Men Who Could Be Pope," *National Catholic Reporter*, March 11, 2013, https://www.ncronline.org/blogs/ncr-today/papabili -day-men-who-could-be-pope.

139 "whispering . . . generates": Andrea Tornielli quoted in ibid.

140 "two cardinals . . . religious sisters": John L. Allen Jr., "Papabile of the Day: The Men Who Could Be Pope," *National Catholic Reporter*, February 25, 2013, https://www.ncronline.org/blogs/ncr -today/papabili-day-men-who-could-be-pope-6.

141 "easily the most . . . cardinals": Allen, "Papabile of the Day: The Men Who Could Be Pope" *National Catholic Reporter*, March 11, 2013, https://www.ncronline.org/blogs/ncr-today/papabili-day-men-who -could-be-pope.

141–42 "such an obvious . . . apartments": John L. Allen Jr., "Papabile of the Day: The Men Who Could Be Pope," *National Catholic Reporter*, March 2, 2013, https://www.ncronline.org/blogs/ncr-today /papabile-day-men-who-could-be-pope-11.

142 "the notion of . . . hemisphere": John L. Allen Jr., "Papabile of the Day: The Men Who Could Be Pope," *National Catholic Reporter*, February 19, 2013, https://www.ncronline.org/blogs/ncr-today/papabile -day-men-who-could-be-pope-0.

142 "Conservatism's Cape crusader": Peter Popham, "Cardinal Peter Turkson: Conservatism's Cape Crusader," *Independent* (UK), February 15, 2013, https://www.independent.co.uk/news/people/profiles /cardinal-peter-turkson-conservatisms-cape-crusader-8497539.html.

143 "if it's the will . . . pope": Lizzy Davies, "Catholic Church Ready for Non-European Pope, says Ghanaian Cardinal," *Guardian* (UK), February 13, 2013, https://www.theguardian.com/world/2013/feb /13/catholic-church-pope-ghanaian-cardinal.

143 "African traditional . . . tendency": Samuel Burke, "Meet the Man Who Could Be the First Black Pope," CNN, February 12, 2013, http://amanpour.blogs.cnn.com/2013/02/12/meet-the-man-who -could-be-the-first-black-pope/.

144 Great Asian . . . Curia: John L. Allen Jr., "Papabile of the Day: The Men Who Could Be Pope," *National Catholic Reporter*, February 22, 2013, https://www.ncronline.org/blogs/ncr-today/papabile -day-men-who-could-be-pope-3.

147 **"Prepare yourself, dear friend"**: Elizabetta Piqué, *Francis: Life and Revolution: A Biography of Jorge Bergoglio* (Chicago: Loyola Press, 2013), p. 23.

147 **"after many . . . Holy See"**: Matthew Fisher, "Canada's Marc Ouellet Came Close to Becoming Pope, Media Reports Say," *Global News* (Canada), March 15, 2013, https://globalnews.ca/news/409907/canadas-marc-ouellet-came-close-to-becoming-pope-media-reports-say/.

147 **"seemed very . . . happening"**: Associated Press, "So What Really Happened Inside the Papal Conclave that Selected Pope Francis? Here's a Cardinal's-Eye View," *New York Daily News,* March 14, 2013, http://www.nydailynews.com/news/world/papal-conclave-article-1.1288950.

148 **"he felt a deep . . . day"**: Antonio Spadaro, S.J., "A Big Heart Open to God: An Interview with Pope Francis," *Jesuit Review,* September 30, 2013, https://www.americamagazine.org/faith/2013/09/30/big-heart-open-god-interview-pope-francis.

148 **After the sixth . . . house"**: Associated Press, "So What Really Happened Inside the Papal Conclave?"

148 **"Don't forget the poor"**: Cindy Wooden, "Pope Francis Explains Why He Chose St. Francis of Assisi's Name," Catholic News Service, March 17, 2013, http://www.catholicnews.com/services/englishnews/2013/pope-francis-explains-why-he-chose-st-francis-of-assisi-s-name.cfm.

148–49 **"Do you accept . . . Assisi"**: Ivereigh, *The Great Reformer,* p. 363.

7. A DIRTY SECRET

150 **"not follow the . . . disappeared"**: Telegram from American ambassador to Argentina Robert Hill to Secretary of State Henry Kissinger, "Ambassador's Conversation with Admiral Massera," March 16, 1976, U.S. Department of State Argentina Declassification Project (1975–1984), August 20, 2002 (Digital National Security Archives Accession Number NSAEBB185), https://nsarchive2.gwu.edu//NSAEBB/NSAEBB185/19760316%20Ambassadors%20conversation%20with%20admiral%20massera%200000A005.pdf.

150 **"probably the best . . . history"**: Telegram from Ambassador Robert Hill, "Vileda's Moderate Line Prevails," March 30, 1976, U.S. Department of State Argentina Declassification Project (1975–1984), August 20, 2002 (Digital National Security Archives Accession Number NSAEBB185), https://nsarchive2.gwu.edu//NSAEBB/NSAEBB185/19760316%20Ambassadors%20conversation%20with%20admiral%20massera%200000A005.pdf.

150 **"chance they [the junta] have"**: Quotes taken from U.S. Department of State Argentina Declassification Project (1975–1984), August 20, 2002 (Digital National Security Archive Accession number NSAEBB185), https://nsarchive2.gwu.edu//NSAEBB/NSAEBB185/19760326%20Secretary%20of%20Stet%20Kissinger%20Chariman%20apgesl%201-39%20-%20full.pdf.

151   For example . . . council: Marguerite Feitlowitz, *A Lexicon of Terror: Argentina and the Legacies of Torture* (Oxford: Oxford University Press, 1998), p. 79.

151   "the total capacity . . . 5,000": Ibid., p. 17.

151   "Heil Hitler": Daniel Feierstein, "Political Violence in Argentina and Its Genocidal Characteristics," *Journal of Genocide Research* 8, no. 2 (June 2006): 151.

151   "They put on . . . us": Uki Goni, "Pope Francis and the Missing Marxist," *Guardian* (UK), December 11, 2013, https://www.theguardian .com/world/2013/dec/11/pope-francis-argentina-esther-careaga.

153   "encourage the Vatican . . . law": Department of State confidential cable from U.S. Embassy, Buenos Aires, "The Tactic of Disappearance," September 26, 1980 (National Security Archives, Washington, D.C.), https://assets.documentcloud.org/documents/3010645/Document-08-Department-of-State-The-Tactic-of.pdf.

154   "given their friendship . . . I could": Sam Ferguson, "Pope Francis and the 'Dirty War,'" *New Republic,* March 19, 2013, https:// newrepublic.com/article/112692/pope-francis-and-argentinas-dirty -war-video-testimony.

154   "We know . . . subversion": Vallely, *Pope Francis: Untying the Knots,* p. 68.

155   "Do not tell . . . meet": Interview transcripts published in "Bergoglio, a Witness in the ESMA Supertrial," *Clarin,* March 2013, https://www.clarin.com/pope-francis/bergoglio-witness-the-esma -supertrial_0_H1Prwg9swQe.html.

155   "tremendous pressure . . . Church": Vallely, *Pope Francis: Untying the Knots,* p. 74.

155–56   "he [Bergoglio] . . . in the matter": Ivereigh, *The Great Reformer,* p. 158.

156–57   "very formal . . . seriously": Interview transcripts published in "Bergoglio, a Witness in the ESMA Supertrial."

157   "almost certain . . . ugly": Ferguson, "Pope Francis and the 'Dirty War.'"

157   "I've already told . . . know": Ibid.

157   "Look, Massera . . . left": Ibid.

157   "one of the most . . . information": Daniel Satur, "Jorge Bergoglio, la dictadura y los desaparecidos," *La Izquierda Diario,* March 24, 2017, https://www.laizquierdadiario.com/Jorge-Bergoglio-la-dictadura -y-los-desaparecidos.

158   "Zamora: . . . navy": Ferguson, "Pope Francis and the 'Dirty War.'"

158   "Why not the legal . . . hierarchy": "Bergoglio, a Witness in the ESMA Supertrial."

159–60   "On November 15, 1976 . . . field": Cardinal Jorge Mario Bergoglio, ed., *Iglesia y democracia en la Argentina* (Conferencia Episcopal Argentina: Buenos Aires), March 6, 2006, p. 652.

159   "Contrary to the . . . out": Sergio Rubin and Francesca Ambrogetti, *El Jesuita* Ediciones B: Argentina, 2010), p. 191.

160–61 **OBJECT OF THE MEETING . . . unofficially:** Full memorandum published by Horacio Verbitsky, "Omissions and Intentions," *Página/12* (Argentina), April 11, 2010, https://web.archive.org/web /20130316043549/http://www.pagina12.com.ar/diario/elpais/sub notas/143711-46189-2010-04-11.html.

161   "At the beginning . . . later on": Rubin and Ambrogetti, *El Jesuita*, p. 188.

161   "cede anything . . . War: Vallely, *Pope Francis: Untying the Knots*, p. 56.

162   "it gives . . . in that pit": Horacio Verbitsky, "Preguntas sin respuesta," *Página/12* (Argentina), May 6, 2012, https://www.pagina12 .com.ar/diario/elpais/1-193425-2012-05-06.html.

162   "his interrogators . . . have known": Vallely, *Pope Francis: Untying the Knots*, p. 81.

163   "I don't have . . . contrary": Horacio Verbitsky, *L'isola del silenzio: Il ruolo della Chiesa nella dittatura Argentina* (Rome: Fandango Libri, 2006), p. 61.

163   "since [he] . . . over and over": Vallely, *Pope Francis: Untying the Knots,* p. 80.

164   *"Bergoglio's silence . . . trial":* Estela de la Cuadra, quoted in "El silencio de Jorge Bergoglio," *Página/12* (Argentina), September 4, 2007, https://www.pagina12.com.ar/diario/elpais/1-90784-2007-09- 04.html.

166   "He [de la Cuadra] . . . can do": Letter from Jorge Bergoglio to Mario Picchi, October 28, 1977, published by Daniel Satur, "La Carta Que Oculta Bergoglio," *La Izquierda Diario* (Argentina), September 20, 2014, http://carga.laizquierdadiario.com/La-carta-que -oculta-Bergoglio.

166   **His chief was Colonel Ramón Camps:** Camps went on to head the Argentine Federal Police and was later convicted of twenty-one counts of premeditated murder, twenty-one counts of unlawful imprisonment, and twenty-eight counts of torture in a trial of military generals in 1986. He was sentenced to twenty-five years in prison but served just three years before he was, staggeringly, given a presidential pardon by Carlos Menem in 1989.

166   "The sins of the . . . children": Marcela Valente, "RIGHTS-ARGENTINA: Priest Faces Judgement Day," Inter Press Service News Agency, July 9, 2007, http://www.ipsnews.net/2007/07/rights -argentina-priest-faces-judgement-day/.

167   "The attitude . . . either": Testimony quoted in Alexei Barrionuevo, "Argentine Church Faces 'Dirty War' Past," *New York Times,* September 17, 2007, https://www.nytimes.com/2007/09/17/world/americas /17church.html.

167 "No, it must have . . . [which began in 1985]:" Mark Dowd, "Pope Francis and Argentina's 'Disappeared,'" *BBC News Magazine*, April 11, 2013, https://www.bbc.co.uk/news/magazine-22064929.

168 "Bergoglio's telephone calls . . . banishment: Elisabetta Piqué, *Pope Francis: Life and Revolution*, p. 92.

169 "the man . . . was sick, crazy": Cámara and Pfaffen, *Understanding Pope Francis*, p. 149.

169 "I lived . . . in Córdoba": Fr. Antonio Spadaro, "Interview with Pope Francis," Libreria Editrice Vaticana, August 19, 2013.

169 "What hurts me . . . learned": Rubin and Ambrogetti, *El Jesuita*, p. 47.

169 "a time of . . . my inner life": Cámara and Pfaffen, *Understanding Pope Francis*, p. 151.

170 "Between feelings . . . this hope": Ibid., p. 153.

170 "My authoritarian . . . problems": Spadaro, "Interview with Pope Francis."

170 "the lack of . . . [among men and communities]": Cámara and Pfaffen, *Understanding Pope Francis*, p. 184.

171 "the grace of silence": Jorge Mario Bergoglio, "Silencio y Palabra" (Silence and Word), in *Reflexiones en Esperanza* (Reflections of Hope) (Buenos Aires: Ediciones Universidad del Salvador, 1992), p. 143.

8. HABEMUS PAPAM . . . ITERUM

172 "It's not carnival time": Elizabetta Piqué, *Pope Francis: Life and Revolution*, p. 31.

173 "He met with us . . . is different": Cardinal Timothy Dolan, "Inside the Conclave," *GoodNews* (UK) 225, May/June 2013, http://www.ccr.org.uk/old/archive/gn1305/part_a.pdf.

173 "exchanging good . . . mutual prayer": Vallely, *Pope Francis: Untying the Knots*, p. 164.

173–74 When a microphone . . . your welcome": "First Greeting of the Holy Father Pope Francis," Libreria Editrice Vaticana, March 13, 2013.

174 "First of all . . . keep him": Ibid.

174 "Now I would . . . over me": Ibid.

174 "You can't imagine . . . one of us": "Secrets of the Vatican," *Frontline*, PBS, February 25, 2014.

175 "to follow . . . his footsteps": *Regula primitiva*, Saint Francis of Assisi (Encyclopædia Britannica, 1999).

175 "one of the . . . deep humility": St. Francis of Assisi, F. L. Cross and E. A. Livingston, eds., *The Oxford Dictionary of the Christian Church* (Oxford: Oxford University Press, 2005), p. 636.

176 "The cardinalate . . . hiding inside them": "Careerism and Vanity: Sins of the Church," *La Stampa*, February 24, 2012, https://www.lastampa.it/2012/02/24/vaticaninsider/careerism-and-vanity-sins-of-the-church-pSPgcKLJ0qrfItoDN5x35K/pagina.html.

177 "We have come . . . together": Vallely, *Pope Francis: Untying the Knots,* p. 166.

177 "May God . . . down": Lizzy Davies, "Pope Francis Eschews Trappings of Papacy on First Day in Office," *Guardian* (UK), March 14, 2013.

177 "Startled officials . . . celebrating crowds": Vallely, *Pope Francis: Untying the Knots,* p. 171.

177 "had to set a good example": Statement by Vatican spokesman Father Federico Lombardi, quoted by Peter Walker, Paul Owen, and David Batty, "Liveblog: Pope Francis—First Day After Election," *Guardian* (UK), March 14, 2013, https://www.theguardian.com/world/2013/mar/14/pope-francis-first-day.

178 Journeying . . . no solidity: "Homily of the Holy Father Pope Francis," Libreria Editrice Vaticana, March 14, 2013.

178 Journeying, building . . . forward: Ibid.

179 The United States . . . of the population: "America's Changing Religious Landscape," Pew Research Center, May 12, 2015, http://www.pewforum.org/2015/05/12/americas-changing-religious-landscape/.

180 a poll in . . . religious person": Ahmed Benchemsi, "Invisible Atheists," *New Republic,* April 24, 2015.

180 "Jorge Mario Bergoglio . . . come together": Vallely, *Pope Francis: Untying the Knots,* p. xi.

9. THE SUPERSTAR POPE

183 "I felt I . . . to weep": "Visit to Lampedusa—Homily of Holy Father Francis," Libreria Editrice Vaticana, July 8, 2013.

183 "for those who . . . tragedies": Ibid.

184 "immoral . . . Catholic values": Philip Pullella, "Exclusive: Pope Criticizes Trump Administration Policy on Migrant Family Separation," Reuters, June 20, 2018, https://www.reuters.com/article/us-pope-interview/exclusive-pope-criticizes-trump-administration-policy-on-migrant-family-separation-idUSKBN1JG0YC.

184 "deep concern . . . Jerusalem: "Pope Francis General Audience," *Libreria Editrice Vaticana,* December 6, 2017.

184 "not Christian . . . border: Jim Yardley, "Pope Francis Suggests Donald Trump Is 'Not Christian,'" *New York Times,* February 16, 2016, https://www.nytimes.com/2016/02/19/world/americas/pope-francis-donald-trump-christian.html?hp&action=click&pgtype=Homepage&clickSource=story-heading&module=first-column-region&region=top-news&WT.nav=top-news.

184 In a year when . . . and injustices: World Bank, *Poverty and Shared Prosperity 2016: Taking on Inequality* (Washington, D.C.: World Bank, 2016), https://openknowledge.worldbank.org/bitstream/handle/10986/25078/9781464809583.pdf.

184 "exclusion and . . . the powerless": Apostolic Exhortation *Evangelii Gaudium* of the Holy Father Francis, Libreria Editrice Vaticana, November 24, 2013, chapter 2, p. 53.

184 "Some people . . . purchasing power": Ibid., chapter 3, pp. 54 and 56.

185 "no to a financial system . . . reforms: Ibid., chapter 3, pp. 55–57.

186 "The pope is . . . cardinals": Carlo Fantappiè, "Papacy, Sede Vavante, and 'Pope Emeritus': Ambiguities to Be Avoided," *Chiesa, L'Espresso* (Italy), March 9, 2013, http://chiesa.espresso.repubblica.it/articolo/1350457bdc4.html?eng=y.

186 "Resigning means losing . . . pope": Professor Enrico Maria Radaelli, "Perché Papa Ratzinger-Benedetto XVI Dovrebbe Ritirare le sue Dimissioni: Non è ancora il tempo di un nuovo papa perché sarebbe quello di un antipapa," *Aurea Domus*, Section 8–9, February 18, 2013; republished in English by Sandro Magister, "Last-Ditch Appeal: The Pope Should Withdraw His Resignation," *Chiesa, L'Espresso* (Italy), February 20, 2013, http://chiesa.espresso.repubblica.it/articolo/1350437bdc4.html?eng=y.

187 "Francis/bishop of Rome": *Annuario Pontifico* 2013, p. 23, in Magister, "Vatican Diary: The Identity Cards of the Last Two Popes." *Chiesa, L'Espresso* (Italy), May 23, 2013, http://chiesa.espresso.repubblica.it/articolo/1350523bdc4.html?eng=y.

187 "supreme pontiff emeritus": Ibid., p. 1.

187 "bishop emeritus . . . not to oppose it": Ibid.

188 "Thank you for . . . temperament": Edward Pentin, "Vatican Reveals Full Text of Benedict XVI's Letter to Msgr. Viganò," *National Catholic Register*, March 17, 2018, http://www.ncregister.com/blog/edward-pentin/full-text-of-benedict-xvis-letter-to-mons.-vigano.

189 "The manipulation changed . . . and assessment": Nicole Winfield, "Vatican Doctors Photo of Benedict's Praise for Francis," Associated Press, March 14, 2018, https://apnews.com/amp/01983501d40d47a4aa7a32b6afb70661?__twitter_impression=true.

189 "the letter in its entirety": Pentin, "Vatican Reveals Full Text of Benedict XVI's Letter to Msgr. Viganò."

189 "I don't feel . . . made": Ibid.

190 "Only as an aside . . . theologians": Ibid.

190 "thunderous . . . news": Sandro Magister, "Two Popes, Two Churches, the 'Fake News' of Francis and Benedict's Big No," *Settimo Cielo, L'Espresso* (Italy), April 1, 2018, http://magister.blogautore.espresso.repubblica.it/2018/04/01/two-popes-two-churches-the-fake-news-of-francis-and-benedicts-big-no/.

190–91 "It is a cry . . . defenseless": "Celebration of Palm Sunday of the Passion of the Lord—Homily of His Holiness Pope Francis," Libreria Editrice Vaticana, March 25, 2018.

191 "fake news . . . human sin": "Message of His Holiness Pope Francis

for World Communications Day," Libreria Editrice Vaticana, January 24, 2018.

192 "He meant . . . is he on?'": Nicole Winfield, "Reflections on Pope Francis from 35,000 Feet," Associated Press, September 8, 2015, https://www.businessinsider.com/ap-reflections-on-pope-francis -from-35000-feet-2015-9?IR=T.

192 "So much is written . . . to judge?": "Press Conference of Pope Francis During the Return Flight, Apostolic Journey to Rio de Janeiro on the Occasion of the XXVIII World Youth Day," Libreria Editrice Vaticana, July 28, 2013, http://w2.vatican.va/content /francesco/en/speeches/2013/july/documents/papa-francesco _20130728_gmg-conferenza-stampa.html.

192 "You know . . . people say": Delia Gallagher and Hada Messia, "Pope Francis Tells Gay Man: 'God Made You Like That and Loves You Like That,'" CNN, May 21, 2018, https://edition.cnn.com/2018 /05/21/europe/pope-francis-gay-comments-intl/index.html.

192 "contrary to the essence . . . wanted": Pope Benedict XVI, *Light of the World*, p. 152.

192 "an intrinsic moral evil": Cardinal Joseph Ratzinger, "Letter to the Bishops of the Catholic Church on the Pastoral Care of Homosexual Priests," Libreria Editrice Vaticana, October 1, 1986.

193 "acts of great . . . be avoided": Catechism of the Catholic Church Approved and Promulgated by John Paul II, part three, section two, chapter two, article 6, 2357 and 2358, Libreria Editrice Vaticana, August 15, 1997.

193 "many observers insist . . . Church": James Carroll, "Who Am I to Judge? A Radical Pope's First Year," *New Yorker,* December 23, 30, 2013, https://www.newyorker.com/magazine/2013/12/23/who-am-i -to-judge.

193 "all those in . . . sanctifying grace": "Post-Synodal Apostolic Exhortation *Amoris Lætitia* of the Holy Father Francis—Chapter Eight/301," Libreria Editrice Vaticana, March 19, 2016.

194–95 "One of his most . . . opposite": Andrea Tornielli, "Pope Francis: An Intimate Portrait," *Sunday Times* (London), April 16, 2017, https:// www.thetimes.co.uk/article/pope-francis-an-intimate-portrait -0rx6nbs6h.

195 Francis's desire . . . in their outlook: *Correctio Filialis de haeresibus propagates* (A filial correction concerning the propagation of heresies), August 11, 2017, http://www.correctiofilialis.org/wp -content/uploads/2017/08/Correctio-filialis_English_1.pdf.

195 "It is the conservative . . . loudest": Tornielli, "Pope Francis: An Intimate Portrait."

195–96 "It's a decisive move . . . Holy Spirit": Susy Hodges, "Pope at Mass: Be Bishops for Your Flock, Not for Your Career," *Vatican News,* May 15, 2018, https://www.vaticannews.va/en/pope-francis/mass-casa -santa-marta/2018-05/pope-mass-santa-marta-bishops-flock.html.

197 **Madonna of Humility . . . went indoors:** Associated Press and Agence France-Press, "Pope Meets Pope: Francis Tells Benedict 'We're Brothers,'" *Telegraph* (UK), March 23, 2013, https://www .telegraph.co.uk/news/worldnews/europe/vaticancityandholysee /9949839/Pope-meets-Pope-Francis-tells-Benedict-Were-brothers .html.

198 **"I cannot live alone . . . people":** "Press Conference of Pope Francis During Return Flight."

198 **Benedict passed Francis . . . commissioned:** Edward Pentin, English transcript of Archbishop Gänswein's EWTN Germany interview, *National Catholic Register,* July 5, 2016, http://www.ncregister .com/blog/edward-pentin/full-english-transcript-of-archbishop -gaensweins-interview-with-ewtn-german.

198 **when Francis turned eighty . . . pontiff:** Catholic News Agency, Pope Francis Visits Benedict XVI to Wish Him a Happy Birthday, *Crux Now,* April 15, 2017, https://cruxnow.com/vatican/2017/04/15 /pope-francis-visits-benedict-xvi-wish-happy-birthday/.

198–99 **And when Benedict turned ninety . . . birthday:** John L. Allen Jr., "Benedict XVI Shares a 90th Birthday Beer with Family and Friends," *Crux Now,* April 17, 2017, https://cruxnow.com/vatican/2017/04/17 /benedict-xvi-shares-90th-birthday-beer-family-friends/.

199 **"on a pilgrimage toward home":** Letter from Pope Emeritus Benedict to Massimo Franco, dated February 5, 2018, published by *Corriere della Sera,* reprinted by Joseph Ratzinger–Benedict XVI Vatican Foundation, February 7, 2018, http://www.fondazioneratzinger.va /content/fondazioneratzinger/en/news/notizie/la-lettera-di -benedetto-xvi-al-corriere-della-sera.html.

199 **"that he's a serene . . . heart":** Father Georg Gänswein interviewed by Franca Giansoldati, "Padre Georg Gänswein: Benedetto, grande Papa che non è stato ascoltato," *Il Messaggero,* April 14, 2017, https://www.ilmessaggero.it/pay/edicola/benedetto_grande_papa _non_ascoltato-2379824.html.

199 **These days, Benedict . . . he replies":** Ibid.

EPILOGUE

202–3 **"For the death . . . have mercy":** Bergoglio's address quoted in "Carlos Mugica, the Martyr of the Villas Miserias," *La Stampa* (Italy), May 11, 2014, http://www.lastampa.it/2014/05/11/vaticaninsider/carlos-mugica -the-martyr-of-the-villas-miserias-HjIuvlyHfCKya8ZPNviq4M /pagina.html.

204 **"Since someone will . . . lie round":** Philip Larkin, "Church Going," *The Less Deceived* (Hessle, UK: Marvell Press, 1955).